A GAME

A GAME FOR DANCERS

Performing Modernism in
the Postwar Years, 1945–1960

GAY MORRIS

WESLEYAN UNIVERSITY PRESS
Middletown, Connecticut

Published by Wesleyan University Press, Middletown, CT 06459
www.wesleyan.edu/wespress
© 2006 by Gay Morris

Printed in the United States of America
5 4 3 2 1

Text by George Balanchine used by permission of The George Balanchine Trust.
Balanchine is a trademark of The George Balanchine Trust.

Library of Congress Cataloging-in-Publication Data
Morris, Gay, 1940–
A game for dancers : performing modernism in the postwar years, 1945–1960 /
Gay Morris.
    p. cm.
Includes bibliographical references and index.
ISBN–13: 978–0–8195–6804–5 (cloth : alk. paper)
ISBN–10: 0–8195–6804–x (cloth : alk. paper)
ISBN–13: 978–0–8195–6805–2 (pbk. : alk. paper)
ISBN–10: 0–8195–6805–8 (pbk. : alk. paper)
1. Modern dance—History. I. Title.
GV1619.M67   2006
792.809'045—dc22   2006000181

For G. G.

CONTENTS

ILLUSTRATIONS

ACKNOWLEDGMENTS

In a research project that spans many years, the number of people who contribute to it grows accordingly. This project lingered in the back of my mind for most of a career that has involved both art and dance criticism. It began to come to fruition with a dissertation in the Sociology Department of Goldsmiths College, University of London, that was overseen by Helen Thomas. During those happy years I often lived in a flat, which overlooked an eighteenth-century square, that was loaned to me by Sue Merrett, my editor at the *Dancing Times*. It is safe to say there would be no book today without the aid of these two remarkable women. Helen was a mentor and became a close friend; Sue is now retired and floats about the canals and rivers of England on her barge. Other colleagues in the United Kingdom who have given advice and encouragement over the years include Stephanie Jordan, Stacey Prickett, and especially Dee Reynolds, who read parts of the book manuscript as it developed.

In the United States I must particularly thank Marcia Siegel and Mark Franko, who have each in important ways helped sort out my thoughts over the course of the project and have been friends as well as colleagues. Others who have helped with information and advice include Claudia Gitelman, Dawn Lille, Murray Louis, Ze'eva Cohen, Joe Nash, George Dorris, Jack Anderson, Doris Hering, Donald McKayle, Susan Buirge, Phyllis Lamhut, Janet Soares, Deborah Jowitt, Lynn Garafola, Joan Brown, Delores Brown, David Vaughan, Naima Prevots, George Jackson, Elizabeth Zimmer, Don McDonagh, and Leslie Getz.

The staffs of research libraries and archives are the unsung heroes of scholarship, and my work was aided immeasurably by them. This was especially the case with all the people at the Dance Collection of the Library for the Performing Arts and the Schomburg Center for Research in Black Culture, both of which are research arms of the New York Public Library, where much of my research was done. Phil Karg at the Dance Collection was particularly helpful with all aspects of locating and obtaining photographs. I also must thank David Vaughan (this time in his role as archivist) and Stacy Sumpman at the Cunningham Foundation Archives; Stephen McLeod at the University of California–Irvine Library where Donald McKayle's archives are housed; Steve Siegel, archivist at the 92nd Street Y; Beth Olsen and Robert Tracy at the Alvin Ailey Dance Theater; and the staff of the New York City Ballet, its archives, and the Balanchine Trust. No scholar could do her work without these dedicated and generous people.

I would like to thank my editor, Suzanna Tamminen, production editors Jessica Stevens and Elizabeth Rawitsch, marketing manager Leslie Starr, and the staff at Wesleyan University Press for their unstinting support throughout the course of this book. A special thanks, too, to John Bennett, computer guru extraordinaire.

Three chapters in *A Game for Dancers* include material from articles that appeared elsewhere: chapter 1 includes sections from "Bourdieu, the Body, and Graham's Postwar Dance" that appeared in *Dance Research* 19:2 (Winter 2001); chapter 2 includes substantial material from "Balanchine's Bodies" that was included in *Body and Society* (December 2005); chapter 3 is an enlarged and revised version of "Modernism's Role in the Theory of John Martin and Edwin Denby" that appeared in *Dance Research* 22:2 (Winter 2004). I thank these journals for permission to reprint.

Finally, I would like to thank my family. There must be a special corner of heaven for these much-put-upon people who listen for years to stories and complaints of an arcane nature and who patiently take in stride lunches cancelled and events missed. As for spouses, they are in a saintly class all their own.

INTRODUCTION

When I first imagined *A Game for Dancers*, I thought it would deal with the shift in aesthetics that occurred in American modern dance after World War II, a time during which dancers moved away from the idea of communicating essential emotions to a so-called pure dance. I wanted to investigate this shift, which seemed to have had much to do with the advent of the Cold War and the resulting chill on overt political expression. However, compelling as this topic was, I eventually realized that it was only part of a larger and more troubling issue. This concerned modernism itself and what was possible in that late modernist moment. Modernism, which largely had been intended to give artists control over their work, was by 1945 being actively co-opted by the very forces it had been meant to counter. During the 1940s and '50s, dancers did not yet question the rules of the game they played; they continued to attempt to find solutions within it. Yet how could modern dancers fulfill the aims of a modernism that was ever more compromised? And how could modernism serve the needs of a genre that was itself facing institutionalization? It is the postwar dancers' struggles to solve their considerable problems within the framework of modernism that is finally the subject of this book.

Although American postwar modernism has received a great deal of attention in fields such as art history, cultural studies, and social criticism, the emphasis has generally been on the impact larger social forces have made on art. *A Game for Dancers* differs from these studies in that it considers a specific art field's history and dispositions as crucial factors in how that field intersects with broader social issues. In particular, competition for position within the field is a key element.

In dance studies itself, neither the postwar period nor the problems of late modernism have received extensive investigation. The majority of dance research has dealt with issues across a spectrum of modern dance rather than those particular to the postwar period.[1] The few works that have dealt specifically with these years have tended to emphasize dance's relationship to the Cold War.[2] Although Cold War politics figure prominently in the coming pages, they are viewed in relationship to modern dance's position in the dance field and the struggles that went on there in the 1940s and '50s. As for the topic of modernism, it also has been viewed predominantly from the standpoint of American modern dance as a whole, as in Julia Foulkes's recent *Modern Bodies: Dance and American Modernism from Martha Graham to Alvin Ailey* (2002).[3] *A Game for Dancers* instead draws attention to the problems surrounding the body of modernist ideas and practices that postwar dancers and commentators adhered to, manipulated, and exploited, but never overtly challenged.

In attempting to come to grips with modernism in American postwar dance, several sources have oriented my study.[4] The first is John Martin's theory concerning the aims and methods of modern dance as a modernist genre, which he formulated during the 1930s and which serves as a base from which to speak about dance modernism. His work will be examined in detail in chapter 3. Briefly, however, it called for a dance that communicated abstracted emotion through movement forms developed individually by each dancer. This "authentic" dance was available to everyone because all humans shared physiological mechanisms that allowed them to intuitively assimilate meaning in movement. Such a dance was characterized by new, independent, functional forms that were developed to deal with the ever changing demands of modernity (Martin [1939] 1965: 42–55, 121–126). Martin's ideas of the processes and goals of modern dance were generally shared by the field at large and here serve as a baseline for speaking of modern dance.

The second element to set the course of my study are the debates that have taken place over the last three decades in art history and criticism. Art critics and historians have emphasized the relationship between art and capitalist ideology after the war, which is crucial to any analysis of late modernism.[5] Among the key questions they have asked is whether modernism was simply an enforcer of the status quo in the disguise of a revolution of form or whether it was able to work, at least to some degree, as social critique. In addressing this issue I have given considerable thought to T. J. Clark's description of modernism as "a kind of skepticism, or at least unsureness, as to the nature of representation in art" (Clark 1984: 10).[6] In modern dance this doubt was manifested in an imperative to embody rather than represent meaning, a subject I take up in chapter 1. The notion of embodied meaning contributed to dance's sense of its own autonomy and, significantly, set it apart from painting and literature.

As Clark points out, the need for autonomy, as a distinctive feature of modernism, reached its apotheosis in Clement Greenberg's 1960 essay, "Modernist Painting," in which he stated that an art that was not independent was liable to be assimilated into entertainment or therapy (Greenberg [1960] 1993b: 86). However, Greenberg had developed his ideas on autonomy much earlier than 1960. He initially laid them out in his two much-quoted essays, "Avant-Garde and Kitsch" ([1939] 1986a) and "Towards a Newer Laocoon" ([1940] 1986b). Here Greenberg traced modernism's beginnings to nineteenth-century France when artists were forced into the marketplace as a result of the rise of bourgeois power and shifts away from aristocratic and church patronage after the revolution. Some artists, as a means of protest and to gain their freedom from outside political and economic control, rejected market institutions and methods. In this way they defined themselves as separate from, and in opposition to, the dominant class ([1939] 1986a: 7). According to Greenberg, artists then turned their backs on politics to focus their attention on preserving art, for art's task had become to guard the highest achievements of Western civilization from the onslaughts of the ruling class. Artists preserved art by making it its own justification ([1940] 1986b: 28). That is to say, they intended art to be seen for what it was—a painting, a drawing, a piece of sculpture—rather than an imitation of some aspect of the external world. In order to give art this independence, they engaged in self-criticism, in which they eliminated from their medium all elements that were foreign to it, including anecdotes, messages, and ideas. "Content is to be dissolved so completely into form that the work of art or literature cannot be reduced in whole or in part to anything not itself" ([1939] 1986a: 8). Art thus took a defensive position against the dominant order by retreating into a reductive formal purity.

Most of Greenberg's theory lay within the realm of generally accepted modernist claims. However, he took to extremes the artist's independence from society and the limitations of artistic concerns. An important aspect of the recent art historical debates has had to do with the degree of separation from life called for in Greenberg's theory and how it related to postwar art and politics. The place of autonomy in postwar modern dance is also a central point of inquiry in *A Game for Dancers*. I will suggest that dance's embodiment played a crucial role in how dancers and theorists conceived of autonomy and consequently of how that affected their ideas of dance's relationship to society.

In addition to looking to art historical debates to help unravel postwar dance modernism, I have turned to elements of Pierre Bourdieu's theory of practice. Bourdieu posits that social agents (be they individuals, groups, or institutions) tend to think, perceive, and act according to webs of durable, transposable, and generative dispositions that he calls "habitus" (1990b: 52–65, see also 1990a, 1993b, Bourdieu and Wacquant 1992). Habitus is inscribed in bodies and constituted in practice. Bourdieu sometimes explains habitus as "a feel for the game." Agents occupy positions within fields that they defend or contest. Bourdieu conceptualizes fields as social microcosms that have their own structures and laws (1993a: 181). At the same time that fields are governed by objective relationships, they are also governed by their own history, which agents both assimilate and respond to.

Bourdieu put his theory to work in numerous empirical studies, including that of the seminal period of nineteenth-century French modernism (1993a, 1996). While concurring with historians on the general outline of events that led to modernism, as a sociologist Bourdieu emphasizes the developing structures and processes of modernism rather than artists' careers or works, or the evolution of forms and styles. He particularly calls attention to the strategy artists developed to gain independence from the market, referring to it as "turning the economic world upside down." Instead of producing art to meet demand, artists claimed a disinterest in the market. They attempted to create an art that for them was more truthful because it was not corrupted by market concerns. At the same time, however, as Bourdieu points out, the artists were themselves bourgeois in the sense that they came from the bourgeois or petty bourgeois class. Bourdieu calls them a dominated fraction of the dominant class in that they had little power within their own milieu. However, as members of the dominant class their position toward that class was ambivalent. That is to say, even as they ridiculed it and battled against it, they could not completely sever their ties from it. Some part of them still yearned for acceptance. And some did, in fact, garner a certain recognition by standing against society and in time became known and successful because of the status they had earned through their opposition. As Bourdieu points out, their disinterest became understood and even respected, then became expected and eventually rewarded (1996: 61). As consecration occurred, a new generation of artists appeared to take the place of their elders and to renew their oppositional aims. This rejection of the past by young artists and their gradual assimilation into the mainstream became a hallmark of modernism. It ensured an opposition to the art establishment and a market-oriented society while at the same time providing an opportunity for success within that world. Thus, the very processes of modernism demonstrated an ambivalence that was similar to the artists' own class attachments.

Although one might argue that artists' work was simply co-opted by the ruling order, such a case becomes more difficult to make when at least some artists were rewarded with recognition and/or money. Wealth, of course, is relative. Few dancers who did not participate in the commercial theater or films became wealthy in the postwar period. Nonetheless, dancers such as Martha Graham, Alwin Nikolais, Paul Taylor, and Merce Cunningham did in time become consecrated and were rewarded with grants, honors, and other benefits of legitimation. Surrendering to commercial interests may have been reprehensible to vanguard artists, but few rejected the seduction of consecration, of becoming either "a modern classic" or, in today's advertising jargon, "a cutting-edge must-see."

Although artists attempted to free themselves from the market, it is important to note that, following Bourdieu, fields never gain complete autonomy from larger social forces; rather they are semiautonomous, having their own histories through which they refract outside influences (1993a: 176–183). This means that art cannot be viewed either as fully independent from, or as an unmediated reflection of, society at large. This idea is particularly important with respect to the Cold War. Although Cold War pressures were certainly felt in the dance field, how it responded was dependent on its own history and internal needs. I will argue that history and need were bound to modernism and its demand for a renewed vanguard.

Although Bourdieu's study of modernism deals only with nineteenth-century France, it is clear that modernist structures and practices endured into mid-twentieth-century America, where dancers assumed that a modernist vanguard existed and that it functioned much as outlined here. The enduring nature of modernist structures and processes helps explain why dancers did not question the rules they played by, and why they did not understand the co-opting of modernism itself. To this extent, what had begun as a response to a particular situation had become an unquestioned set of rules. Yet at the same time, core aspects of that predicament remained. Artists still sought independence from the market and from capitalist values while at the same time being inextricably tied to the social order they opposed. Walter Benjamin described this opposition from within as being like a secret agent in one's own camp. Speaking of Baudelaire he said, "Baudelaire was a secret agent, an agent of the secret discontent of his class with its own rule" (quoted in Marcuse 1978: 20). A key question in this study is whether it was possible to continue to carry out this subversive activity.

Modernist ambivalence showed itself in numerous ways during the postwar years, none more so than in the debates that circulated around issues of freedom. The rules of modernism required independence from the market, and modern dancers were obsessed with the dangers both of co-option and selling out. Yet they also argued endlessly over the need to enlarge audiences and gain a more secure financial footing. While they worried over economic freedom, dancers were also concerned with political freedom. Historian Eric Foner, in his study of American freedom (1998) points out how concepts of freedom shifted between the 1930s and the postwar years. During the '30s, he writes, freedom was reconceived from the old notion of freedom from government control to freedom from the worst vagaries of the market. This idea was manifested in the New Deal, which provided a larger role for government in guaranteeing the rights of labor and providing a social safety net in innovations ranging from old-age pensions to unemployment insurance. During the postwar years, Congress blocked expansion of New Deal policies and pushed through legislation such as the Taft-Hartley Act that weakened earlier gains made by labor. Historian James Patterson notes that "the 1940s, a time of significant expansion of governmental social welfare in many western European countries, in fact solidified the privatization of social welfare in the United States" (1996: 46). Paralleling shifts in attitudes toward social welfare were shifts in ideas of what constituted freedom. Once again liberation became defined as freedom from government control. The irony was that at the same time, federal institutions gained increasing power, particularly those that relied on surveillance, such as the FBI, the newly created CIA, and investigative arms of Congress—notably the House Un-American Activities Committee (HUAC). The dance field's responses to these contradictory pressures are a continuing theme throughout the book.

Yet to see modern dance only in terms of larger social issues would be to lose sight of its internal struggles. These centered on the need to renew itself in order to retain its vanguard position in the field. Until the 1950s, modern dance defined itself as a genre that sought to communicate emotional essences. To use John Martin's term, modern dance was "expressional" ([1939] 1965). Its techniques and point of view were based on those founded by the pioneers of the 1920s and '30s. For modern dance to achieve a renewal, somehow those original assumptions had to be challenged without also destroying modern dance itself. It is no secret that by the end of the 1950s "objectivist" modern dance was declared the new vanguard.[7] One of the questions I explore is why objectivism succeeded over competing strategies. Where did it go for support, and why was it embraced? Most important, was it able to fulfill any kind of oppositional role at that late stage of modernism? Was opposition still possible, or was it a kind of residual ghost that could be invoked but no longer manifested?

In considering the problems I have outlined on postwar dance, I have been particularly interested in the relationship between dancing and writing, in how discourse and practice were intertwined in a variety of ways and how that connection helped define what dance was at that moment. To begin with, many dancers in the 1940s and '50s explained themselves in print. They declared their positions in manifestos, they wrote at length of their aims, and they voiced their concerns. These declarations, made despite the fact that dance was considered transparent to any open minded spectator, demonstrates to what extent dancers sought to shape the reception of their work. Another manifestation of this intent was the ubiquitous lecture-demonstration, an integral part of modern dance practice. Most often dancers expressed their views in *Dance Observer*, which regularly ran their articles. Dancers' supporters also wrote articles. John Cage, Remy Charlip, and Carolyn Brown described Merce Cunningham's work processes; Murray Louis explained Alwin Nikolais's philosophy; David Vaughan defended James Waring's choreography. Dancers who could muster this kind of support had their work more widely discussed than those who could not, which aided their exposure, always an important aspect of the modernist process. This discourse was an essential part of definition that accompanied the dances themselves and established a way of seeing those dances.

Then there were the critics, the authoritative voices of interpretation and legitimation. It is striking how close the connections were between critics and dancers and how small the number of critics was, despite more extensive dance coverage compared with the 1930s.[8] This made the power relations between dancers and critics particularly complex. Few critics held the view, common today, that it was a conflict of interest to be personally involved with artists. Walter Terry of the *New York Herald Tribune* studied ballet and modern dance before becoming a journalist and was a personal friend of many of the most celebrated dancers. John Martin of the *New York Times*, although he professed a determination to keep his distance, had given lecture series at Bennington College in the 1930s, where he had close contact with many of the first-generation dancers and which in turn helped him develop his own dance theory. Edwin Denby danced in Europe before he began to write dance criticism for *Modern Music* and, as a replacement for Walter Terry, at the *New York Herald Tribune* during the war. More important, there is evidence that he helped write George Balanchine's articles for Anatole Chujoy's *Dance Encyclopedia* and perhaps others, as well (Mac-Kay 1986: 31).[9] Considering that Balanchine's English at the time was little more than functional, it wouldn't be surprising that he (or, more likely, Lincoln Kirstein) sought out a sympathetic critic to help express the choreographer's thoughts in written form.

Certainly the most powerful postwar critics were John Martin and Walter Terry, the only full-time dance critics for New York daily newspapers. *Dance Observer* never tired of lamenting that the dailies rarely covered concerts beyond Broadway or theaters close by, such as the Met and City Center. Although it is true that Martin and Terry were obliged to focus on productions in the Broadway area, they did manage to cover more concerts outside it than might be expected. Yet these limitations had their effect on where modern dance was performed. When possible, dancers tried to appear in Broadway theaters on the Sundays when regular Broadway shows were closed. Although a crushing expense and one that many could not afford, it was among the few ways modern dancers could be certain to be covered by the *Times* and *Herald Tribune*, as well as the other dailies.

There were three American magazines of the postwar period that were dedicated to dance: *Dance Observer, Dance Magazine*, and *Dance News*. During the 1940s, *Dance Observer* was the most important, serving as an arena for dancers and their supporters to air their views. *Dance Observer*, however, was not a neutral space in which debate took place. It had been started by Louis Horst in 1934 as a means of supporting modern dance in general and Martha Graham in particular. At the time Horst started the magazine he was Graham's music director, her mentor, and her lover. Although Horst and Graham's relationship changed over the years, *Dance Observer* continued to support modern dance as Horst and others had defined it in the 1930s. Considering that it was a part-time operation run out of various New York apartments, the magazine wielded a surprising amount of power within the New York dance field. The editors of *Dance Observer* were often aligned with dancers or were dancers themselves. Gertrude Lippincott, for example, was a dancer as well as an editor who wrote several defining articles in the 1940s. Doris Rudko, an associate editor in the 1950s, was a dancer and assistant to Horst in his composition classes.

Non-dancers associated with *Dance Observer* included Joseph Campbell, who was an editor for several years. In addition to being married to Jean Erdman, Campbell was a close friend of Martha Graham and a respected scholar of mythology who had considerable influence on modern dance in the 1940s. Horton Foote was also a *Dance Observer* editor in the 1940s. He arrived in New York with an acting career in mind and, in addition to the writing he did for *Dance Observer*, soon began to work with dancers who were attempting to develop dance-drama as a new form of modern dance. *Dance Observer* critics also wrote for other publications. Robert Sabin, a music as well as dance critic, wrote dance criticism for *Musical America* in addition to his work for *Dance Observer*. His sister, Evelyn, had been a member of Martha Graham's early group. George W. Beiswanger, a philosopher and aesthetician, was also the dance editor of *Theatre Arts* magazine. In addition, he wrote a monthly column on modern dance for *Dance News* beginning in 1943. He was married to dancer Barbara Page Beiswanger, who served for a time as a *Dance Observer* editor.

While *Dance Observer* dominated the dance press in the 1940s, *Dance Magazine* gradually came to the fore in the 1950s. *Dance Magazine* did not include the lively editorials and reader debate that characterized *Dance Observer* in the 1940s and that died in that magazine, as well, in the 1950s. *Dance Magazine* was particularly aimed at dance students, and included many articles on educational activities and columns on such topics as dancers' health. The magazine was also directed toward advocates of ballet as well as of modern dance. In all then, *Dance Magazine* was a less specialized publication than *Dance Observer,* and it rarely engaged in controversy or took strong stands on issues. Its very blandness, coupled with attention to advertising and sophisticated layout and photography, may have been major reasons it came to dominate the dance scene in the 1950s. During the 1940s, *Dance Magazine* ran few reviews, but that changed in 1952 when Doris Hering was hired as a permanent member of the staff.[10] During the 1950s, she covered an extraordinary number of concerts each month, nearly as many as *Dance Observer* with its half-dozen critics. However, this also meant that with rare exceptions *Dance Magazine* had only one critical voice for most of the postwar years. Although often more flexible than *Dance Observer* critics, Hering shared a similar expressional viewpoint.

The other dance publication of those years was *Dance News,* founded by Anatole Chujoy in 1942, which had a tabloid format and came out monthly. Chujoy, a native of Latvia who had received a law degree in St. Petersburg, was a knowledgeable devotée of ballet and particularly dedicated to Balanchine; he wrote the first book on the New York City Ballet when the company was barely eight years old. In 1951, Chujoy hired P. W. Manchester, an English critic, to help him cover the dance scene. Although *Dance News* always favored ballet, Manchester reviewed a number of modern dance performances. Like most of her colleagues, she viewed modern dance through expressional eyes. The other critic of note during that time was Margaret Lloyd. Lloyd wrote for the *Christian Science Monitor,* which was available throughout the country. But of particular importance was the book she published in 1949 entitled *The Borzoi Book of Modern Dance.* Like Sally Banes's *Terpsichore in Sneakers* several decades later, it went far in anointing certain modern dancers and in arranging them into categories of pioneers, which she called revolutionaries, and new leaders. Martin and Terry also wrote general dance history books that similarly accomplished the task of categorizing and consecrating various dancers.

Although most of the dance press supported an expressional aesthetic, toward the end of the 1950s, several critics appeared who advocated objectivism, among them David Vaughan, Selma Jeanne Cohen, and Jill Johnston. Denby must also be counted in this camp. Although he wrote little during the latter part of the 1950s, he had long supported Cunningham and had even longer been an advocate of objectivism through Balanchine's choreography. It should be added that although the dance press was predominantly male by a small majority, with the exception of Doris Hering at *Dance Magazine* the most powerful critics were men. *Dance Observer* usually had slightly more men than women critics, but those who wrote most often during the 1940s and '50s—Robert Sabin, George Beiswanger, and Nik Krevitsky—were men, and of course Louis Horst maintained control over the magazine as well as writing reviews.

One could find dance coverage in magazines outside the dance press, especially in *Theatre Arts* and *Musical America*. Occasionally more general interest magazines covered dance, such as *Time, Newsweek*, and *Life*. As would be expected in conservative magazines, these extolled ballet, most often in the form of attractive girls, while generally ridiculing modern dance. This kind of opposition was necessary if modern dance was to retain its vanguard status. To have been accepted by the popular press would have called into question the genre's rebelliousness and its position as the advanced guard of high-art dance.

As for race, the dance press (here referring to critics who specialized in reviewing high-art dance) was exclusively white. The general-readership black press rarely dealt with dance unless it was a concert by a major performer, such as Katherine Dunham, or Broadway musicals that featured African Americans, such as *Show Boat* or *Cabin in the Sky*. The *Amsterdam News, New York Age*, and *People's Voice* (all in New York), the *Afro-American* in Baltimore, the *Norfolk Journal and Guide* in Virginia, and the *Chicago Defender* occasionally covered high-art dance, but in the 1940s and '50s they focused the majority of their attention on Dunham and Pearl Primus. These publications were most interested in success gained and racial barriers broken by black performers rather than having any particular commitment to art forms that showed little interest in black venues or black audiences and in which black artists were not widely represented.

The leftist press that had been so active in the 1930s in reviews and discussions of dance slowly died as the Cold War set in. Most publications were gone by the end of the 1940s. *New Masses*, which had provided lively dance coverage for years, succumbed in 1948. Its last review, which appeared in March 1948, was of an Anna Sokolow concert by its long-standing dance critic Edna Ocko, named by Jerome Robbins as a communist in his appearance before the House Un-American Activities Committee in 1953.

In all, then, dance coverage was more extensive than it had been in the 1930s, but the group who actually did the writing was small, and the vast majority of critics honed to an expressional aesthetic. However, above and beyond defenses of one aesthetic or another, writers of all stripes were notable for their willingness to invoke elements of modernism that supported their cause while deemphasizing, eliding, or ignoring aspects that did not. In addition, they drew on modernism to support broader agendas related to race, class, and gender and to either disrupt or fortify the status quo. Thus modernism, although constituting what Michel Foucault would have called a discursive formation, was flexible in the sense that it was employed for a variety of purposes, many of which were at odds with each other.

Where, it might be asked, does this abundance of writing leave dancing? Does discourse simply write over bodily practice, or is there some less unequal relationship between them? That is a question that is confronted throughout *A Game for Dancers*. I treat dancing as a socially significant, embodied practice, and as such its analysis plays a central role in the book. In general I follow a tradition that is based on a notion of the "lived body," the idea that human beings and their consciousness are embedded in the body (Nettleton and Watson 1998: 9). This tradition is represented by such theories as Marcel Mauss's techniques of the body ([1934] 1973), Erving Goffman's concepts of bodily presentation and communication (1959, 1963, 1979), Bourdieu's idea of bodily intelligence, and Susan Foster's notion of the theorizing body. Mauss showed how common activities like walking and swimming are learned and culturally specific, while Goffman demonstrated how bodily movement is used to communicate meaning in everyday life. Bourdieu's ideas relate to his theory of practice, in which the body is necessarily key. He describes what he calls bodily "hexis," as "political mythology realized, em-bodied, turned into a permanent disposition, a durable way of standing, speaking, walking and thereby of feeling and thinking" (1990b: 69–70). Hexis is a crucial part of Bourdieu's concept of habitus, that is, dispositions that seem natural but are aspects of learned behavior that, in this case, literally embody social position and attitudes and that influence not only the thinking and feeling of the actor but of others. This view of bodily practice offers the possibility of dance not only ordering thoughts and feelings through choreography but through the very way in which bodies confront the world.

Bourdieu's notion of the social as bodily practice extends to a concept of theory as practice. He argues for there being a bodily intelligence that lies outside the realm of conscious reason. He writes: "There is a way of understanding which is altogether particular, and often forgotten in theories of intelligence; that which consists of understanding with one's body" (1990a: 166). Foster enlarges this idea when she contends that through corporeal intelligence dance cultivates a body that is capable of generating ideas as bodily writing (1995: 15). This is especially evident in an area of dance such as the rehearsal process, where give-and-take between choreographer and dancers forms the basis of dance production. In the course of this activity, movement queries are raised and solutions offered that produce particular bodies on the stage. That is to say, something like a physical conversation goes on between dancers and choreographer. The choreographer shows the dancers a movement segment, the dancers adjust the movement to their own bodies, frequently offering movement alternatives, which the choreographer accepts or changes again. The process continues in this way until the dance is finished. Foster notes that recent critical studies in dance have begun to treat bodies as not only written on but as capable of writing. Such bodies, endowed with agency, have the capacity to theorize. However, "the theoretical, rather than a contemplative stance achieved afterwards and at a distance, becomes embedded (embodied) within the practical decisions that build up, through the active engagement of bodies, any specific endeavor" (1995: 16). Although Foster's language is Foucaultian and therefore implies a discursive body, the process she describes is a material one of bodies informing bodies. Bourdieu would say these practical decisions, filtered through the habitus or bodily dispositions of the dancers and the dance, embody the social. The body generates ideas through habitus, that is, the ideas are socially constructed and limited.

For both Bourdieu and Foster, then, the body is capable of generating ideas or theorizing through practice rather than through conscious thought. This is not to say that dance has no relationship to language, that it is somehow ineffable, or that choreographers don't engage in rational deliberation. But it does mean that dance also functions in a way that is different from language and conscious thought. Bourdieu and Foster's concept of bodily theorizing is important for a social analysis of dance because it makes it possible to see the social not only in who sponsors the dance or views it, or what kinds of narrative themes dance embraces, or how dance might serve a broader social function, but to see the social as embedded in the practice of dance, in the dancers' comportment and the steps they do, in how the dance movement is assembled and how the dancers are arranged on the stage, and in how dancers are trained and developed. It is therefore dance as a social practice that informs the analysis of works in this book.

A Game for Dancers is organized around a set of problems and attempted solutions. It follows a more or less chronological path, although there is time overlap between chapters. However, although the book is to my knowledge the first to look closely at dance within the context of postwar modernism, it is in no way meant to be a survey of postwar dance. To begin with, it defines postwar in narrow terms as the years between 1945 and 1960 and does not stray far beyond those bounds. It also focuses exclusively on New York, both because of space constraints and because New York was the center of American dance at that time. Even so, many important choreographers who performed in New York are hardly mentioned, including Sybil Shearer, Katherine Litz, Erick Hawkins, Mary Anthony, Louis Johnson, Daniel Nagrin, and many others. A number of dancers who emerged in the latter part of the 1950s also have been omitted in favor of artists whose careers were more fully developed within the temporal framework of this study. The choreographers whose works were chosen for analysis were pertinent to the particular problems I outline. In some cases, too, they greatly influenced the generation of dancers who came after them, and their legacy is still discernable today. I hope that now that the postwar period has been opened to investigation, studies of the work of many choreographers active during those years will follow. Some, like Shearer, Litz, Hawkins, Johnson, Nagrin, and Anthony, are familiar names whose dances deserve more sustained analysis within the context of postwar concerns, while others, such as Iris Mabry and Ronne Aul, have been nearly forgotten but also warrant attention.

A brief note on the photographs that appear in the book: wherever possible I have used photographs of original casts and productions. However, that has not always been possible for a variety of reasons. When I have used photographs from later productions, I have noted it. Photographs are at best personal and artistic interpretations of what the photographer sees within the limitations of technical possibilities. The 1940s and '50s were still the days of light meters and flashes. Most photographs were not made on the stage during performances but in studios, and often in poses that had little to do with the choreography of the work being portrayed. Production shots were far less frequent than they are today, owing to cost and technical difficulties. The photographs included here are therefore meant simply to suggest dances rather than to be precise documents of them.

The first chapter of *A Game for Dancers* sets out the difficulties modern dancers faced at the conclusion of the war. It discusses their predicament within the dance field and examines their relationship to ideas that were circulating in the broader intellectual field. It also looks at one highly controversial solution to modern dance's problems, which involved what was seen as a new form of dance-drama.

Chapter 2 deals with ballet, a seemingly quixotic sidetrack in a book focusing on modern dance. But in Ballet Society, Lincoln Kirstein and George Balanchine challenged modern dance's vanguard position and sought to replace it with a modernist ballet. This was not the only competitor from the world of ballet; Antony Tudor took on many of the elements of modern dance, as did Agnes de Mille and Jerome Robbins to a lesser extent. However, Tudor, de Mille, and Robbins were aligned with expressional models, while Balanchine offered an aesthetic that was closer to an alternative to expressional dance. It should be added, though, that this alternative was in form alone, since ballet had no real oppositional aims to the status quo. In the 1950s, a young generation of modern dancers used elements of the kind of objectivist aesthetic Balanchine advocated to develop a new modern dance vanguard.

The third chapter of the book looks closely at the dance theory of three men—John Martin, Edwin Denby, and John Cage—all of whom influenced the dance field in the postwar years. Although they were at odds on specific issues, I point out their shared modernism and how they theorized an authentic dance as a solution to modernity's technological and bureaucratized rationalization.

Chapter 4 explores the relationship of dance modernism to issues of community and difference in light of consensus ideology. In some instances choreographers from minority constituencies attempted to define communities distinct from a dominant culture. This chapter looks at Jewish dancers who sought to essentialize their identity in the wake of the Holocaust and the founding of the state of Israel. In trying to deal with difference, dancers put pressure on the boundaries of modernism and at the same time demonstrated modernism's limits. This chapter also examines works by Anna Sokolow that called attention to a society in which collective life had disintegrated. In carrying out this task she introduced innovative approaches to form that allowed her to encompass social critique through non-dance movement associated with neurosis and madness. Continuing an examination of community and difference, chapters 5 and 6 focus on African-American choreographers who saw modernism's demand for universal experience used against them in contradictory ways, even as they gained greater access to the modern dance genre.

The final chapter of *A Game for Dancers* considers objectivist modern dance, focusing on the work of Alwin Nikolais and Merce Cunningham. I contend that at least in these two cases objectivist choreographers attempted to tie formal innovation to elements of resistance, resistance that went unrecognized.

At this point one might well ask why it is of interest to investigate modern dance at the end of a period of pioneering optimism and growth, a time when, as a genre in transition, it presented more problems than solutions and when it was beset by doubt and struggle. The answer is the obvious one—that the problems of the postwar years are still with us, in fact exist with particular force today. Not only are we experiencing an oppressive conservatism and attacks on civil liberties that recall the postwar era, we also face the ever increasing power of global capitalism, raising questions of resistance and how it is expressed. Postwar dancers faced an increasingly centralized and oppressive power in a variety of ways, and there are lessons to be learned in the complexity and difficulty of their predicament, as well as in the solutions they offered.

A GAME FOR DANCERS

THE TROUBLE WITH MODERN DANCE

Horton Foote wrote in October 1944 that modern dance had reached a crisis in its development.[1] The twenty-eight-year-old *Dance Observer* editor noted that modern dancers had begun by fighting for aesthetic goals. Now, he said, they faced another kind of battle, one against commercial forces that threatened their artistic independence. "Every day on the Theatrical Page we read of one more well-known dancer going to Broadway or Hollywood. It has become a mammoth exodus, a giant trend" (1944: 98). Foote warned that modern dance consorted with show business at its peril. The economic bottom line was all that mattered in the commercial theater, killing "individualism of taste, daring, experiment." Quoting novelist James Farrell, he continued: "This is a culture which does not serve men; on the contrary it makes men its servants" (ibid.).

Certainly Foote was right in saying that the borders between modern dance and the commercial theater were porous.[2] Although dancers had long supplemented their small earnings by performing in commercial shows and nightclubs, commercial work for high-art dancers increased markedly after the war. This occurred primarily because a ballet-based dance began to compete with tap as the major form on Broadway and in films, giving modern and ballet dancers new opportunities to work in shows and Hollywood (Moulton 1957; Feuer 1993; Steyn 1997).[3] George Balanchine had used ballet in the shows he did for Broadway and films in the 1930s and early 1940s, but it was Agnes de Mille who was credited with sealing ballet technique for Broadway musicals in 1943 with *Oklahoma!* By 1945, ballets and ballet-based dance were part of many Broadway musicals. The majority of these dances were not done on pointe and could be managed well by modern dancers, who were also more available than ballet dancers because they seldom worked under extended contract obligations. Also, several major modern dance choreographers turned to the commercial theater during the 1940s, most notably Hanya Holm and Helen Tamiris. Balanchine also continued commercial work into the 1940s, and Jerome Robbins began his Broadway career in 1944 with *On the Town*. Ballet and modern choreographers who were doing Broadway shows often engaged high-art dancers. Balanchine and Katherine Dunham joined forces for *Cabin in the Sky* in 1940; Agnes de Mille hired Erick Hawkins to dance in *Oklahoma!* (1943); Helen Tamiris used Daniel Nagrin in most of her shows and gave Pearl Primus a starring dance role in *Show Boat* (1946), which also included Talley Beatty and Joe Nash in the cast; and there were many others.

Films, too, began to integrate ballet into musicals more thoroughly than they had earlier. Gene Kelly and Fred Astaire added ballet to their films, bringing to prominence a number of ballet-trained dancers, including Vera Ellen, Cyd Charisse, Taina Elg, and Leslie Caron. Both modern and ballet dancers were hired to perform in the new ballet-oriented films that ranged from *Seven Brides for Seven Brothers* (1954) to Kelly and Astaire hits such as *An American in Paris* (1951) and *Silk Stockings* (1957). *The Red Shoes*, which was released in 1948, also fed the taste for ballet in films. In addition, high-art dance was appealing to television, which was just beginning to emerge as a major commercial genre. Dancers appeared primarily on variety shows to add a touch of sophistication to the various acts. Ballet dancers were far more in demand than modern dancers since they were what most of the general public thought of as high-art performers; they were also more glamorous and could convincingly be billed as stars. Modern dancers, at least to judge from announcements in the press, tended to be seen most often on religious programs where perhaps their seriousness of purpose and relative austerity were not considered a deterrence to audiences. It is significant, too, that after the war the dance press routinely covered Broadway shows, films, and television appearances by high-art dancers. *Dance News*, Anatole Chujoy's monthly, not only reviewed these events but included news and gossip, especially about Broadway shows.

The symbiotic relationship between high-art dance and the market was actually built into dance practice, since it enabled many dancers to have high-art careers. If dancers did not work in the commercial theater, their only means of support outside of performances was teaching, often sporadic and not well paid, or taking menial jobs such as waiting tables, which would not unduly interfere with rehearsals and perform-ances.[4] Commercial employment allowed dancers to continue to per-form and choreograph high-art work even as it enticed some of them away permanently.

Considering the amount of traffic that circulated between high-art and commercial forms, much of it advantageous to high art, one might ask why Foote was so alarmed. There were several reasons. To begin with, as has been pointed out, modern dance's position vis-à-vis the dominant order was always ambivalent, but by the mid-1940s the bal-ance had started to tip. As Foote noted, the lure of entertainment was killing the spirit of experiment that was necessary for modern dance to remain a modernist form. This in turn jeopardized the genre's position in the field. However, the fear that commercialism threatened high art was also part of a larger phenomenon that obsessed artists and intellec-tuals in the postwar years. Commercialism was an element of ration-alization, a central issue of modernity. Early in the twentieth century, Max Weber had predicted that the use of rational calculation by busi-ness, the state, science, and technology, would increasingly infiltrate all aspects of life (Weber [1904–5] 1999; 1946; 1978). Rationalizing processes were spurred by capitalism and by state, military, and corpo-rate bureaucracies. Although art was not Weber's central concern, his theory posited that rationalizing processes penetrated everywhere, so art, too, was at risk. Weber himself wrote an essay, published shortly after his death in 1920, showing how the development of the piano, its music, and practice were directly related to market forces and bourgeois domestic demand (1978: 378–382).

In the 1940s, artists and intellectuals became particularly concerned with the market in terms of the relationship of high art to mass culture. Among the early indications of this was Greenberg's "Avant Garde and Kitsch," published in 1939 in *Partisan Review* ([1939] 1986a: 5–22). In his essay Greenberg not only defined the goals of what he called the avant-garde, he examined its opposite, kitsch. He defined kitsch as the mass-produced imitation of high art consumed by mass society. Con-trolled by market demand and produced for the many wage-earners needed for the capitalist system, kitsch was meant to provide easily di-gestible distraction. Where genuine art demanded a viewer's reflection to make its effects, kitsch had effects built into it, a message, as it were, ready-made and controlled by capitalist interests. Greenberg's idea of mass culture would soon receive more thorough analysis in Theodor

Adorno and Max Horkheimer's "The Culture Industry" ([1944] 1979), written during the war while the two members of the Frankfurt School were living in New York. For Adorno and Horkheimer the culture industry controlled the mass production of products, including entertainment, and it in turn was controlled by those who had the greatest economic hold on society (ibid.: 121). As the power of the culture industry grew, it ever more fully produced consumers' needs, controlling and disciplining them (ibid.: 144).

Although for Adorno and Horkheimer there was little way to escape the grip of the culture industry, Greenberg was somewhat less pessimistic. Opposing kitsch or mass culture was the avant-garde, the segment of the art field least subject to the market. As indicated in my introduction, Greenberg saw the task of the avant-garde as one of protecting genuine culture in the face of overwhelming rationalization and capitalist decline. However, Greenberg argued that once the avant-garde had defined itself in opposition to bourgeois culture, it abandoned politics for the rarefied atmosphere of pure art. Significantly, he felt the primary function of the avant-garde "was not to 'experiment,' but to find a path along which it would be possible to keep culture *moving* in the midst of ideological confusion and violence" ([1939] 1986a: 8). This would be art's position until the triumph of socialism.

Foote, in his *Dance Observer* article, echoed Greenberg's position on high art's relationship to mass culture. Represented by Broadway and Hollywood, mass culture was a threat to the authentic art of a modern dance, which Foote characterized as individual, daring, and experimental. Foote felt the need to reiterate modernist principles at a moment when high-art dance was particularly vulnerable to commercial interests. However, he did not advocate that artists stop experimenting, turn their backs on society, and assume the defensive position Greenberg called for. On the contrary, it was experiment that needed protection and the answer was not to go into hiding but to fight back. He called for artists from all fields—he mentions Tennessee Williams, Leonard Bernstein, and Katherine Anne Porter, among them—to band together to demand they be given the means to do their work. "Together we must force our society to recognize our intrinsic worth as builders of a better and more healthy future as assets of the national life just as the scientist, the university or the scholar" (1944: 98). Foote did not specify how society would compensate the artist. However, he did say that if it was not possible in the present system, "then our energies must go to rid ourselves of this system" (ibid.: 99). Seven months after his initial article, Foote wrote another in which he clarified his thinking. He now referred to a "Society of Artists," an association that would not remove the artist further from society, he said, "but would more securely make him a part of it" (1945b: 56). This stake in society would come in the form of government subsidies to artists.

Foote's two articles are a bridge between thinking derived from New Deal principles of the 1930s and what would become dominant postwar ideas. His articles were written in 1944 and 1945, as the war turned definitively in favor of the allies and the United States prepared for world leadership once peace was achieved. New Deal thinking was still common currency, although in fact Congress had stalled much legislation after Roosevelt's reelection in 1936. Funding for the Federal Theater Project ceased in 1939, and the Works Progress Administration as a whole was formally disbanded in 1942. Although President Truman proposed numerous social welfare projects in his first budget, he was able to carry out few of them in the face of determined congressional opposition. Arts subsidies were not even among his proposals. The idea of banding together in a community to change society, so much a part of 1930s strategies, would seem increasingly impossible as the postwar period took hold. Dancers became distrustful of any idea of government support, seeing it as compromising their independence. Even in 1944, Foote's ideas of communal action and government support were being consigned to the past. However, his concern with the problem of a rationalized art and the need for a modernist vanguard to stand against mass culture were sure signs of the future.

As early as 1946, an article appeared in *Dance Observer* advocating an approach different from Foote's to the problem of modern dance's relationship to commercialism. It was written by another editor, Gertrude Lippincott, who was a dancer and educator. Lippincott's article, titled "Pilgrim's Way" (1946: 84–85), typified the thinking that would come to dominate during the postwar period, although the article was controversial at the time.

Beginning, like Foote, by defining modern dance's predicament, she compared the artist to a pilgrim who is constantly tempted by commercialism to win success. She said that Broadway choreographers had incorporated modern and ballet techniques into their dances, and in order to attract audiences, modern dancers had increasingly studied ballet and added its virtuosic elements to their own techniques. Modern dancers were substituting virtuosity for experimentation and invention in their dances, and they were making their works less complex and easier to understand in order to appeal to the uninitiated. She reminded readers that the aim of modern dance was not to entertain.

She then went on to say, in opposition to Foote, that politics had no place in modern dance because when it did, dance ceased to be art and became propaganda. "The arts have a life of their own, and although they are sometimes influenced by existing social and political happenings, more often they are not" (1946: 84). Art deals with timeless and universal themes, not local, transient ones, she said. Lippincott ended by stating that the vanguard artist "cannot expect easy popularity unless he is willing to lower his standards by becoming 'chi-chi,' Broadway-theatrical, or downright cheap" (1946: 85). Then, reiterating modernist rules, she stressed that the artist must accept the fact that audiences would remain limited because only a small number of people were able to understand "so strenuous an artistic experience" (ibid.).

Much of Lippincott's article dealt with the threat of mass culture as a corrupting influence on authentic art. Broadway had stolen modern and ballet techniques, and modern dancers had been lured into adding entertainment elements to their work in order to profit from larger audiences. As such, she echoed Greenberg's warnings on kitsch and Adorno and Horkheimer's views on the insidious power of the culture industry. She also came down on the side of Greenberg when she asserted that art must distance itself from politics in order to retain its independence from the field of power. In her view, political subject matter compromised the autonomy of modern dance because it placed the dancer under the control of external ideological forces. For Lippincott, politics and commercialism both threatened the artist's freedom to work according to her own conscience. Artists could not afford to turn their art into propaganda anymore than they could afford to bow to the whims of current fashion. She concluded, "The way of the artist, in our western society, is a lonely one. He must remain primarily an individual creator, although he works under the shadow of current social events and artistic trends" (1946: 85).

Lippincott's modern dancer was very different from Foote's. Gone was Foote's community and in its place was the lone artist, who separated herself from direct social influence in order to remain independent and true to herself. Like Foote, she did not imagine the artist giving up experiment, but she restricted it to a timeless world of abstraction.

After the war, few dancers took on Foote's idea of a community of artists demanding government subsidies. It was clear that government support was unlikely and that the kind of political action Foote advocated would fall on deaf ears. But in 1946, some dancers still argued that art could and should have a political purpose, at least implying that it was possible to change institutions and policies. Lippincott's article received responses in this vein from Mary Phelps (1946b: 110–111) and Elizabeth Wiggins (1946: 125). Phelps, who was also an editor for *Dance Observer*, argued that art and politics had long been at home together, and listed a number of artists from Shakespeare to Beethoven whose works were political in nature. The artist who shunned politics, she argued, gave up the chance of influencing society: "To expose falsity and meanness on whatever ground; to confront the terror; to vindicate a truth and see it grow; to make fun; to call for hope and pay with joy that comes to no one alone—these are in the power of art" (1946b: 110).

Although some, like Phelps and Wiggins, argued for a political dance, dancers and their supporters increasingly tended to center the debate on issues of accessibility versus vanguardism rather than a political versus apolitical binary. The question they most often argued was, should dancers try to make their work more accessible to a mass audience or preserve their modernism by producing experimental work for themselves and their peers? When the notion of politics appeared, it was pushed onto the side of accessibility. For example, dancer Joseph Gifford, in answering an article written by another dancer, Juana de Laban, characterized socially conscious dance in this way. In her original article, Laban had deplored modern dance's emphasis on "the intellectual and the abstract" and called for a more dramatic form that would draw on American subject matter and rhythms and thereby appeal to wider audiences (Laban 1945: 55–56). In his excoriating response, Gifford said he found in statements such as hers "an almost frightening emphasis on such things as audience acceptance" (Gifford 1945: 66). The real problem with modern dance, he said, was not lack of accessibility but that youngsters were copying the innovations of their elders, whose work had already been absorbed into the mainstream. Shaping a dance to conform to audience expectations, he said,

> created the almost ludicrous examples of "folksy" art that is neither of the folk nor art. It created the bastard "blues-y" art, wherein the dancer develops one superficial aspect of the people called, The Negro, and feels

he or she is prancing in the democratic rhythm of our times. And, more recently, it has created the amusing examples of Modern Dance being interpolated into Broadway musical comedy—its note up high but one eye always looking down to make sure that its feet stay clear of the producer's toes. (1945: 66)

For Gifford, trying to identify with or defend "the people" was not a political act but merely one more example of attempting to be accessible, which he equated with commercialism. In addition, Gifford said, modern dance's acceptance by "liberal" political groups meant that it was now capable of being used as a facile propaganda tool. Although Gifford didn't define what he meant by liberal, one assumes it was a euphemism for leftist groups and the Communist Party in particular. Gifford argued that serious modern dancers must reject all outside influence and look to themselves when making dances. Gifford saw the artist, as would Lippincott, as a lone soldier battling against institutionalized forces. However, it should be mentioned that unlike Greenberg, neither Gifford nor Lippincott suggested that the task of modern art was simply to guard the fortress of civilization against the philistines. Experiment, as they both stated, was necessary to guarantee art's independence. The kind of defensive position advanced by Greenberg would merely reinforce the status quo, and as such signify defeat.

Another important theme that Gifford touched on was that of nationalism versus internationalism. Gifford was contemptuous of Laban's suggestion that dancers draw on American sources, which he viewed as a form of nationalism. In the 1930s, high-art dancers had turned to American subject matter to attempt to establish an American artistic identity. Humphrey's *The Shakers* (1931), Graham's *Frontier* (1935) and *American Document* (1938), Tamiris's *Negro Spirituals* (1928–1944), and numerous other works exemplified dancers' interest in American sources. During the war such subject matter reinforced American patriotism and continued to be popular. However, once the war was over, this view changed markedly in most quarters. The notable exceptions were the remaining leftist dancers, many of whom were associated with the New Dance Group and were the ones who came under attack from Gifford.

The shift toward internationalism was at first linked to antifascism. During the 1930s and war years, American newspapers had run numerous articles and cartoons that depicted the Nazis as destroyers of

Western art and culture. This was particularly the case in the face of the "degenerate" art exhibition of 1937 (which toured Germany and Austria for four years) and the influx of European vanguard artists into the United States (Hoelterhoff 1975; Hinz 1979; Barron 1991). However, as Serge Guilbaut has pointed out, the fascists were not destroying all Western art, just modernist art, and so as an enemy of fascism the United States was also obliged to defend modernism. In addition, Guilbaut asserts that the United States, now a world leader, needed an art that took a comparable leadership position (Guilbaut 1983: 54–55; see also Saunders 1999; Caute 2003). As such, the old national themes and motifs that had been so important in defining an American art were no longer acceptable. Not only were they too provincial, they were considered too close to the kind of nationalism that had characterized Nazi Germany. Now an international viewpoint was called for that could play on a world stage. Typical of this postwar stance was an article written by art historian H. W. Janson in the *Magazine of Art*, which attacked the American regionalist artists, who during the Depression had gained fame painting scenes of American life in a social realist manner.[5] Janson accused these painters of being dangerous nationalists, then went on to say:

> The great artists of the past and present, no less than the great philosophers and scientists, have always conceived of themselves as servants of mankind, rather than of particular nations or groups. Their work has been based upon the acceptance of ethical and religious values embracing all members of the human family, regardless of origin or nationality. Nationalism cannot possibly take the place of this allegiance to humanity as a whole. Wherever such a substitution is attempted, whether by force or by guile, it will inevitably produce the same sad results. (1946:186)

In Janson's article, regionalism, with its focus on American themes, became associated with nationalism and fascism and by extension with propaganda and the manipulation of mass society.

Although Gifford did not tie Americana dance works to fascism, he did speak of their easy use as a propaganda tool. In this case the villain was the political left, which would soon enough be subject to widespread attack. During the early postwar years it was common to conflate fascist and communist aims (Adler and Paterson 1970). As Janson connected regionalist art with nationalism and easily manipulated mass society, so Gifford made similar connections among Americana dance, nationalism, leftist political propaganda, and the culture industry. For Gifford, it was the dancer's task to keep art independent of both political and commercial appropriation.

Another dance commentator, Margaret Lloyd, also linked internationalism and modern dance in a revealing fashion when she wrote that American modern dance "becomes more international, with no loss of patriotism, as it becomes more liberal, as it leaves the confines of early modernism, narrow national and class consciousness, for the timeless, universal realm of dance, and the one world of people" (1949: 186). Lloyd's remarks, published in 1949, stressed the idea that modern dance had been narrow in focusing on national and class identity. She included in this narrow category the socially conscious work of dancers such as Sophie Maslow and Jane Dudley. In place of these interests, Lloyd called for a dance that would be timeless and universal. She attached the word "liberal" to such a dance, presumably because it reflected "the one world of people." Thus, she linked internationalism, modernism, and liberalism. She also equated nation and class with the specific, and internationalism with the universal, which accorded with American postwar aspirations.

During 1945 and 1946, President Truman had not yet solidified his foreign policy; in that time, as has been seen in the responses to Lippincott's article, at least some dancers were still able to conceive of an art that had a direct relationship to politics. But by mid-1947, the Truman administration had put a policy of communist containment into place, and the Cold War had hardened into reality (Lacey 1990; Hamby 1976; Whitfield 1991; Chafe 1999). It put the United States once again on a wartime track, and with it came an increased centralization of power. The FBI greatly expanded its sphere of influence in the immediate postwar years. Truman feared J. Edgar Hoover and was unable to do much to curb him. The Republicans took both houses of Congress in the 1946 elections, bringing Richard Nixon and Joseph McCarthy to Washington and helping to set the stage for the anticommunist witch hunts that would soon follow. By mid-1946, a number of leftists had joined the anticommunist ranks, including prominent union leaders and such intellectuals as Irving Howe and Arthur Schlesinger Jr. Early

1947 brought Executive Order 9,835, intended to keep the civil service free of "disloyal" elements. It outlawed, among other things, subversive organizations or those associating with them, without specifying which organizations fell into this category.

Several liberal publications protested vigorously: an unsigned editorial in the *Nation* stated that Truman's executive order "reflects a fear of totalitarian communism that is driving us to use totalitarian methods" ("The Shape of Things" 1947: 346). Further stories in the *Nation* bore such titles as "Liberals Beware!" (5 April 1947), "Washington Witch-Hunt" (5 April 1947), and "Warning All Scientists" (2 August 1947), which told of the dangerous turn taken in Washington and the victims of various purges. The cover of the 11 August 1947 issue of the *New Republic* had SUBVERSIVE! stamped across such names as Thomas Jefferson, Abraham Lincoln, and Oliver Wendell Holmes. The cover headlined a report on the state of civil liberties in the country. Numerous articles followed, among them "Cry Shame . . . !" by Martha Gellhorn, which chronicled the goings-on at HUAC (1947), and "Guilt by Gossip" by Daniel S. Gillmor (1948), which deplored the witch hunting and atmosphere of paranoia that had swept far beyond the borders of Washington. Considering the political climate in the late 1940s, it is not surprising that dancers were less optimistic than they had been even a year or two earlier about art's ability to bring about social and political change, at least through confrontation.

Another event that influenced dancers' views of a political art came in early 1948 when word reached the United States that officials of the Soviet Music Union had denounced Russia's most respected composers, charging them with formalist tendencies. Among those named were Dimitri Shostakovich, Aram Khatchaturian, and Sergei Prokofiev. Alexander Werth, reporting in the *Nation*, quoted a Music Union official who had defined formalism as "the lack of ideas, lack of content, emptiness of form, without reference to reality" (1948b: 209). In this report and an earlier one on 10 April (1948a: 393), Werth noted that the Soviets wished to have an art that was connected to real life, that was clearly understandable to the masses, and that was in no way "pure" or abstract, qualities that appealed only to aesthetic elites (ibid.). The answer was socialist realism, which would be the only sanctioned approach to art behind the Iron Curtain. This attack on formalism was, by extension, an attack on the United States, where modernism (construed in Soviet terms as formalism) had been defended since the rise of fascism and where New York was in the process of becoming the capital of the modernist advanced guard.

The politicizing of modernism in this manner was another element of the escalating Cold War, and a number of artists quickly rose to defend the American Way. Gertrude Lippincott wrote an editorial for *Dance Observer* entitled "Freedom and the Arts" (1948: 44–45) that encapsulated this viewpoint. She began by saying that dancers had long worked to promote the idea of arts subsidies and had looked with envy on other countries that provided them. Many were stunned, she said, when the fascists had taken over the arts in Germany and Italy and used artistic organizations and activities for propaganda purposes. Americans had hoped for more from the Soviet Union, but that hope had been shaken in 1936 when Shostakovitch had been censured. Now all remaining hope had vanished with news of the newest denunciations. Lippincott disingenuously found it difficult to understand how political characteristics could be ascribed to art in the first place, when true art could not be political because "it transcends national and political boundaries and appeals to all mankind" (ibid.: 45). Lippincott was most shocked by the Soviet composers' public confessions and their recanting of modernism. Since they were not allowed to leave Russia, they were, she said, virtually artist-slaves who functioned at the will of their masters. Then she argued that although American artists were ignored, they were free to produce what they wished. Their neglect "may be a blessing in disguise, because no artist can ever serve any master other than himself" (ibid.).

Lippincott's editorial accomplished several things. It summarized the modernist viewpoint that authentic art dealt with essences and universals that appealed to all humanity rather than being tied to specific ideas and situations; it presented the official American position that Western art was free and Soviet art was not; and it made the case that American neglect of the arts was actually positive. American dance, then, should be nonpolitical in content to show that it was free, and it should not demand political action to ensure its place in the social sphere because neglect also kept it free. That a dance that did not deal directly with political subject matter could in itself indicate a political position, that it supported Washington's desire for a critique-free art and had the added bonus of asking nothing of Washington in return, escaped her notice. In their concern to be free from control, dancers in the postwar years rarely asked what they were free to do.

The result of all these pressures on dance from both the domestic and international arenas was that the political element of the debates surrounding commerce and artistic freedom almost disappeared by mid-1948. However, while external conditions contributed to dancers' sense of powerlessness to effect social change through overt confrontation, and an acceleration of the Cold War further froze discussion of a political dance, the internal problem of modern dance's institutionalization remained an immediate, crucial issue, and the argument over how best to ensure modern dance's future continued even as talk of the pros and cons of a political dance faded.

One of the major points of Gifford's 1945 article was that in order to be more accessible, young modern dancers were not revolting against the older generation but rather were imitating it. Gifford differentiated between what I call the intergeneration of dancers, such as Maslow, Sokolow, and Dudley, who began their careers in the 1930s and continued to do socially conscious work (some of these dancers will be discussed in chapter 4), and a second generation of artists who came of age in the mid-1940s. The evidence suggests that Gifford was correct in his concerns about this younger generation and that much of the imitation he perceived in their work was related to the direction in which Martha Graham was moving during the 1940s. Graham, the most consecrated of the first-generation pioneers, was turning toward an ever more theatricalized dance. Her concerts now included sophisticated lighting, costumes, and props, as well as orchestral music rather than the piano and percussion scores of her early career. As for her dances, they had begun to resemble ballets in their length and complexity. This trend stood in marked contrast to her early dances, which had been notable for their austerity. Now Graham even arranged her programs like ballet performances, usually with three works to a program separated by two intermissions. In addition, she made her technique more complex and virtuosic by adding balletic elements to it. She also began to tell stories in some of her dances. This trend led to the descriptive title "the theater of Martha Graham," implying her work was less about dance than it had been in the past and more about an integrated theatrical experience.

Although Graham's move into theater was the result of a number of factors, it is worth noting that she, like so many other modern dancers, wrestled with the problem of vanguardism and accessibility. An unsigned

"The Theater of Martha Graham," a photograph taken in the early 1960s of Martha Graham as Jocasta, Bertram Ross as Oedipus, and company in Graham's *Night Journey* (1947). *Photo: © Martha Swope.*

Newsweek article published on 17 January 1944 under the headline "Doom Eager Dance" mentioned that three years earlier Graham had promised a new kind of work that would differ from the more austere dance she had offered in the 1930s. The magazine quoted her as saying, "We must win back our audiences. We have alienated them through grimness of theme and a non-theatrical approach. . . . We must prove that our theatre pieces have color, warmth, and entertainment value" ("Doom Eager Dance" 1944: 85). Yet while Graham was taking a stand for greater accessibility, she continued to draw on her status as a vanguard rebel, a status she had earned from her years of struggle and that had led to her consecration. For example, she was quoted in a *Life* magazine article of 17 March 1947 as saying: "Some people like me, some don't. Many consider me a menace" ("She Is Priestess of Intellectual Ballet" 1947: 101). Although audiences were likely to find Graham far less a threat to society than they had a decade earlier, a hint of danger could be scintillating.

Among the changes that Graham helped bring to modern dance in the 1940s was a new attitude toward ballet technique. Ballet had hitherto been anathema to modern dance since it was assumed to be at odds with modern dance's mission of creating innovative forms that could confront the issues of modernity. When Graham began to develop her modern dance in the 1920s, she, like the other first-generation dancers, conceived her own technique in opposition to ballet. But in 1938, when Erick Hawkins joined her company, he arrived as a ballet dancer, having come from Lincoln Kirstein's Ballet Caravan. In the early 1940s he taught ballet classes at the Graham studio, and in time Graham's dancers noticed that her technique was becoming more balletic. Jean Erdman spoke of the addition of new movements that used ballet turnout and an immobile torso, particularly in turns. These, she said, presented problems of balancing and centering without impulse from the center, which were difficult for the dancers (Horosko 1991: 78–79; see also Helpern 1991: 22). When Merce Cunningham joined the company in 1939 as the second male, Graham suggested he take ballet classes at the School of American Ballet, and Cunningham did. Other dancers also took ballet classes outside the Graham school on their own.

In the 1940s, Graham also began to hire dancers with bodies that were lighter and more balletic than the dancers she had employed in the 1930s, such as Sophie Maslow, Anna Sokolow, and Jane Dudley. Mark Ryder noted the difference these new bodies made in the dance movement when he returned from the war to rejoin the company. "What had been slow and powerful became lightning fast, like quicksilver," he said (Horosko 1991: 81). Critic Margaret Lloyd agreed. She contrasted the 1936 performances of *Primitive Mysteries* to the 1947 revival. In the '30s, she said, dancers like Dudley, Maslow, Sokolow, May O'Donnell, and Gertrude Shurr "imparted the virility, or 'guttiness,' the work demands" (1949: 53). Now, she said, the piece was not nearly so well performed, in part because the girls were "thin." "They are young and attractive; they are so light they could be mistaken for ballet dancers" (ibid.). In Lloyd's view, they lacked "the full-blooded vigor of the concert group of the mid-thirties" (ibid.). These new dancers not only gave the company a lighter, more balletic appearance, their increased range of movement made it possible for Graham to add more complexity and technical virtuosity to the dances. Graham may well have seen this as a way of enriching her choreography, but at the same time it also allayed some of the grimness of modern dance she had spoken of in the

Newsweek article, and of adding "entertainment value." Although Graham was not alone in absorbing ballet elements into her technique, she was a leader in that trend.

The majority of young dancers who came of age in the mid-1940s did not question Graham's move toward ballet or any of the other elements of her new theatricalism. Young dancers generally had no access to major theaters, and they had no funding to mount complicated productions. They did not have companies, but only small, unpaid groups that met occasionally to put together a concert. Yet instead of turning these apparent drawbacks to advantages by casting themselves as purists and the older generation as sell-outs to "bourgeois" demands for entertainment, something like the opposite occurred; they attempted to compete with the new theatricalism.

First, they expanded technique by insisting on the right to study and use any technical language that suited a particular dance, including ballet. Jean Erdman, who danced in the Graham company from 1938 to 1942 before becoming a choreographer in her own right, reflected the general trend among second-generation dancers when she wrote in 1948 that, as opposed to their elders, young choreographers were less interested in forming personal vocabularies and styles. Nor did they want to devote themselves to only one modern dance technique. Rather, they preferred to study a variety of techniques, including ballet and ethnic forms, and to draw on whatever sort of movement was appropriate for each individual dance (Erdman 1948: 40–41).[6] By using varied techniques, the young modern dancer sought to depersonalize and objectify what for the first generation had been a highly personal movement language. This was a significant shift in goals from that of prewar dancers.

Critics contributed to this shift by attacking dancers for transferring their personal styles to movement for groups. This transfer occurred despite the fact that the dancers themselves were attempting to depersonalize their dance vocabularies. Nik Krevitsky's review of Iris Mabry's *Counterpoint* was typical: "It is nothing more than an extension of Miss Mabry's personal style, which doesn't fit a group of sixteen dancers. Movements and gestures which become her, just don't suit others" (1948: 57). And Mary Phelps ended her review of a Valerie Bettis concert with: "So with Valerie Bettis' problem of extending her talent from the solo to the group field we have about the status quo ante. Group work cannot be gone at as multiplication of the soloist's impulse. It has to be done by true addition: new substance of movement when more figures are concerned" (1948: 19). These reviews illustrate the confusion of goals that was evident within modern dance. Modern dance demanded new forms that in the past had been developed through personal vocabularies and styles, but now dancers were criticized for not being able to depersonalize movement to fit more ambitious group works. At the same time, dancers were also attempting to objectify their movement.

In addition, many of the second-generation dancers studied composition with Louis Horst or Doris Humphrey. Although the courses gave the dancers structural principles with which to work that the pioneering generation of the 1930s had needed to develop for themselves, they also tended to stifle experimentation. No longer did the student have to ask what an appropriate subject or form might be; she was taught it. Horst's classes in particular stressed specific kinds of dances. Many of the solos that were performed at concerts resembled dances composed for Horst's courses in preclassic and modern forms—galliards and minuets, primitive and medieval studies. Solos in this vein were often first cousins of classroom exercises, a situation that critics increasingly complained of as the postwar years wore on. One has only to look at *Transformations of Medusa* (1942), an early dance by Jean Erdman, to understand the degree to which academic forms found their way onto the stage. Erdman has said that the three-part solo was inspired by her classes with Horst. This dance has the static quality of a well-executed exercise in Horst's archaic form.

In a review of the field in 1953, John Martin wrote of the results of the dangerous trend toward accessibility that Gifford had warned of ten years earlier. Martin noted that modern dance "has forgotten its reason for being in its efforts to take on the forms of theatrical effectiveness" (1953: 3; see also 1955b). He went on to say that because young dancers merely executed movement rather than experiencing it, "the result is a kind of ersatz ballet, pieced together from 'Graham technique,' 'Holm technique,' 'Limón technique' (all of them utterly without significance when separated from their context) and lacking both the impersonality and the traditionalism which make the genuine ballet classic." His list continued with laments about the quality of the dances presented. "The study of composition is admirable and necessary, but it does not automatically produce works of art. How many of the young dancers are simply presenting us with their classroom exercises in composition!"

(ibid.). As a solution to these problems, he called for a return to the basic principles on which modern dance had been built.

Certainly by the mid-1940s, many second-generation dancers were working at cross-purposes with the aims that had put modern dance in a vanguard position in the interwar period. They attempted to exchange personal languages for impersonal ones, which undermined the modernist goal of developing new forms for a new age and which also served to differentiate individual dancers from their rivals. Yet at the same time they learned to create movement on their own bodies, which hindered them from successfully choreographing group dances. Then, through the institutionalizing of composition, they learned to make dances in a way that hindered experimentation, the means through which challenges to the old guard were issued. And that wasn't all. Among the most damaging trends in 1940s modern dance was an increasing use of narrative (in the sense of plot lines or the detailing of specific sequences of events) at the expense of plotless form.

Narrative was problematic for several reasons and as such became a highly contentious issue for dancers and critics as the 1940s unfolded. First, it brought modern dance closer to traditional forms of ballet and drama, in theory making it more understandable and thus accessible to larger audiences. In this sense it suggested commercialism. Narrative also countered important modernist principles that left modern dance open to attack on a number of fronts. As noted in my introduction, T. J. Clark has described modernism as centering on an uneasiness or doubt about the nature of representation in art (Clark 1984: 10). In a modernist dance this doubt was most clearly manifested in a demand to embody rather than represent meaning. This is the view expressed in Martha Graham's well-known statement: "Why should an arm try to be corn; why should a hand try to be rain? Think of what a wonderful thing the hand is, and what vast potentialities of movement it has as a hand and not as a poor imitation of something else" (Graham [1937] 1985: 107). A modernist dance was authentic to the degree that it embodied rather than imitated or represented experience. Narrative, whether in the form of plot or pantomime, was representation rather than embodiment.

Modern dance's original goals had espoused an autonomous art that placed embodied movement, as dance's essential element, at its center. Communication was crucial, but it was communication through abstracted corporeal movement, not through literary, that is, representational means. John Martin wrote that it was in movement that dance's power lay: "With this discovery the dance became for the first time an independent art—an absolute art, as they like to say in Germany—completely self-contained, related directly to life, subject to infinite variety" ([1933] 1972: 6). Although movement may seem the obvious basis of dance, Martin argued that ballet made movement incidental, favoring instead the poses between movement. Ballet did not treat movement as a unified entity but rather as a series of distinct elements that were assembled like a language to create meaning. Modern dance brought attention back to dance's essential component and in doing so once again unified movement and meaning (ibid.: 6–7).

The drive to keep literary elements at bay in modern dance was emphasized repeatedly in the 1930s. Two of Graham's most quoted remarks were: "If you can write the story of our dance, it is a literary thing but not dancing," and "My dancing is just dancing. It is not an attempt to interpret life in a literary sense" ([1937] 1985: 102). While modern dance's avoidance of language reflected its desire to eliminate dependence on other art forms, which was necessary to its modernist goals, there were even deeper motives for distrust. Modernists also perceived language as dangerous to art because it could control through its power to define. Pierre Bourdieu notes in his analysis of nineteenth-century French modernist painting that artists fought to make art "irreducible to any gloss or exegesis" so it could not be appropriated by writers or writing. "It is a strategy which consists of denouncing and methodically thwarting—in the conception and the very structure of the work, but also in an anticipated metadiscourse (the obscure and disconcerting title) or in a retrospective commentary—any attempt at annexation of the work by discourse" (1996: 137). Martin reflected this viewpoint when he pointed out that the task of the artist was to express irrationally what others would later rationalize in writing. So strong was his sense of the need to keep dance free from the dominating power of language that he added: "It is safe to say that when any art form has got itself to the point where it can be translated into words, it is dead as an art form" ([1933] 1972: 11). Modernists generally distrusted language and its power to define meaning, largely because they associated language with rationalized thought, which, in turn, was linked to the market and thus to ruling-order ideology. Postwar vanguard dancers were consumed with the dangers that language posed to the genre's independence, not just from the other arts, but also from the field of power with its weapons to control and consume. Yet as the 1940s advanced, modern dance works increasingly told stories, and Graham, as the leading exponent of modern dance, was in part responsible for it.

In the interwar years, Graham's works had generally conformed to the rules of modernism she espoused. For example, *American Provincials* of 1934 consisted of two parts, a solo for Graham, "Act of Piety," and a group dance, "Act of Judgment," which pitted Graham against the group. Although critics saw the work as an attack on the forces of Puritanism, the piece included no narrative story line nor program notes to explain it (McDonagh 1973: 102). Other works were treated similarly: *Perspectives* (1935) consisted of two independent studies, *Perspective No. 1: Frontier* (Graham's famous solo) and *Perspective No. 2: Marching Song*. *Panorama* (1935) was made up of dances entitled "Theme of Dedication," "Imperial Theme," and "Popular Theme." In all these dances subject matter was kept generalized.

However, in the 1940s, Graham added to her repertory a number of works with much more specific topics. By 1945 she had composed such ballets (as she herself called them) as *Letter to the World* (1940), based on the life and poetry of Emily Dickinson, and *Deaths and Entrances* (1943), inspired by the lives of the Brontë sisters. Between 1946 and 1948, Graham produced some of her best-known works, several of which dealt with Greek mythological themes. These included *Cave of the Heart* (1946), based on the story of Medea, and *Night Journey* (1947), which concerned the Oedipus myth. When she first presented *Cave of the Heart* she called the protaganist One Like Medea, then changed it to the more generalized Sorceress. *Night Journey* retained the names of the characters in Sophocles' play. During the 1940s, Graham did not abandon plotless subject matter. *Dark Meadow* (1946), for example, depicted a ritualized event that was not made specific, and *Diversion of Angels* (1948), which she made for the company and in which she did not appear, was entirely without a story line. Nor did Graham stop dealing in metaphor and ambiguity in her narrative pieces; these elements remained crucial in all her work. However, as the 1940s advanced and Graham became more involved in dealing with literary themes, she made dances that incorporated far more mimetic gesture than she had in the past, in order to support the stories she was telling.

A comparison of a solo from the 1930s, *Frontier* (1935), and one from the 1940s, the opening dance in *Night Journey* (1947), provide examples of the shifts that took place in Graham's work. *Frontier* is plot-less, and Graham did not provide program notes that told viewers what she was trying to do or what she wanted them to think about the dance. The movement for *Frontier* is not specific. It consists primarily of ges-tures in which the dancer stretches her arms in great arcs and of steps in which she sweeps one leg high to the side as she moves forward, or executes big skips that take her forward and back from the railing up-stage center that forms a locus for her movement. At one moment she bends her arms and joins her hands in front of her while moving her arms from side to side. This could indicate any number of things, from the rocking of a baby to the motion of a wagon heading west, or it could be simply a gesture that for Graham communicated something about the way one moved in, or was moved by, the West. Graham's alert posture and the largeness and openness of her movement may convey attitudes about the frontier, but these are movement metaphors that suggest without becoming specific. Throughout the dance Graham kept mean-ing open, full of multiple possibilities that the spectator resolved or al-lowed to stand as he or she wished.

The opening dance of *Night Journey* is considerably different. Here Graham, as Jocasta, is seen resisting a confrontation with her past. We know this is the situation because her written program notes have told us and because Graham executes certain pantomimed gestures in the dance that reinforce the written text. For example, Jocasta approaches the wedding bed and recoils in horror. She repeatedly touches her head, a gesture both in daily life and in the theater that indicates thought. She repeatedly touches her breasts and pubic area to indicate the sexuality that is the source of her problem (also revealed in the program notes). This is not to say that the dance includes no abstract movement. There are steps that would qualify as "pure" movement as well as others that are suggestive rather than specific. Certainly, Graham did not give up metaphoric movement in the 1940s, but she did make meaning more explicit in some of her works both through movement and through the narratives that she chose to relate.

The fact that Graham's dances dealt with specific characters and nar-ratives in a way they had not done before the war was certainly evident to contemporary critics, who differentiated between Graham's former "pure dance" and the new "theater of Martha Graham." Cecil Smith, writing in *Theatre Arts*, commented on the changes in Graham's work in a 1947 season at the Ziegfeld Theatre: "Not a single dance composed

Martha Graham in *Frontier* (1935). *Photo: Edward Moeller. Courtesy of Jerome Robbins Dance Division, The New York Public Library for the Performing Arts, Astor, Lenox and Tilden Foundations.*

Martha Graham as Jocasta in *Night Journey* (1947). *Photo: Arnold Eagle. Courtesy of Jerome Robbins Dance Division, The New York Public Library for the Performing Arts, Astor, Lenox and Tilden Foundations.*

between 1931 and 1939, the date of *Every Soul is a Circus*, was given a place in her schedule. Clearly she now regards herself as a theatre artist, and does not feel that the early pieces—many of which were magnificent examples of 'pure dance'—are suited to her present following" (1947: 29). Smith, however, did not use this shift toward theater to attack Graham; rather, he defended her theater work as a new development in vanguard dance. He wrote that although Graham's dances were narrative, they did not deal with outer reality but with the "veiled and perplexed world of the inner consciousness" (ibid.: 30). She conveyed this world, he said, with pure movement, an evocative prop or two, and costumes, and in doing so transfigured the turmoil of personal emotions. Thus, according to Smith, Graham accomplished the task of a modern art.

Critic Margaret Lloyd was even more intent on stressing the vanguard nature of Graham's new dance, which, she said, put pure movement at its center. She wrote that in Graham's theater, "movement is still paramount, in spite of remote literary, mythological, or pantomimic references" (Lloyd 1949: 64). However, as much as supporters defended Graham's new theatricalism, they nonetheless perceived it as moving away from abstraction rather than toward it, a step that put a vanguard genre at risk. It was on this point—the use of narrative as an element foreign to dance—that several generations of dancers would attack Graham in the 1950s and '60s. However, in the 1940s, Graham's dances were still seen as vanguard productions that in their concern with myth and the unconscious revealed universal aspects of human existence.

Where Graham led, others followed, and many did not have Graham's nuanced approach to literature or the complexity of her vision. For example, Valerie Bettis choreographed a work entitled *Daisy Lee* (1944) in which she danced out a story of "the frantic remorse of a woman who destroyed not only her husband's but also her sister's life through her own pride, possessiveness and emotional dishonesty" (Sabin 1945a: 70). While Bettis performed the central role, voices offstage represented the other characters. When the work premiered in 1944, it was listed as a dance-play with a libretto by Horton Foote. In another dance Bettis drew on sections of William Faulkner's novel *As I Lay Dying* (1948) in which she interspersed portions of spoken text with movement to create portraits of two southern women. The characters in the piece included nearly a dozen members of the Bundren family and their friends and acquaintances. Bettis performed some of her works under the auspices of the Choreographers' Workshop, which billed itself as "interested in presenting not only pure dance, but works of theatre that include a dance viewpoint and works of dance that include a theatre viewpoint."[7] There were many other examples of dance dramas at this time, from William Bales's *Judith* (1949), described as a "theatre piece based on the story of Judith and Holofernes" (Krevitsky 1949: 98) to Jean Erdman's *The Fair Eccentric, or The Temporary Belle of Hangtown* (1951), which, according to one critic, approximated the oleos of vaudeville and included extended sections of pantomime (Krevitsky 1951b: 42). In other instances, dancers simply quoted a poem or story in a program note, and then danced it.

Since modernism required artists to produce new forms, it is not surprising that a number of second-generation choreographers wished to develop dance and drama into a new amalgam. However, they had difficulty reconciling the antiliteral aspects of modernism with narrative. Valerie Bettis attempted to address the problem by dividing what she called theater dance into two types, one based on plot, which was developed narratively, the other on an emotional idea, which was developed thematically. "It must be realized that only in the former [narrative dance] can theatrical devices such as literal costuming, special props, definitive sets, and stylized acting or mime be used freely, if intelligently" (1945: 82). In addition to theater dance, with its narrative and thematic forms, there was "pure" dance. Bettis continued: "Free dance movement must be studied and understood; and it is the dancer's obligation to distinguish for his audience between the theatre dance, in which the idea is developed thematically, and the 'pure' dance, both of which may employ this kind of movement" (ibid.). This not altogether lucid explanation suggests that Bettis had difficulties defining how the various forms of pure, thematic, and narrative dance related to each other.

By 1948, Nina Fonaroff was better able to argue the case for dance drama (1948: 52). She began by stating that pure dance was theatrical because acting and pure movement came from the same root, that is, an emotional source. There was a difference, she said, between sensory movement and explanatory movement. Pantomime was explanatory movement and so was ballet, which, at least in Fonaroff's view, explained itself through costumes, scenery, and mimetic gesture. After mentioning several actors who incorporated pure movement into their work, such as Jean-Louis Barrault and Laurence Olivier, she went on to say

Valerie Bettis and Duncan Noble in Bettis's *Daisy Lee* (1944). *Photo: Tripp and Dellenback. Courtesy of Jerome Robbins Dance Division, The New York Public Library for the Performing Arts, Astor, Lenox and Tilden Foundations.*

that actors who used pure movement distorted drama beyond the literal to reveal its essence: "When the intention demands extremities; when the drama is the epitome of what it is about—then its working material can, by distortion rise to that epitome and fulfill the furthest possibilities of the mediums, movement approaching dance, and speech, poetry. But if the intention of the play stops at the naturalistic, the representational, there is no call for distortion" (1948: 52). Pure movement was what made it possible to reveal essential elements of drama. When a choreographer used words, she had to be sure the dance did not merely illustrate the text. Rather, she had to create a structure that needed both while at the same time keeping them separate. Fonaroff advocated using a common rhythmic structure that would allow each medium to remain independent. Conceding that the vast majority of dance theater conformed to word illustration, Fonaroff nonetheless said she would devote herself to developing a form that would allow for the autonomy of both media.

A year later, Katherine Litz made a similar argument regarding the common emotional source shared by dance and drama. She suggested that dancers study acting because "every movement, no matter how arbitrary, can be given dramatic quality through an understanding of emotional values" (1949: 67). The dancer who studied acting came to a "deeper understanding of the dramatic basis of movement" (ibid.). In this statement Litz, like Fonaroff, argued that dance had a dramatic base; accordingly dance was not opposed to drama but related to it.

However, as much as dancers attempted to combine two existing forms into a new one, both on paper and on the stage, they were ultimately working against modernist prescriptions, and as such they put the vanguard status of modern dance at risk. This held true despite the fact that in some cases they succeeded in producing works that merged drama and dance with marked success. One of the best examples was José Limón's *The Moor's Pavane* (1949), which became a signature work for the Limón company. Limón had been a leading dancer with the Humphrey-Weidman group since the early 1930s. Humphrey-Weidman disbanded in 1945 while Limón was serving in the army. After his discharge he decided to form his own company, and Humphrey agreed to become artistic director. Although Limón's earlier choreography had not received a great deal of praise, once under Humphrey's tutelage, his work became stronger, and he soon emerged as the great hope of the postwar generation. Critics from John Martin to Doris Hering to the

Dance Observer writers looked to Limón as the best chance of carrying on the work begun by the first-generation pioneers.

The Moor's Pavane, based on Shakespeare's *Othello* and set to music by Purcell, premiered in 1949.[8] Limón reduced the number of characters in the plot to four, telling in succinct fashion the story of Othello's jealous love and the tragedy to which his unbridled emotions led.[9] Like Graham, Limón had to use pantomime to tell his complicated story, but he also enclosed the drama within a framework of courtly dances, which controlled narrative and constantly led the viewer's attention back to the dance itself. The work opens with the four characters in a circle, their arms held high, hands joined. As the dance progresses they circle, bow, advance and retreat, in the formal patterns of the dance. These patterns, in addition to being "pure" dance movement, also suggest the characters' interconnected relationships. At the same time, the dance also incorporates within its overall structure many of the gestures and movements that will typify the characters' relationships in more specific ways: Othello and Iago lock their arms together in silent struggle; Desdemona holds out her handkerchief; Emilia and Iago hover closely and give each other meaningful glances as they watch Desdemona and Othello embrace. The next dance deals with the relationship between Iago and Othello. Iago clings to and wraps himself around Othello, while Othello wards him off with large, impetuous gestures. The dance ends with Iago executing a series of low, cringing bows. And so the work progresses, through dances for Iago and Emilia, Othello and Desdemona, Iago and Othello, until the final dance in which Desdemona's murder is hidden behind Emilia's voluminous skirt. The piece ends with a tableau of the four dancers, Iago and Emilia framing Othello, who is seen stretched across Desdemona's body.

The Moor's Pavane interweaves pantomime, metaphoric movement, and the formal designs of court dances with unusual finesse. Nonetheless, Limón's choreography depended on mimetic gesture to a degree seldom seen in the pioneering modern dance of the 1920s and '30s. As Marcia Siegel has noted, Limón's gift was "to explain, to dramatize, to become a hero for a while and play out that hero's role" (1979: 168). The desire to specify and explain, successful as it may have been in a work like *The Moor's Pavane*, was a problem for modern dance, a problem that caused a clash that reverberated through the dances and debates of the period.

Joseph Campbell, a respected scholar of mythology, sounded the

From left, Lucas Hoving, José Limón, and Pauline Koner in Limón's *The Moor's Pavane* (1949). *Photo: Gerda Peterich. Courtesy of the Jerome Robbins Dance Division, The New York Public Library for the Performing Arts, Astor, Lenox and Tilden Foundations.*

alarm in articles in *Dance Observer* in 1944 and 1945. Campbell deplored the trend toward literary means in modern dance, writing that "... unhappily, the entire Modern Movement is going over to little plays, and to a horrendous bastard-art of poem-dancing" (1944a: 31). Dance was not a discursive art but an embodied one, he argued:

> The dancer, that is to say, is not a semaphorist, but a work of art in the flesh; her function is not the [*sic*] flash messages back and forth from brain to brain (that is the role of the discoursive [*sic*] paragraph), but to embody Significant Form. And what is Significant Form? It is the rhythm of life projected in design; the invisible pattern of the psyche reflected in time and space; a profoundly inspired disposition of feeling-charged materials stemming from, and addressed to, that creative center where human consciousness and the unconscious fruitfully touch. (1944b: 66)

In making this argument, Campbell, like Martin a decade earlier (Martin [1933] 1972: 10–11), was pointing out that modern dance's purpose was to embody those hidden realities that language could not convey. The ability to embody the human experience that words could not touch was dance's unique strength, and modern dance was in the process of giving it away.

Campbell blamed the literary trend on Graham's dance-dramas, but explained that the influence was ironic, as Graham had actually developed a new dance form. Her works were legitimate because she did not attempt to illustrate stories but to inhabit "the timeless realm of dream" that was linked to the unconscious. In addition, Campbell said, Graham depicted her characters as archetypes, characteristic of certain psychological states and situations, which in Campbell's view gave them universal significance. Both Campbell and Graham were followers of Carl Jung, and as such accepted archetypes as the content of the collective unconscious (Jung 1971: 59–60). Campbell, like other critics, was loathe to hold Graham in any degree accountable for the direction that modern dance was taking. It must be remembered, too, that he and Graham were close friends, and he was writing in a magazine that wholly supported her work.

The need to communicate was a liability for modern dance because it was always in danger of illustrating or imitating rather than embodying authentic states of mind through movement alone. Campbell began another article the next year by making this point and attempting to provide an answer through myth, which the surrealists, those certified avant-gardists, had also used as a path to the unconscious. Myth and legend, Campbell wrote, provided archetypal images that were universal and that were keys to the unconscious (1945: 52–53). Citing Freud, Jung, and the mythologist Stith Thompson, he asserted that the episodes and personages of myth, legend, fairytale, and fable were timeless and essential. For every aesthetic element there was a psychological one identical with a psychological value of a mythological element. If the dancer could fully understand the implications of the images and render them with appropriate aspects of her craft, she could successfully fuse form and content. What was necessary was to find the correspondences between the psychological effects of the aesthetic form being used and those of the archetypes of myth and symbol. Campbell had no advice on how the dancer was to locate those links; that apparently was her task. However, in his argument he attempted to provide an answer to modern dance's predicament through means that actively sought to maintain art's independence from causal logic by plumbing the unconscious and bringing authentic experience to the surface.

Campbell's attempts to offer at least one way out of trouble for modern dance only served to point up the problem, and arguments continued well into the 1950s over whether or not dancers should employ literary means. These debates had much to do with dancers' ambivalence about the field's relationship to the market and hence the culture industry. Narrative made dance more accessible to spectators, which meant, for some, larger audiences and greater success. As such, narrative became an element in modern dance's assimilation into the mainstream, because, as Gertrude Lippincott and others argued, vanguard art was aimed not at a broad public but at a small group of peers who chose to ignore the market.

Writers' views on the use of literary devices in modern dance were as complicated as dancers'. Some commentators were outright supporters, as were Bernice J. Wolfson (1947: 88–89) and Winthrop Palmer (1949: 112), who wrote articles tracing a history of literary means used in dance, and which were intended to legitimize the dual form. On the other hand, there were also numerous articles that supported the pure dance viewpoint, and critics as a whole subscribed to the idea that detailed storytelling was not good for modern dance. One of the ways they manifested their antinarrative stance was to brand works they felt illustrated a story as literal. For example, Nik Krevitsky wrote that Patricia

Newman's *Green Mansions* was "a lengthy, literal interpretation of Hudson's beautiful novel . . . and when it ended with Abel's anguish, there was a feeling of rejoicing in that it was over" (1948: 57). Yet, in fact, critical response to narrative was largely arbitrary because once the idea of a theater-dance had been accepted as a new form, critics then had to distinguish between dramas that appeared literal and those that did not. Trying to decide at what point a theme left the realm of the universal and became specific depended on the personal opinion of the critic. Consequently, while some writers praised a work like Bettis's *As I Lay Dying*, with its biographical sketches of two southern women, others found it dangerously close to illustration.

The debates and the confusion that tore at modern dance in the 1940s were indicative of a genre in transition, but they also suggested the ambivalent position artists held in relation to the dominant order. Most wanted to save modern dance's floundering vanguardism, but they couldn't agree on how to do it. And hovering over the arguments and proposed solutions was the specter of the market with its seductive possibilities for larger audiences and greater success. In addition, other major pressures from outside the arena of dance came to bear on the field in the immediate postwar years, further tangling dancers' and critics' motives for support of one position or another. Foremost among these were the rise of the Cold War and the repressive atmosphere that accompanied it. Accusations of literalism were thus used, not just as a way to reinforce modern dance's position in the field, but as a means of condemning social and political protest. For example, Joan Brodie found Patsi Birsh's *In the Mines of Avondale*, which dealt with a mining disaster, "a little too literal" (1948: 44), while Doris Hering warned in *Dance Magazine* that José Limón's *El Grito* was perilously close to a polemic in its defense of a Mexican Indian uprising (1953a: 54).

In other instances, dancers were less overt in their politics, veiling their critique in various ways that needed decoding. For example, as the anticommunist hysteria of the late 1940s gained momentum, dancers choreographed a number of works that dealt with the New England witch hunts of the seventeenth century. These included Mary Anthony's *The Devil in Massachusetts* (1952), Miriam Pandor's *Salem Witch Hunt* (1952), James Dalgleish's *Salem Witchhunt* (1952), and Marion Scott's *The Afflicted Children* (1953). (Arthur Miller's *The Crucible* appeared on Broadway in 1953.) José Limón's *The Traitor* (1954), which dealt with Judas's betrayal of Christ, also was choreographed in these years. Yet critics did not decode such works. They either ignored any connection to contemporary life in the dances, or if that proved impossible, they labeled them literal. The critical response to protest narrative, whether through silence or an accusation of literalness, was used as a means of censoring material that might bring unwanted attention from the field of power; as such it became complicit with that power.

Although the anticommunist witch hunts of the postwar years centered on government employees, they also invaded the arts and entertainment fields, the academy, unions, business, and many other areas. A number of dancers had been involved with left-wing causes in the 1930s and suffered for it after the war. The most notorious case was that of Jerome Robbins, who was called before the House Un-American Activities Committee and named names, among them Edna Ocko, critic for several left-wing publications, including *New Masses* and the *Daily Worker* (Bentley 1971; Jowitt 2004). Others who came under scrutiny included Pearl Primus, who was called before the committee and whose passport was revoked for a time; Anna Sokolow, who was interviewed without being called; and Bella Lewitzky, who was kept under FBI surveillance for a number of years (Barber 1992: 10; Warren 1998: 96; Craig 2001). Such direct encounters with official repression were rare among high-art dancers, but the threat of them sent a chill through the field.

In addition, dancers had another reason to fear outside social forces: that was homophobia, which was rampant in the postwar period. It is difficult to know exactly what percentage of men in the dance field were gay, as such information did not enter written discourse. As John D'Emilio has pointed out in his study on the emergence of the gay liberation movement in the 1960s (D'Emilio 1998), homosexuality in the 1940s and '50s was generally thought to be a personal, individual issue. There was as yet little concept of a unified homosexual minority; this idea developed only gradually over the course of the next several decades. In the postwar period, heterosexual norms were enforced on the stage, and heterosexuality was assumed offstage in written accounts. Yet if homosexuality did not enter dance's written record, it is generally agreed that the percentages of gay men working in the dance field—including dancers, choreographers, designers, composers, administrative personnel, and critics—have been high since early in the twentieth century. During the postwar years, for example, a large number of male choreographers were gay or bisexual, including Robbins, Tudor, Weidman, Limón, Cunningham, Nikolais, Taylor, and Ailey (Jowitt 2004; Chazin-Bennahum 1994; Siegel 1987; Burt 1995; Louis 1973; Taylor 1987; Dunning 1996; DeFrantz 2004). Important dance critics were also gay or bisexual, as were a number of company directors, administrators, and supporting personnel. Both women and gay men found a haven in the dance field where they could garner support from like-minded individuals and where, too, they could gain power. However, being dominated by women and gay men gave dance less stature than the other arts. Read through feminist theory, dance was a feminized site in a society of heterosexual male domination. Within the field there was much anxiety about dance's effeminacy, as witnessed in articles that appeared in the dance press. These generally ran along two lines: a case would be made for the masculinity of dance by comparing its physical demands to those of other physically taxing activities, or a case would be made for why parents should allow their sons to study dance. In an interview in the 1950s, George Balanchine combined both points (Balanchine 1954: 504). To the question of whether or not boys should be allowed to take ballet classes Balanchine replied that he understood that parents were hesitant to send their sons to ballet school because they were afraid they would become "sissified" or would not develop the strong muscles that other activities would give them. However, he argued, ballet builds strong, flexible bodies that have a great deal of endurance. Then, appealing to manly patriotism, he added, "this is the reason many of our best dancers were good soldiers during the war" (ibid.). Balanchine was a convincing spokesman for the virility of male dancing, since his numerous marriages to beautiful ballerinas apparently demonstrated his heterosexuality. However, public perceptions, as Balanchine noted, were that dance was for "sissies," and this was attested to by the low numbers of boys compared with girls taking dance classes and by the advanced age at which boys entered the field compared with girls (Kirstein [1953] 1983: 97–106; [1959] 1983: 398–400). The low economic rewards and short careers of dancers also must have made dance unattractive to all but the most determined men.

Homophobia was tied to anticommunist rhetoric to an extraordinary degree in the postwar period. As historian Stephen Whitfield has noted, "If only through innuendo, nothing in the political arena in the 1950s was more convenient than establishing some sort of connection between political and sexual 'perversion'" (Whitfield 1991: 43). The casualness with which communism and homosexuality were linked is remarkable. For example, in 1946 President Truman fumed privately that "All the 'Artists' with a Capital A, the parlor pinks and the soprano voiced men are banded together. . . . I am afraid they are a sabotage front for Uncle Joe Stalin" (quoted in Griffith 1981: 298), while Arthur Schlesinger Jr. noted in *The Vital Center* that communism "perverts politics into something secret, sweaty and furtive like nothing so much, in the phrase of one wise observer of modern Russia, as homosexuality in a boys' school" ([1949] 1998: 151). Communists were routinely equated with effeminacy and homosexuality on a metaphoric level, while actual homosexuals were viewed as a threat to national security and the moral fiber of the country. According to a Senate report commissioned in 1950 to investigate homosexuality in the federal civil service, the stigma of their lifestyle left homosexuals open to blackmail and therefore made them dangerous if they held jobs in the government or military. On the subject of morality the Senate report continued: "These perverts will frequently attempt to entice normal individuals to engage in perverted practices. This is particularly true in the case of young and impressionable people who might come under the influence of a pervert" (quoted in D'Emilio and Freedman 1997: 293).

Homophobic hysteria may well have been aided by the Kinsey report on male sexuality, which appeared in 1948 and revealed that homosexuality was far more widespread than previously realized. Kinsey reported that at least 37 percent of the male population had engaged in some overt homosexual activity between the onset of adolescence and old age. Among those unmarried to age thirty-five, 50 percent had some homosexual experience, as had 10 percent of married males between the ages of sixteen and twenty-five. The report also countered ideas of stable sexuality, showing that sexuality was often flexible and changing throughout a person's life. Kinsey said that his research found that homosexuality existed in every age group, social level, and occupation, and in both cities and rural areas. He added that his statistics were, if anything, understated because of the stigma of homosexuality (1948: 168–172, 610–656).

Another factor in the growth of homophobia during the postwar years was the religious revival that swept the country. Between 1940 and 1959, church-going in the United States rose from 49 to 69 percent, while men like Bishop Fulton Sheen and the Reverend Billy Graham became household words. In the 1950s "one nation under God" was added to the Pledge of Allegiance, recited each morning by school-children throughout the country, and "In God We Trust" was added to the U.S. currency. Godless communism and perverted homosexuality were anathema to an organized religion that grew ever stronger during the 1940s and '50s (Oakley 1986: 319–327; Silk 1988: 15–107; Whitfield 1991: 82–84; O'Neill 1986: 212–215). These various sources of homophobia had real consequences as gays and lesbians were increasingly barred from the civil service and the military, academia, and other fields such as businesses with government contracts. In addition, local police routinely harassed homosexuals by raiding gay bars and meeting places (D'Emilio and Freedman 1997: 293–294). Newspapers often published the names of homosexuals detained by the police, and should a gay man be exposed, his working life, even as a dancer, would likely be over. Considering this political and social climate, the last thing the dance field needed was close scrutiny from government agencies and institutions that linked social protest with communism, communism with homosexuality, and homosexuality with perversion and treason.

Modern dance, then, faced troubles on several major fronts in the postwar years. These included most importantly its own institutional-ization, which put its vanguard position in jeopardy, and increasing pressures from inside and outside the field alike, which sought to elim-inate or suppress any element of critique. The rules of modernism de-manded solutions to both sets of problems, yet modernism itself was problematic as elements of it were co-opted for Cold War use. In the meantime, another challenger appeared from outside the genre in the unlikely guise of ballet. Although modern dancers had long worried about the power of ballet, the assumption generally had been that bal-let would overwhelm and assimilate modern dance. George Beiswanger's view was typical. Writing in 1942, he stated: "It is quite possible that the final and only lasting service of the modern dance will be the rejuvena-tion of ballet. Let us face the facts. Ballet has the money, the organiza-tion, the repertory and the audience. And, like all established institutions, it has a flexible conscience" (1942: 116). Having devoured its own past, Beiswanger said, ballet looked for new sustenance: "Whenever it begins to see something fresh and exciting in the new impulses of its own day, it takes them over, babbling all the time about the eternal verities of the five positions and the turn-out of the thigh" (ibid.). Although Beiswanger had cause for concern, as ballet choreographers such as Antony Tudor and Agnes de Mille appropriated aspects of modern dance, this did not prove to be the major threat. Rather, it arrived in the guise of Lincoln Kirstein, and through him George Balanchine, who did not so much absorb modern dance as attempt to compete with it. Kirstein's audacious plan was to wrest from modern dance its vanguard place within high-art dance. The extent of this challenge will be taken up in the next chapter.

BALLET'S CHALLENGE

In the fall of 1946, Lincoln Kirstein issued a manifesto. The occasion was the inauguration of Ballet Society, the subscription series he had undertaken and funded with his own money. It stated, in part:

> The Ballet Society will present a completely new repertory consisting of ballets, ballet-opera and other lyric forms. Each will have the planned collaboration of independent easel-painters, progressive choreographers and musicians, employing the full use of advance-guard ideas, methods and materials. . . . Since ballet in the U.S. is relatively new, our interest has been primarily in the revival of productions already famous, or the creation of works based on national themes. Now, with the close of a second world war, broader directions are possible and desirable.[1]

Although Kirstein's remarks would seem to be aimed at other ballet companies, his intentions went beyond challenges to the Ballet Russe de Monte Carlo and the six-year-old Ballet Theatre, the major American companies at that time.[2] His intention in using advance-guard ideas, methods, and materials was also to provoke modern dance. Kirstein planned to carry out his conquest of the vanguard through the choreography of George Balanchine, whose work Kirstein viewed as a reformation of the classical *danse d'école*. Kirstein's notion of "advance-guard ideas" was primarily aesthetic. He was not interested in opposing institutionalized art but in building large, knowledgeable audiences. Nevertheless, the fact remains that in the 1940s ballet briefly attempted to compete with modern dance for position in the field, and this competition came at a time when modern dance was particularly vulnerable. The real danger in Kirstein's challenge was not that ballet would become a true modernist vanguard, but that it would expose the fault lines in mod-

Lincoln Kirstein and George Balanchine in the 1950s. *Photo: Tanaquil LeClercq. Courtesy of the Tanaquil LeClercq Collection, New York City Ballet Archives.*

ern dance and so further weaken, if not destroy, the genre's already vulnerable status and position. For through Balanchine, ballet offered an aesthetic based on an antiliteral dance that was more stringent than much of what modern dance was offering by the mid-1940s. The Kirstein-Balanchine enterprise is examined here not only because it set itself up as a rival to modern dance, but because Balanchine's neoclassicism helped encourage a young generation of modern dancers to devise an objectivist dance of their own that, in the 1950s, was declared a new modernist vanguard.

Kirstein's antipathy to modern dance was long-standing; he had begun to write polemics against it in the 1930s and remained opposed to it for the rest of his life (Reynolds 1983: xvi–xvii).[3] His argument, laid out in several early articles, was that ballet had a better chance of fulfilling the requisites of a modernist vanguard than modern dance. Modern dance's failure, he said, was that it was a full-scale revolt from the accepted form of high-art dance, and as such was a dead-end because it had no way to remake itself. Kirstein compared ballet's position to that of cubism, the innovations of which had not killed the tradition of painting but renewed it ([1937] 1983: 253). Cubism was a method of self-criticism that reconsidered the tradition of painting. Ballet, too, built on and renewed tradition rather than dismantling it.[4] Modern dance, on the other hand, constituted a complete break with the past; as such it had no basis for further development. Compounding the problem in Kirstein's view was the fact that modern dance was not founded on an impersonal vocabulary that could be expanded or refreshed, but on a dancer-choreographer's personality. The subject of Graham's dances was not dance, but Graham herself. For this reason, each modern dance choreographer was forced to reinvent the genre. Kirstein saw little future for modern dance under such conditions ([1934b] 1983: 38–41).

One might well ask why Kirstein wanted to challenge the existing vanguard, especially when the two most prominent American ballet companies saw no need to do so. The obvious answer was to differentiate Ballet Society from other ballet companies, and it is likely this was one of his reasons. However, additional answers come to mind.

The first has to do with Kirstein's own background and dispositions, beginning with his Harvard education and contacts (Weber 1992; Kirstein 1994; Jenkins 1998). During his student days in the 1920s, he had been attached to several important modernist projects. These included *Hound and Horn*, a literary magazine he helped found, which published some of the most advanced modernist writing of its day. Authors included James Joyce, Gertrude Stein, T. S. Eliot, William Carlos Williams, e.e. cummings, and Ezra Pound. He also started the Harvard Society for Contemporary Art with his friend Edward Warburg of the banking family. The gallery showed the work of a host of modern artists ranging from Americans such as Georgia O'Keeffe, Arthur Dove, and Edward Hopper, to School of Paris painters such as Matisse, Braque, and Brancusi, and a number of surrealists. The society was an acknowledged precursor of the Museum of Modern Art. Among Kirstein's uni-

versity friends were Alfred H. Barr, who would become the first director of the Museum of Modern Art, and Philip Johnson, the modernist
architect who in the 1960s designed an addition to the Museum of
Modern Art and who also designed the State Theatre at Lincoln Center, the eventual home of New York City Ballet. In the 1930s, Kirstein
also had been on the junior advisory committee for the Museum of
Modern Art and established a dance archive there. He had close ties
to many of the surrealists, neoromantics, and other vanguard European
émigré artists who lived in New York during the war and who designed
sets and costumes for his projects. This world of modernist movers and
shakers in which Kirstein circulated may well have made him feel that
his ballet company had to fit a modernist model if it were to garner the
kind of prestige he sought.

By the end of the war, Kirstein, with his connections and well-honed
feel for the game, also may have realized that taking an advanced-guard
position could reap more than the limited, if rarefied, status of the
prewar years. As powerful elites within the United States came to view
modernism as a weapon, first against fascism and then communism,
there were larger prizes to be had. Granted, modernism in 1946 was
controversial, but Kirstein had influential friends, such as Nelson Rockefeller, who were backing it.[5] Certainly he understood that the Americana subject matter he had favored in his concert group, Ballet Caravan,
in the late 1930s was no longer viable. That small concert group, which
Kirstein had assembled two years before his more ambitious American
Ballet expired in 1938, had been devoted to works that dealt primarily
with America's past or with a vernacular scene of the present. *Pocahontas* (1936), *Yankee Clipper* (1937), *Billy the Kid* (1938), and *Filling Station*
(1938) were just some of the works that Ballet Caravan presented in its
five-year existence.[6] These ballets paralleled the paintings of regional
artists and the works of many modern dancers of the same period. By
1946, Kirstein realized it was necessary to take a different path. The
"broader directions" he spoke of in his manifesto would be toward the
internationalism that was emerging at the time, and the vehicle would
be Ballet Society, led by Balanchine.

Kirstein had attempted to cast Balanchine in several guises since he
had brought him to the United States in 1933, each designed to bene-
fit from current trends. An article for the leftist periodical *New Theatre*,
written the year after Balanchine's arrival, depicted him as a revolutionary with communist sympathies (Kirstein 1934a: 12–14). Kirstein

mentioned that Balanchine's father, a musician, had recently been honored by a jubilee in the Soviet Union while neglecting to mention that Balanchine had left his native country in 1924 with no intention of going back. In the article, Kirstein did not emphasize abstract classicism, which was to become the basis of Balanchine's postwar style, but rather his interest in renewing the relationship between dance and drama. In support of this, he pointed to an early Balanchine piece in the USSR set to a poem by Alexander Blok. He went on to say that Balanchine had been interested in dance-drama at the Ballets Russes, perhaps thinking of *Prodigal Son* (1929), and in 1933 had set *The Seven Deadly Sins* by Bertolt Brecht, who Kirstein described as a "superb young communist artist." Balanchine, Kirstein wrote, "knows ballet as 'ballet' is dead." Instead he had reinstated another term, "choreodrama," and according to Kirstein, planned a revolutionary kind of theater around it. The form would be that of the old ballet—Kirstein argued that revolutions preserve the best elements of the past, which included balletic form—with new content delivered in new ways. "The workers need a demonstrated subject matter," he wrote, "a dramatized, legible spectacle, far more than they need a new *form* of expression" (1934a: 14).

Choreodrama, and the accompanying image of Balanchine as a communist-inspired revolutionary, soon disappeared from Kirstein's writing, but he still did not emphasize classicism or abstraction. Rather, he now stressed the neoromantic aspects of Balanchine's choreography. Neoromanticism, which like surrealism dealt with the irrational—with dreams, visions, hallucinations, and the unconscious—was associated with artists like Pavel Tchelitchev and Eugene Berman, both of whom designed interwar Balanchine ballets. In *Blast at Ballet*, Kirstein described Balanchine in neoromantic terms:

> His choreography is not ever literally narrative; it seldom tells a consecutive story. It weaves, however, a dominating but eventually a climactic and profound atmosphere which is frequently romantic, but just as often so odd in its romance as to seem a genre of romanticism the like of which has seldom been seen before. It is the poetic romanticism not of a Rousseau or Chateaubriand, but of the cruel tales of E. T. A. Hoffmann, Grimm or Andersen; the somber verses of Lenau, Heine and Hölderlin, the cynical self-contempt of Byron and Poushkin. It is a romantic attitude divested of sentimentality. It is an atmosphere at once nervous, individual, spoiled, tender and tragic. ([1937] 1983: 178)

Kirstein, himself, was partial to neoromanticism, as well as surrealism. For many years Tchelitchev, in particular, was a friend and consultant to both Kirstein and Balanchine (Taper 1984: 163; Buckle 1988; Kirstein 1973, 1994). Ballet Society choreographers also used some of the subject matter that concerned the surrealists and neoromantics, namely myth and legend. John Taras created a ballet entitled *The Minotaur* (1947), and Balanchine produced *The Triumph of Bacchus and Ariadne* (1948) and *Orpheus* (1948).

However, by 1947 Kirstein was no longer promoting Balanchine as a neoromantic, even though neoromantic and surrealist-inspired works made up part of Ballet Society's repertory. Kirstein now pronounced Balanchine a neoclassicist who had developed an American style of ballet through a nonnarrative, or abstract, dance. In two articles written for *Theatre Arts*, Kirstein traced a history of Balanchine's work that saw him first as inheriting the mantle of Marius Petipa, the father of classical ballet (Kirstein 1947a: 37–41; 1947b: 37–41). Balanchine received this inheritance through his training and association with the Imperial Ballet of St. Petersburg and his dedication to the *danse d'école*. Next, Balanchine had advanced his classical heritage into pure-dance ballets that he had evolved in the United States through such works as *Serenade* (1935), *Concerto Barocco* (1941), *Ballet Imperial* (1941), and *The Four Temperaments* (1946). Kirstein's linking of plotless ballet to America suggested that neoclassical abstraction was an American form.

Yet, however eager Kirstein was to have Balanchine seen as the creator of a new American form, the opinion of most critics from the time of Balanchine's arrival in the United States had been that his work was part of a decaying Franco-Russian ballet. Few denied Balanchine's choreographic facility, but they considered him glib and superficial. Walter Terry (1941: 10) of the *New York Herald Tribune* compared Balanchine unfavorably with Martha Graham, while John Martin spoke of Balanchine's "anemic aesthetics" ([1939] 1965: 207). In a 1937 review of the American Ballet, Martin wrote:

> When dealing with Balanchine's compositions, it is necessary always to accept the fact that for him the dance, as he has expressly stated, is purely spectacular and should strive only for the attainment of sensuous pleasure. That he believes such pleasure is best attained by tenuous rather than robust means is apparently characteristic of his personal approach.
>
> It should not be surprising, then, to discover that the three ballets he

has presented, two of them newly created, should be without substance and trivial. (1937: 7)

Of the same American Ballet program Gervase Butler wrote in *Dance Observer:* "His [Balanchine's] chief error lies in the choice of movement and concept so foreign to the American idiom. In a world wherein we find ourselves the youngest and most vital nation, the European cachet has long lost its potency on the arts it dominated before the war. In other words, we have not yet attained American Ballet" (1937: 67).

As late as the mid-1940s, *Dance Observer* critics were still accusing Balanchine of superficiality and foreign glamour. Robert Sabin wrote: "Mr. Balanchine suffers from his own cleverness. He is such an artist to his finger tips, so witty and ingenious that he can say practically nothing with an air of having said a great deal. *Dances Concertantes* is a case in point, for it contains few passages of memorable choreography, yet one cannot resist its glittering facility" (1944: 101). A year later, Sabin spoke of Balanchine's *Concerto Barocco* as "neo-classic chi-chi" (1945b: 97). It was clear that if Balanchine were going to be seen as the inventor of a new American style, some minds would have to be changed. And change, they did. Between 1945 and 1955 Balanchine was transformed from a foreign interloper out of touch with American dance into the creative genius of a native American ballet. This is not to say that Balanchine did not have his supporters early on. Anatole Chujoy, editor of *Dance News*, wrote intelligently of Balanchine's work and published a book on the New York City Ballet in 1953. Even more important was Edwin Denby, who almost single-handedly defined what would become Balanchine's American style. But it may have been John Martin's capitulation more than anything else that shifted the tide of opinion. In the late 1940s, Martin, the great defender of modern dance, began to see in Balanchine many of the qualities to which modern dance had hitherto held sole claim. These included experimentation, an American style, and a dance that put movement at its center. As such this ballet challenged modern dance's position on several fronts.

What was Balanchine doing in the mid-1940s that encouraged critics to change their opinions, and why did his ballet come to be so appealing to postwar observers? It is time to look at Balanchine's work of those years, in this case his most radical ballet and one that set the style for other "experimental" endeavors. Balanchine chose to choreograph *The Four Temperaments* for the first Ballet Society program on 20

November 1946. The ballet represented only one of several styles in which Balanchine worked simultaneously, and it must be emphasized that it remained only one such style. Throughout his career Balanchine made narrative works, and for many years he continued to produce neo-romantic ballets. However, *The Four Temperaments* would come to epitomize what for critics was Balanchine's American style.

Balanchine had commissioned the score for *The Four Temperaments* from Paul Hindemith in 1940 with money from his work in films and on Broadway.[7] Hindemith supplied a chamber piece entitled *Theme with Four Variations (according to The Four Temperaments)*. The temperaments were associated with the four humours of medieval physiology and the corresponding temperaments they were supposed to produce in humans: black bile (melancholic), blood (sanguinic), phlegm (phlegmatic), and yellow bile (choleric). The score for *The Four Temperaments* consists of a three-part theme and four variations, the latter entitled Melancholic, Sanguinic, Phlegmatic, and Choleric. In *Balanchine's New Complete Stories of the Great Ballets* the work is described as follows:

> Subtitled "A Dance Ballet without Plot," *The Four Temperaments* is an expression in dance and music of the ancient notion that the human organism is made up of four different humours, or temperaments. Each one of us possesses these four humours, but in different degrees, and it is from the dominance of one of them that the four physical and psychological types—melancholic, sanguinic, phlegmatic, and choleric—were derived. Greek medicine associated the four humours and temperaments with the four elements—earth, water, fire, and air—which to them composed the human body as well as the world. (Balanchine 1968: 171)

The author adds that "neither the music nor the ballet itself make specific or literal interpretation of the idea" (ibid.).

The Four Temperaments is divided according to the score with three duets stating the three-part theme.[8] The duets are followed by the four variations. The first, Melancholic, features a male soloist and corps de ballet; the second, Sanguinic, is a duet with corps; the third, Phlegmatic, is for male soloist and corps; and the fourth, Choleric, is for a female soloist and corps. Balanchine also generally followed the score in aspects such as tempo and pulse drive, and he took his cue from the

The Phlegmatic variation with Todd Bolender and corps de ballet in the original Ballet Society production of George Balanchine's *The Four Temperaments* (1946), © The George Balanchine Trust. *Photo: Peter Campbell. Courtesy of Jerome Robbins Dance Division, The New York Public Library for the Performing Arts, Astor, Lenox and Tilden Foundations.*

composer in the plotlessness of the ballet, using the notion of temperaments simply as a point from which to begin. Balanchine's close following of the score is not surprising since he was an expert pianist who had studied to be a composer as well as a dancer. For him dance was always inextricably tied to music.[9]

Ballet movement, derived from the vocabulary and comportment of the classical dance or *danse d'école*, makes its effects through such elements as pattern and dynamics, but also through what are commonly called movement images. Sally Banes has defined such images as "suggested characterization which appears, disappears, and reappears through the articulation of posture and gesture" (Banes 1995: 350). The most prosaic version of such movement images is pantomime, an imitation of movement from everyday life, such as recoiling in fear. A step removed from pantomime is what theater director William Ball calls connotative movement, those conventionalized gestures and movements that are used on the Western theater stage and that are understood to have general meaning (Ball 1984: 110–112). A person kneeling before another to suggest supplication is one example, as is a couple holding hands to suggest romance. At a less mimetic level, dance imagery may draw on other encoded systems to suggest associations, such as baroque sculpture or military drill. Or dance imagery may derive from movements and gestures that have no specific meaning in themselves but that suggest meaning through formal processes, including such devices as repetition, symmetry, and recontextualization.[10]

Looking at *The Four Temperaments*, it is clear that despite the moods that are indicated in the various section titles, little of the movement makes clear reference to them. Occasionally a dancer performs an action that derives from daily life and is immediately recognizable. So, in the Melancholic variation, the male soloist circles down into a tight heap, his head lowered in what is a virtual cliché for dejection. But such images are rare. Far more common are movements that are suggestive, but less specific. The Melancholic soloist pushes through the "obstructing" arms of the female supporting dancers. In the Sanguinic duet the man lifts the woman in a series of low split lifts that encircle the stage and in which she seems to be pushing through the air in slow flight. In other instances movement derives from encoded systems within painting and sculpture that refer to medieval imagery. The Phlegmatic figure at one point resembles an unhappy jester, his knees turned in, his body drooping, while at another, he executes a courtly bow. Lincoln Kirstein described Todd Bolender, the original dancer of the Phlegmatic variation as "a fluidly sluggish acrobatic mendicant" (1973: 82). The women in the ballet recall medieval painting and sculpture, as well as twentieth-century showgirls and fashion models, when they stand with their hips thrust forward and their body weight back.

There are many dance images in the ballet that could suggest multiple meanings, such as the women's pose just mentioned. Another example occurs in the Choleric variation, which centers on a female soloist. The dancer enters from upstage left and moves horizontally across the space in a series of fast, tight turns. At center stage she whips to a kneeling position with her head and arms stretched downward as if she were diving toward the floor. Although this speed might be interpreted as anger, one of the dominant traits of the choleric temperament, or associated with fire (the Greek counterpart of the medieval

The Melancholic variation from George Balanchine's *The Four Temperaments*, © The George Balanchine Trust. New York City Ballet production, 1969. *Photo: © Martha Swope.*

humour), it could just as easily be seen simply as speed, since there is little else in the dance that attaches itself to clear cues of anger or flames in everyday movement. The opening music, however, is in a fast tempo that suggests speed, and Balanchine, faithful to the music, has followed its suggestion. Music, therefore, also plays a role in accounting for dance images.

Added to these various movement images are others that seem simply mysterious. In the second duet of the theme (repeated in the finale) the man and woman exit across the stage in sharply pointed walking steps while their heads and torsos face front like Egyptian bas-reliefs. As they step, they flip their arms, bent at sharp right angles, up and down in opposition to each other as if engaging in an untranslatable kind of semaphore. At other moments the women make cat's paw–like gestures with their hands curled softly in front of them, or execute stiff arm movements out to the side as if demonstrating the kick of the Australian crawl.

The Four Temperaments, then, offers an array of movement images to which a viewer's eye can attach and make fleeting connections yet can never organize into a narrative or even into a unified mood. As critic Walter Terry noted in an early review, the various images emerge and then are immediately dissolved into the larger framework of abstract classicism (1951b: 17). However, while classicism ultimately unifies the disparate dance images, the *danse d'école* itself is constantly disrupted by anticlassical elements. These include the use of a flexed as well as the pointed foot of the *danse d'école*, turning the leg in as well as out, shifting the weight down as well as up, and allowing the torso to collapse as well as assume the held-up position that is a basic part of ballet comportment. Most important among these disruptive elements is a recurring decentering of the body, which forms a leitmotif through the ballet. So, for example, in the many *grands battements* that are included, the body is not centered and straight, but is pushed front, back, or sideways. In another repeated pose, the body is cantilevered back over the supporting leg, which is bent in a *demi-plié*, while the working leg points forward. The Melancholic variation is filled with backbends, giving the impression that the soloist is on the edge of gravity, that if he were to move another inch he would collapse—and these are only a few examples of decenteredness that could be mentioned.

Dancer Merrill Ashley has spoken of having difficulties with a step in the Sanguinic variation in which, unsupported, she was supposed to look as if she were falling backward, although the fall was in fact controlled. She explained: "In *The Four Temperaments* the body is frequently at an oblique angle. It's a very unusual type of movement which takes some getting used to. I think all of the dancers in 'Four T's' have experienced some difficulty in learning to move in such a unique way" (Ashley et al. 1987: 27; see also Ashley 1982: 384–386). Patricia Wilde agreed: "I found Sanguinic difficult. Very difficult. It's that strange, off-balance thrusting and then moving back again to another off-balance position and then having to right yourself and go into the many multiple turns and things. That does create problems" (Wilde et al. 1987: 28). The steps may have been difficult because they occurred neither in the *danse d'école* nor in usual human comportment. Being off-balance was therefore unusual and uncomfortable. However, although the use of such anticlassical elements as turn-in, flexed feet, a collapsed torso, and decenteredness disrupt and fragment the unity of the *danse d'école*, it should be emphasized that they are not allowed to dominate the dance, which

Mary Ellen Moylan and Fred Danieli in the Sanguinic variation from the original Ballet Society production of George Balanchine's *The Four Temperaments* (1946), © The George Balanchine Trust. *Courtesy of Ballet Society Collection, New York City Ballet Archives.*

continually returns to the ballet vocabulary and comportment. The significance of the dominance of classicism will be discussed shortly. First, however, I want to examine the anticlassical aspects of the ballet in more detail.

At least one commentator in the postwar years saw influences of modern dance in *The Four Temperaments*. Walter Terry wrote in 1951 that "the total effect is quite modern-dance in quality, for fluid torsos, archaic arm patterns and breath rhythms (as opposed to merely musical rhythms) are apparent. . ." (1951b: 17). Terry may well have been correct, since by the mid-1940s Balanchine certainly had been exposed to modern dance.[11] I believe, though, that movement of another kind is more central to the work. Brenda Dixon Gottschild (1996) and Sally Banes (1994: 53–69) have made a case for the use of what Gottschild calls an "Africanist presence" in Balanchine's work. According to Gottschild, this presence is represented most strongly in references to African and African American–derived dance, and in an African-derived aesthetic, which favors such elements as speed and sharp attack, polyrhythm and polycentrism (more than one body part being emphasized at once), omission of transitions, syncopation, and a cool presentation (Gottschild 1996: 11–19). It is important to note that "Africanist" must be thought of here in its broadest terms, since by Balanchine's time such elements often were filtered through the work of white artists and performers to enter a general lexicon of entertainment media as well as white social dance. High-art forms, particularly music, painting and sculpture, had also absorbed Africanist rhythms and imagery. If considered within this broad definition, Gottschild and Banes make compelling arguments for Africanist sources in Balanchine's work. In the 1950s, Edwin Denby, too, noted these sources ([1953] 1986: 438).

Both Gottschild and Banes state that Balanchine had links to Africanist art and culture even before leaving Russia in the 1920s and that he used Africanist elements in his work at least as early as *Apollon Musagète* (1928). More important, Balanchine had worked extensively in the commercial theater and films during the 1930s and '40s, often with black artists such as Josephine Baker, Katherine Dunham, Herbie Harper, and Buddy Bradley. Dunham and other black dancers noted how much Balanchine appreciated their dance, whether it was tap, jazz, or the Haitian-inspired work of Dunham herself. Gottschild includes a photo of Balanchine with Dunham and other dancers in which Balanchine is executing a black social dance move, his left leg lifted high, his right finger pointing skyward. The picture was taken when Balanchine was working with Dunham and her troupe on the Broadway musical, *Cabin in the Sky* (1940).

Both Gottschild and Banes have analyzed Africanist sources specifically in *The Four Temperaments*. They note the focus on Africanist elements such as angular arms, foot flexes, jutting hips, turn-in, and bent knees. They also mention a leaned-back "cakewalk" pose in which the torso is thrown back while the legs execute high-stepping prances, and the little pawlike gestures that were seen in postwar black social dance and in chorus lines. In addition, there is a crouch that the female dancers assume from time to time, which Banes and Gottschild label the "get-down" posture common in Africanist dance. Gottschild points out a lift that is seen frequently in the ballet in which the man lifts his partner from behind as she executes a wide side-split. Gottschild says that this was a popular move in the Lindy Hop and illustrates her argument with a photo. She also notes several other steps that are balletic versions of Lindy moves, including a moment in the second theme duet where the man holds his partner from behind and pushes her hips forward and back as he turns her. Most notable, however, according to Gottschild, is Balanchine's use of decenteredness, which in the duets "deconstruct and defy the ballet's canon of verticality and male support of female centeredness, essentials in the classic *pas de deux*. . . . The males in these duets push, thrust, or manipulate their partners off center. They seem to play with letting the female fall" (1996: 73). Gottschild sees this as "a ballroom dance risk-taking that Balanchine has crafted to meet the needs of the ballet aesthetic and the concert stage" (ibid.).

A number of dancers have commented on the amount of male manipulation of female bodies that goes on in *The Four Temperaments*, as well as the work's emphasis on speed and attack (Reynolds 1977: 73–74; LeClercq 1982: 153).[12] The manipulation of the female body often has to do with holding women so that they can maneuver far off-balance. But in some instances, as in the Choleric variation, the men actually throw or toss the woman into the air, something that they also did in postwar African-American social dances.

Ballet choreographers have traditionally used elements from outside the *danse d'école* as a means of decoration or foreign color. However, Balanchine did not insert African-American steps into *The Four Temperaments* as references or identifying marks of the foreign. Rather he did just the opposite, decontextualizing and abstracting them as he did other dance images. As Banes and Gottschild point out, Balanchine also integrated Africanist aesthetic elements such as speed, attack, and angularity into the ballet medium.

Along with Africanist elements, Balanchine also used methods similar to those of the surrealists to disrupt any kind of sustained narrative or thematic logic in *The Four Temperaments*. Balanchine had connections with surrealism going back to his time with Diaghilev's Ballets Russes, and he had worked with surrealist designers later in Europe and the United States. Important, too, was Kirstein's enthusiasm for surrealism and his understanding of its place in the art world. A number of the surrealists had found their way to New York during the war, including Kurt Seligmann, André Breton, Max Ernst, Man Ray, and Andre Masson.[13] Surrealism represented the current international avant-garde, and during the 1940s, Americans proceeded to absorb its lessons. At the same time, because the United States was now the "leader of the free world," it needed an art that not only stood in opposition to the Soviet Union's, it also needed one that could compete favorably with that of Europe. Surrealism could help place American art within that international milieu. Significantly, when it came time to select a designer for *The Four Temperaments*, Kurt Seligmann was enlisted.

Although Balanchine did not use the kind of subject matter in the ballet usually associated with surrealism, particularly myth and dream, he did employ surrealist devices. This is not to suggest that Balanchine shared the surrealist vision of art's relationship to society, a relationship that called into question the very existence of the institution of art and that Balanchine's dedication to ballet classicism would hardly have allowed. Rather, his assumption of a number of surrealism's means imbued *The Four Temperaments* with an ambiguity and enough disruption of tradition to put it on the side of formal experiment while not challenging the ruling order in any substantial way.[14]

Among the surrealist devices Balanchine used in *The Four Temperaments* were dislocation, contradiction, and incongruity. In surrealism these were often represented in the form of collage, an arrangement of disparate elements that in visual art usually includes cut-outs from mass-produced publications that, in combination, communicate no specific theme or narrative. Balanchine's use of vernacular movement and popular dance steps resembled collage in that they were disparate and unattached to any sort of narrative or thematic framework. Instead, they were decontextualized and arranged formally through visual and temporal elements such as shape and texture, tempo, and dynamics. They were also dissolved into more abstract movements so they lost their specificity or were themselves melded into balletic comportment and style. So, for example, the Melancholic soloist crumples into what may appear to be a pose connoting dejection, but the image is nearly free-floating because it is not reinforced or referred back to narratively by other movement surrounding it. This includes both the movement the soloist does temporally before and after the pose and the movement done simultaneously by the corps dancers surrounding him. However, it must be emphasized that although Balanchine broke up narrative logic, he did not interrupt formal logic. As mentioned above, he related movement through such elements as pattern, texture, and dynamics. He was, of course, also highly sensitive to the musical structure, which served as a strong organizing force in the work.

Manipulation and transformation of the (usually female) body were common in surrealism, especially in photography. In *Primacy of Matter over Thought* (1929), Man Ray depicted a woman melting into a pool of liquid, and Brassai, in *Woman-Amphora* (1935), showed a female figure cropped to resemble a ceramic vessel. Balanchine also used transformation in *The Four Temperaments*. The best-known example occurs in the third theme duet when the man turns the woman in a manner reminiscent of the way in which jazz musicians used to spin the bass viol as part of a virtuosic display. When Balanchine spun a female dancer like a bass fiddle he, too, was making a comment on the transformative possibilities of the human body.

In surrealism, manipulation of the body most often occurred in the artist's manipulation of the image rather than in the subject matter of the work , that is, in one figure depicted transforming or distorting another. Sometimes this manipulation was violent and was especially aimed at women. Man Ray, André Kertesz, and other photographers distorted female body parts, as did Hans Bellmer, who twisted his grotesque dolls into tortured, erotic poses. Balanchine's use of men to handle women never approaches this level of violence, but the repeated placing of female dancers off-balance or lifting them in ways that look strained or painful creates a sense of tension. For example, in the first theme duet, the man holds the woman under the arms, and she hangs in a split, her points touching the ground while the man drags her off stage. In another instance, this time in the third theme duet, the woman clings to the man's back as he drags her after him. Such poses and movements produce a sense of unease that critics have noticed in various ways since the ballet's premiere. The men's handling of the women, although perhaps no more than a means of exploring the choreographic potential of decentering the body, was seen as violent by postwar critics.[15]

On first viewing, Edwin Denby made comments that reflected *The Four Temperament's* closeness to surrealist concerns in its emphasis on fantasy and violence. After noting the denseness and power of the work's dance images, he spoke of the unpredictability and fantastic quality of its sequences, which "crowd close the most extreme contrasts of motion possible" ([1946] 1986: 415). A few months later he expanded on his initial reaction: "It appears to have the dispassionate ferocity of a vital process; its subject is the 'four temperaments' (or humours) of medieval endocrinology and it suggests the grandiose impersonal drama of organic energies. It is an impersonal drama that appears to be witty, cruel, desperate, and unconsoling, like that of our time. Yet all that actually

Jason Fowler and Jennifer Tinsley in the third theme from George Balanchine's *The Four Temperaments*, © The George Balanchine Trust. New York City Ballet production, 2004. *Photo: © Paul Kolnik. Courtesy of New York City Ballet.*

happens onstage is rapid exact ballet dancing in classic sequences that are like none you could ever imagine." ([1947] 1986: 516).

Doris Hering of *Dance Magazine* said of the dances: "They have an almost ruthless quality as though the bodies used in their fabrication should be discarded for new ones after each performance" (1949: 34). Several years later she noted: "*Four Temperaments* [*sic*] is steely and capricious. Balanchine sends his dancers into violent front extensions that end in buttery back falls. He twirls his girls off-center like crooked tops. He pits tension against rag-like relaxation with endlessly exciting results" (1953b: 10). The sense of violence, then, in *The Four Temperaments* could be accounted for through such anticlassical elements as the extreme decenteredness of the movement, which causes a sense of tension in the viewer; the harsh manipulation of the dancers (twirling the girls like crooked tops); the extreme juxtaposition of movement (violent front extensions, buttery back falls; rag-like relaxation and tension); and transformation and distortion of the body (crooked tops).

Aiding the sense of violence and dislocation was the fact that the ballet did not reinforce the moods indicated in the temperaments. Several critics saw this as a failing of the ballet, including Walter Terry, who said that although *The Four Temperaments* was rewarding for its movement design, it did not "mirror the descriptive qualities listed on the program" (1947a: 4). This lack of discernible mood images may well have made *The Four Temperaments* seem impersonal and cold, as Denby commented. However, there were other elements, as well, that contributed to the work's sense of violence—these were the ballet's designs and its finale.

Seligmann's costumes were peculiar assemblages that sometimes looked as if bandages had been added to tights and tutus, at others like ragged medieval clothing with horned or mushroomlike headdresses. According to Kirstein, "Seligmann swathed our dancers in cerements, bandages, tubes, wraps, and tourniquets" (1973: 82). The set, too, suggested twisted bandages painted on a drop that resembled Seligmann's paintings. Altogether, the sets and costumes gave the stage a roiled, uneasy appearance. Then there was the ballet's finale. Kirstein described it as "a volcanic fountain or atomic eruption of bodies" (ibid.). As shown in a 1946 film of a Ballet Society rehearsal, the dancers are grouped in a tight circle. Beginning low to the floor, a wavelike movement sweeps over them, rippling around the circle higher and higher until the dancers are standing with arms raised. In the final moments, a male figure is repeatedly thrown upward from the center in what seems slow motion. If to these elements are added Denby's description of the ballet as "an impersonal drama that appears to be witty, cruel, desperate, and unconsoling, like that of our time," the ballet begins to resonate with the immediate postwar era's concern with the impersonal horror of atomic catastrophe. This aspect of the ballet, choreographed little more than a year after the bombing of Hiroshima and Nagasaki, disappeared in 1951, and with it any trace of timely reference. By that year, Ballet Society had become New York City Ballet and was firmly ensconced in City Center. Balanchine replaced Seligmann's sets and costumes with practice clothes and a plain blue cyclorama, which served to make the ballet less specific. He also changed the finale essentially to the one it has today. In the present version, the female soloists are seen in a series of split lifts in which they soar above the other dancers who form what Arlene Croce called a "runway" for their flight (1977: 190). Croce reflects the general opinion of today's commentators in finding this ending stirring and hopeful, a very different reaction from the dark vision critics saw in the ballet's original form.

Balanchine's use of surrealist elements in *The Four Temperaments*, from collage to corporeal dislocation and the sense of violence it engendered, put his dance on the side of experiment for many viewers; in addition, during the postwar years his ballets came to be seen as uniquely American.

Modern dance had long laid claim to being the only American form of high-art dance. This was in contrast to ballet, which was consistently portrayed as foreign. Martha Graham made pronouncements throughout the 1930s on what an American dance would be, and she assumed that the dance she was describing would be modern dance. This new dance, she said, would not be represented by one technique but by many and would be characterized not by a series of steps but by a unique rhythm and quality of movement, "a characteristic time beat, a different speed, an accent, sharp, clear, staccato" ([1937] 1985: 105). She described the American temperament as young, fresh, exuberant, with an overabundance of youth and vigor. American dancing, she predicted, would be woven from the threads of many old cultures, but "the whole cloth will be entirely indigenous" (ibid.: 100).

Denby attributed many of the traits Graham enumerated to Balanchine's dancers and choreography while at the same time being careful to emphasize the classical form in which they were contained. In 1948, for example, he wrote that Balanchine's American balletic style was strictly classical and supremely musical. His dancers were notable for their long limbs, simple carriage, strength, speed, clarity, animation, and technical and musical exactness (Denby [1948] 1986: 521–522). Denby pointed out that similar traits were seen in "young Americans in a ballroom or in a dance hall" (ibid.: 521). By 1952, he was more explicit about Balanchine's sources. He noted Balanchine's use of "Negro and show steps" and spoke of his "extraordinary absence of prejudice as to what is proper in classicism" ([1953] 1986: 438). Other critics were less specific about Balanchine's Africanist sources, simply ascribing elements that had long been appropriated as "American" to his work and dancers. In 1948, Reed Severin wrote in *Dance Magazine:* "Balanchine has exploited such typical American traits as speed, accuracy, a good ear for rhythm, straightforwardness, athleticism" (1948: 43), while in 1950,

Doris Hering said: "Mr. Balanchine has carefully and intelligently exploited the native speed and high energy of his American dancers" (1950: 12).

Balanchine's use of Africanist elements also introduced a democratic element into the *danse d'école* that may have struck spectators as particularly American. Denby spoke of Balanchine's lack of prejudice in transforming show and ballroom dance elements into classical ballet. As noted earlier, the high art of ballet had always incorporated popular and social dance but had usually separated high and low. Peasant dances, buffoon dances, folk and national dances—all appeared on the stage but were not allowed to mix with the *danse d'école* except as an occasional decorative detail (a hand gesture, a step or two) to remind viewers of the ballet's theme or location. Popular and social dances had their place, but they were not done on pointe and did not incorporate the ballet vocabulary, although they might be balleticized through elements such as comportment and virtuosity. Balanchine mixed low art with high, changing not just steps but the comportment of his dancers. It is here, in the carriage and presentation of the body, that Pierre Bourdieu finds "political mythology realized, *em-bodied*" (1990b: 69–70). Balanchine let torsos bend and sag, hips jut and sway, feet move flat on the floor. At the same time, however, these postures and movements, long associated in Western culture with the "people" or the "folk," were subsumed into a high-art choreography that continued to reinforce the upright, the symmetrical, the balanced, and the light. This movement, democratic but aristocratic, was well suited for America's ascent to world power. It suggested dedication to equality and the common man while embedding these symbols in a courtliness associated with those who rule. At the same time, the ballet's disruption yet extension of tradition made it appear an appropriate heir to European artistic domination. Here was a dance that had not only absorbed all that Europe had to offer but had then reformed the art, giving it new shape and purifying it of contaminating elements, such as plot and pantomime.

Graham had said that American dance would have a sharp, staccato beat. Stephanie Jordan has commented on the fact that pulse was an organizing principle for Balanchine and that pulse drive was reflected in his movement style. The dancers tended to move, in Denby's words, "on top of the beat," with a rhythmic thrust that was quick and exact. Jordan connects this "discipline of pulse" with modernist musical thinking, which played down emotional qualities for control, regularity, and precision (2000: 112–120). Certainly critics commented on the emotional coolness of Balanchine's dances. As late as 1958, the subject was still an issue. *Dance Magazine* published an article by Eugene Palatsky that year in which he wrote that New York City Ballet was controversial in part because of its perceived lack of emotion. In interviews with a number of the company's dancers, Palatsky returned repeatedly to this issue. Balanchine, himself, considered detachment a definitively American characteristic. In an article for *Dance* in 1937 he wrote:

> Superficial Europeans are accustomed to say that American artists have no "soul," no personal or national style. This is wrong. America has its own spirit—cold, crystalline, luminous, hard as light. American dancers have a genuine quality or "soul," but, unfortunately, they rarely possess a technique capable of transmitting it.
>
> It is perhaps the most remarkable soul of all because it is capable of giving an exposition of any material without identifying or diluting it by subjective identification, either national or personal.
>
> Good American dancers can express clean emotion in a manner which might be almost termed "angelic." By angelic I mean the quality supposedly enjoyed by angels which, when they relate a tragic situation, do not themselves suffer.
>
> To be the most perfect instrument without drawing attention to one's personal notion of the chosen composition is not a meager task, but a heroic service, however anonymous. (1937: 13)

Cool detachment was not something that was ordinarily attributed to the American character, and this quality, which Balanchine assigned to the American dance "soul," may actually have been due to more mundane reasons. The early New York City Ballet dancers were young and, except for the principals, had little stage experience. Many were hardly more than students. Tanaquil LeClercq, a sixteen-year-old who had been plucked from the School of American Ballet, spoke about the impossibility of adding interpretation to the Choleric variation while meeting the demanding speed of the steps (LeClercq 1982: 153). The young dancers' inability to charm with stage personality, and perhaps to do little more than master the technical demands being made on them, was transformed by Denby and others into American honesty and straightforwardness, and then into a national style.

Although critics saw elements such as musicality, athleticism, youthfulness, and energy in Balanchine's dance and saw them as uniquely American, he had, in fact, long been interested in youth and virtuosity, as well as Africanist rhythm and movement. As Banes and Gottschild pointed out, Balanchine had inserted Africanist elements into his work while still serving as a choreographer for Diaghilev in the 1920s. As for youth and virtuosity, in 1925 Balanchine had cast a fourteen-year-old Alicia Markova as the Nightingale in *Le Chant du Rossignol* for Diaghilev. When he joined Les Ballets Russes de Monte Carlo in 1932, he had astonished Europe with his virtuosic "baby ballerinas"—Irina Baronova, Tamara Toumanova, and Tatiana Riabouchinska—who were in their early teens and who were said to be able to accomplish amazing technical feats (Kochno 1954: 293; Taper 1984: 136–137; Buckle 1988: 58–59). Thus, Balanchine did not become interested in youth as a uniquely American attribute; he had long favored young dancers.

One of the reasons for his interest in youth was that he was concerned with molding and shaping dancers, and the younger they were, the more likely he was to succeed. On coming to the United States, Balanchine clearly realized that American dancers needed better training if they were to perform his choreography. His insistence on having a school before he began to turn his attention to a company supports the argument for his focus on technique. In the article from *Dance News* quoted above, he mentioned that American dancers for the most part were incapable of transmitting their own native qualities. As both Tanaquil LeClercq and Maria Tallchief have testified (LeClercq 1982; Tallchief 1997) Balanchine spent many long hours working with his young American dancers to improve their technique. In the early postwar years, he was particularly concerned with bringing them to a high degree of technical proficiency quickly in order to be able to compete on an international level. Balanchine nearly always taught the company class each day but, according to LeClercq, before New York City Ballet's first tour to England in 1950, he additionally worked with his leading dancers each night to improve their technique (LeClercq 1982: 167).

In training dancers, Balanchine continually sought greater speed and attack as well as higher extensions (for virtuosity), more precision and greater turn-out (for clarity of body image). Again, these were not interests that originated in the United States but were given impetus in America because he had greater control over his dancers' training and, after 1948, a stable company with which to work. These elements, which Balanchine emphasized as part of his own interests and dispositions, reinforced aspects of what were already considered American attributes. This is not to say that Balanchine also did not view such attributes as typically American, but that they existed in his work long before he entered the United States.

As Balanchine's dance was increasingly seen as American, Balanchine himself became more American in the written discourse of the period. During the 1930s and the early 1940s, he had been treated as a member of the Franco-Russian ballet world, one of several such choreographers who were working in America. His foreignness was emphasized in the popular press through crass imitations of his accent, such as the following quote from an article in *Colliers* magazine: "His name grew, as he puts it, 'more and more famouser'" (Davis and Cleveland 1940: 22). However, as Balanchine came to be accepted as the "creator" of an American ballet, his foreignness was blurred. America's tradition of immigration and assimilation made Balanchine an American through citizenship. It is notable that many of the articles written about him in the postwar period referred to the notion that he had become American through naturalization. For example, Allen Churchill wrote in *Theatre Arts* in 1949: "When America's contribution to ballet is some day added up, the development of ballet as pure dance may be designated as American ballet, just as the contributions of Fokine are labeled Russian. Balanchine, in this country sixteen years, has been an aggressively American citizen for nine" (1949: 35). Churchill tied Balanchine and abstraction to a definitive American dance, and he made Balanchine American. In an even more astonishing sleight of hand, he compared this American choreographer (and the American dance he had developed) to Fokine, a Russian. Not surprisingly, Kirstein, too, promoted the notion of Balanchine's Americanness. In an article written in 1947, he noted Balanchine's American citizenship and said that he had recently mounted a work for the Paris Opera Ballet, the first person from "his country," that is, the United States, to do so (1947a: 37).

Balanchine himself aided the notion of his Americanness in various ways. In 1946, he married ballerina Maria Tallchief, whose father was a Native American. Tallchief speaks in her autobiography about Balanchine's interest in her family and the Oklahoma reservation where she spent part of her childhood. "He claimed that by marrying me he finally felt he was a real American, and he compared us to John Smith and Pocahontas" (1997: 119).

In the late 1940s, some critics saw in Balanchine's ballets a modernism they felt was being compromised in modern dance. However, although Balanchine's work took on some of the attributes of vanguard art, it did not share vanguard goals. For as much as Kirstein spoke out against commercialism and complained of New York City Ballet's poverty, he well understood how necessary it was to find support among establishment institutions in order for a ballet company to succeed. He had spent his life among people of influence, and he knew how to function within that social framework. In 1948, when Ballet Society became New York City Ballet under the aegis of New York City Center of Music and Drama, Kirstein's intentions became clearer. In the 1950s, New York City Ballet proved to be an exemplary representative of an elitist, cultural arm of institutional power. Balanchine's choreography embodied America's new position of world leadership; his choreography built on an imperial past that had been democratized and given youthful energy. At the same time, his emphasis on the lack of specific meaning in his work guaranteed its freedom from the taint of political critique. Balanchine, himself, was the embodiment of the immigrant American who found success on the shores of the land of opportunity. And added to that bit of American mythology was the fact that he had turned his back on Soviet repression for the freedom of the West, part of American Cold War ideology.

Balanchine's dances were exploited in the postwar years as a sign of America's superiority to its European allies in the West and its Soviet enemy in the East. In 1952, New York City Ballet appeared in the Paris festival, "Masterpieces of the Twentieth Century," sponsored by the Congress for Cultural Freedom, a powerful anticommunist organization secretly sponsored by the CIA (Saunders 1999: 113–128; Kirstein 1973: 118; Chujoy 1953: 318–319, 341–345). Among the organizers of the exposition was Nicholas Nabokov, the composer and close friend of Balanchine. City Ballet also was among the early recipients of federal government largesse when, in 1954, the State Department began to sponsor overseas tours by American "cultural ambassadors" (Prevots 1998). Kirstein was conveniently on the committee of dance experts that made recommendations on which companies should be sent abroad. New York City Ballet visited the Soviet Union in 1962, and during the tour the notion that Balanchine had renounced Russia for freedom in the West was a common theme in the American press.

Balanchine choreographed several suites of dances dedicated to American themes in the postwar years, among them *Western Symphony* (1954) and *Stars and Stripes* (1958). *Stars and Stripes* shocked Dag Hammarskjöld, secretary-general of the United Nations and Kirstein's friend, who considered the ballet jingoistic in its exuberant celebration of American patriotism. Kirstein tried to pass off the work as a parody of hyper-Americanism, "but Hammarskjöld judged that the cause of peace among nations was not served by the blatant effrontery of our imperialist gesture" (1973: 151–152). Given that New York City Ballet chose to dance *Stars and Stripes* at Nelson Rockefeller's inauguration as governor of New York in January 1960, it is unlikely that the ballet was meant as a parody of patriotism or that spectators viewed it as such. But by that time, New York City Ballet had long represented establishment culture, both at home and abroad.

Nonetheless, for a time the Kirstein-Balanchine enterprise ruffled the waters of vanguard dance, and it made an impact on the genre with which it chose to compete. Kirstein invited Merce Cunningham to create *The Seasons* for Ballet Society and Iris Mabry to show her work there, and it is notable that both favored an objectivist dance. Cunningham, of course, studied and taught at the School of American Ballet. Other modern dancers who either taught or studied there in the 1940s and '50s included Louis Johnson, Anna Sokolow, Janet Collins, and Paul Taylor. Erick Hawkins danced for Balanchine in the 1930s and taught during that time at the School of American Ballet; in the 1950s, he turned to an objectivist dance after years of working in an expressional mode. Balanchine came in contact with more modern dancers through his musicals, including Katherine Dunham and Talley Beatty. Most important, though, was Balanchine's nonliteral approach to dance, which came at an opportune moment for a young generation of modern dancers who, by developing an objectivist dance of their own in the 1950s, created what would be declared a new modern dance vanguard.

MODERNIST THEORY: JOHN MARTIN, EDWIN DENBY, JOHN CAGE

Three of the most influential dance theorists in the postwar years were John Martin, Edwin Denby, and John Cage. Martin, in addition to his role as critic for the *New York Times*, wrote important theoretical works in the 1930s that helped define the aims of modern dance. In the 1940s, he consolidated this theory and in the 1950s contributed an important study on contemporary ballet. Denby was, with Lincoln Kirstein, the first to promote neoclassicism as an American ballet style, and Balanchine as the exemplar of that style. His writings on dance were published in book form in 1949 and made an immediate and lasting impact on the field. Cage, although best known as a vanguard composer, also was an important influence on modern dance. He wrote only four essays on dance, but he made his ideas known through his musical theory and also directly to dancers, for whom he composed music. While Cage was most closely associated with Merce Cunningham, he provided scores for a wide range of dancers during this period, including Jean Erdman, Nina Fonaroff, Valerie Bettis, Pearl Primus, Marie Marchowsky, Yuriko, Merle Marsicano, Louise Lippold, Iris Mabry, and Alwin Nikolais.[1]

These three theorists are often presented in opposition to each other: Martin promoting a dance that communicated psychological essences, Denby and Cage advocating a dance of so-called pure movement. Denby also is viewed as supporting ballet, in contrast to Martin and Cage, who favored modern dance. However, although they had their differences, I want to suggest that all three shared a modernist vision that differed primarily in degree, and which helps account for who they supported and why. Their modernism led them to advocate a dance that attempted to undermine rationalization through a corporeal intelligence. To this end they shared a faith in the dancing body's ability to demonstrate freedom from systems and processes governed by means-ends calculation.

John Martin (1893–1985) was born in Louisville, Kentucky.[2] His father was a purchasing agent for the Louisville and Nashville Railway, and his mother was a singer. He attended the University of Louisville where his major subject was classics, then studied violin at the Chicago Conservatory. He subsequently worked with the Chicago Little Theatre. After World War I, in which he served in the Army Air Force Signal Corps, Martin moved to New York, where he became editor of a trade publication, the *Dramatic Mirror*. He was the executive director of the Richard Boleslavsky Laboratory Theatre from 1924 to 1926 and occasionally directed summer stock productions in New York and Pennsylvania until 1934.[3] From 1927 to 1962, he was the dance critic for the *New York Times*. In addition to the hundreds of reviews Martin wrote in the course of his thirty-five-year career, he also published a number of influential books.

During the 1930s, Martin had been an outspoken advocate for modern dance, positioning it at the forefront of American high-art dance in *The Modern Dance* (1933), *America Dancing* (1936), and *Introduction to the Dance* (1939). Martin's ideas were similar to those of Louis Horst, with whom he came in close contact during the 1930s. Both taught or lectured at Bennington College, the summer home of the modern dance pioneers. Both sought to legitimize modern dance's place within modernism and to solidify its opposition to ballet, the traditional form from which it had revolted. However, Martin's theory was far more developed than Horst's and less concerned with the craft of dance composition.

Introduction to the Dance includes the major part of Martin's early theory. Like much of Martin's writing, it was aimed not at scholars but laymen. In this instance he had two major purposes: the first was to convince readers that all they had to do to enjoy dance was look at it without obstructing preconceptions; the second was to convince them of the superiority of modern dance to other forms. Consequently, throughout the book he often spoke of dance in general terms when he meant an

John Martin. *Photo: Leo Lerman.*
Courtesy of Jerome Robbins Dance
Division, The New York Public Library
for the Performing Arts, Astor, Lenox
and Tilden Foundations.

authentic dance, best characterized by modern dance or the roots and
aims of modern dance. An authentic dance had a social purpose, which
was to communicate essential truths. Martin posed this authentic dance
against another, which he called by various names but which was one so
dominated by form that it robbed dance of its social element. Formalism was the great destroyer, severing dance's ties to society and driving
artists to an art-for-art's-sake mentality that only reinforced art's separation from its communal source ([1939] 1965: 15–17). Martin credited
formalism's strength to capitalism with its division of labor and its reduction of all relationships to economic ones. Capitalism divided art,
like religion, of which it had been a part, from a daily life now defined
in purely economic terms. It was the task of an authentic dance to re-
connect art and life. Thus, Martin took the modernist position that an
authentic dance stood against rationalizing processes, of which formalism was one result.

Martin's first topic in *Introduction to the Dance* was the nature of
movement. He asserted that dance was "the very stuff of life" (ibid.: 31)
because its medium was human movement and its instrument was the

human body. Martin posited a link between movement and psychic states, which in an earlier volume he had called "metakinesis, . . . this correlation growing from the theory that the physical and psychical are merely two aspects of a single underlying reality"([1933] 1972: 13). Emotions were the result of human needs, drives, and desires. They were a "stirring up" caused by the action of the vital organs and nervous system in response to human contact with the environment ([1939]1965: 36–40).

Dance as art was a mode of human interaction in which the dancer communicated feelings (manifested in movement) that the spectator actively assimilated. The assimilation process did not take place on an intellectual level. Rather, it occurred corporeally without recourse to conscious thought. It was made possible by the fact that all humans possessed what Martin identified as a movement sense. This sense was physiologically based, working through motor and neural mechanisms. It was through these mechanisms that, for example, the body remained balanced as changes occurred in position and weight. But the body did not only respond to environmental encounters in this limited way; Martin claimed that each bodily action also produced an emotion about it. This emotional response to movement embedded itself in a "motor memory of emotion."[4] "Every emotional experience tends to make what we might call records of itself in motor patterns, setting up more of those well-worn paths in the neuromuscular system and adding new phases to those already set up" ([1939] 1965: 47).

Related to this storehouse of emotional memory was what Martin called "inner mimicry." This was a sympathetic motor response that occurred when an individual reacted to an object or another living being's action in a particular way because of having experienced something similar in the past. An individual could also extrapolate from life experience to emotionally relate to other situations not directly experienced. So one might unconsciously tense one's own muscles and then feel a sense of fatigue at the sight of a man or woman carrying a heavy burden. Motor memory and inner mimicry were key to the spectator's ability to respond to meaning in movement.

Dance communication, then, was corporeal; it was carried out body-to-body rather than through any sort of intellectual process. Communication began in life experience. Life experience, for Martin, did not consist of daily events; rather it was made up of the psychic states produced by physiological impulses that occurred when human beings met their environment and that became embedded in the motor memory of emotion. In an authentic dance, dancers drew on their own life experience, which they then abstracted and which spectators, in turn, assimilated through their life experience. Speaking of how a young choreographer might proceed in light of this theory, Martin pointed out that the solution to the problem of choreography "lies in turning directly to the fact that the body reacts to all stimuli first in terms of movement, and that communicative movement suitable for dance can be drawn only from what might be termed his [the dancer's] motor memory of emotion. He must learn how to call upon his emotional associations and translate them into action directly from life experience" ([1939] 1965: 86). However, Martin continued, although the artist communicated feeling or emotion to spectators,

> it is not the dancer's, or any other artist's, purpose simply to arouse us to feel emotion in a general sense, to stir us up to no end. It is his purpose, rather, to arouse us to feel a certain emotion about a particular object or situation. He wants to change our feeling about something, to increase our experience, to lead us from some habitual reaction which he has discovered to be perhaps merely inertia or otherwise limited and restrictive, to a new reaction which has an awareness of life in it and is liberating and beneficent. ([1939] 1965: 53)

An authentic dance challenged the status quo, thereby increasing the viewer's awareness of the possibilities in life in ways that were liberating. It was the dancer's task to introduce into the community an awareness of freedom otherwise prevented by habits, limitations, restrictions, or inertia.

The artist accomplished this vital task through a process of abstraction and formal organization that allowed the dance to communicate to viewers. The assumption here was that if life experience was not organized and abstracted through form, it was not communicable, or as Martin termed it "intelligible." The process of abstraction was a crucial element in Martin's theory because it was the means by which the dance was given universal significance. The artist abstracted from personal life experience, winnowing away inessential elements so that the dance could communicate to others: "The dancer's movements are abstract; that is, they have abstracted the essentials from a particular life experience, omitting all that is merely personal and without universal significance" ([1939] 1965: 89). Although the dancer abstracted specific elements from her movement, the resulting dance was not in itself abstract in the sense of being a purely formal design. The reason for this was, first, that the dance embodied universal experience and, second, that "the body is totally incapable of becoming an abstraction itself or of producing movement that is abstract in the sense of divorced from behavior" (ibid.: 63). The dance was always connected to human life through the body. Those connections may have been obscured, twisted, or otherwise mystified by rationalized theories and academic formulas, but they continued to exist.

Always fearful of such intellectual mystification, Martin contended that the process of imposing form on experience was simply a matter of craft. In the case of dance, the choreographer must understand how to manipulate movement in terms of space, time, and dynamics. The business of form was to shape material so that it fulfilled a specific purpose ([1939] 1965: 57). In this sense the artist was like a workman who knew how to build a functional chair, except that instead of wood or leather the choreographer's material was movement. Although artists had to be well versed in how to shape their materials, spectators needed to know little about it in order to respond to art. In fact, Martin said, complex theories only blocked communication between the artist and spectator.

Martin included sections on materials, music, and drama in *Introduction to the Dance* to give his readers a clearer understanding of the place these elements held in dance making. His discussion of the relationship of dance and drama is of greatest significance here because of the debates on narrative in postwar modern dance. Martin treated drama as narrative in the sense of its being a series of causally related events. He came down strongly against drama in an authentic dance while at the same time conceding drama's ubiquitousness within the dance field as a whole. He noted that although dance and drama were closely related, "dramatic form as such can be said to exist when the dance, instead of presenting the essence of an emotional experience, deals with a specific sequence of events out of which such an experience grows. The more literal its treatment, the less it has of dance about it" ([1939] 1965: 84). Dramatic form was found in many types of dance, but since modern dance dealt with essences, drama was not appropriate to it.[5]

After speaking of form and composition in dance, Martin turned to the subject of style, paying particular attention to what he considered the three major historical styles found on the Western stage. The earliest one of these was romantic, the source of which was the emotions. Romanticism valued feeling, spontaneity, informality; it grew out of the people, was democratic, colloquial, sometimes chaotic. Classicism defined and eventually petrified romantic style; it was concerned with rules, codes, and categories; it organized and defined what had gone before. Eventually classicism became mired in academicism and weakened by lifeless formulas. Then decay set in, or revolution, and the process began again ([1939] 1965: 110–121).

Modernism, the third historical style, combined elements of romanticism and classicism since it was characterized by a drive toward functional form. Modernism was a product of industrial society, in that modern technology relieved the artist of having to imitate visible reality. This allowed the artist to delve below the surfaces of life to seek out "the subjective roots of experience" ([1939] 1965: 123). Then, abstracting from this experience the artist was able to create an autonomous work of art, embodied life experience stripped of irrelevant elements. This embodiment of truth circumvented an otherwise rationalized world. "Here lay the complete answer to representationalism, the complete defiance of the machine in art" (ibid.).

Because the modern artwork was not an imitation, the artist could use materials in a less disguised way than in the past. Sometimes this attention to materials remained focused on finding and exposing essential forms. In this case it was classicist because it was not concerned with life experience. Martin thought that although pure form could perhaps exist in painting and music, it could not in dance because "the body cannot be separated from implied intent" ([1939] 1965: 125). So although Martin's description of an autonomous art in some ways resembled Clement Greenberg's, Martin, significantly, tied dance to life, from which it could not be separated because of its corporeal instrument. This difference suggested that dance had a more necessary relationship to society than did painting. Martin said as much when, as noted earlier, he stated that an authentic dance's function was not simply to stir up feelings for no purpose, but to change the viewer's awareness of the world in a way that was liberating and beneficial (ibid.: 53).

In the second part of his book, entitled "Dance in Action," Martin took up various ways in which Western society uses dance. In his discussion of theatrical dance he made a distinction between "spectacular" and what he called "expressional" dance. The former was meant to be watched objectively, while the latter was participated in vicariously. Spectacular dance was sensuous and intellectual in its appeal; it dealt with surfaces and was part of the category of entertainment in that it was created purely for pleasure. Expressional dance stemmed from the same sources as religion, magic, and social ritual and was meant to awaken emotional perceptions ([1939] 1965: 173–174). Martin placed this dance in the category of art. In the twentieth century, the binary of spectacular and expressional dance was best represented by ballet and modern dance, respectively.

In his chapter on spectacular dance, Martin surprisingly did not argue that ballet, as a form dependent on surfaces, sensuous pleasure, and intellectual appreciation, was incapable of achieving authenticity. Since he had posited that authenticity was dependent on the process of abstraction, which rendered a particular kind of dance autonomous, Martin contended that ballet could become autonomous, and thus authentic, by eliminating its dependence on decor (painting) and narrative (literature) and by returning to a "geometrical-aesthetic basis" of movement. Martin said that ballet's classicism was quite different from purely visual decoration or lifeless mechanics because it idealized the human body. Presumably it was this idealization that set ballet apart, for example, from a chorus line with its mechanical synchronization. Corporeal idealization was at the heart of ballet aesthetics and the source of its drive. Ballet was

> the presentation of its ideal essence freed from the encumbrances of a rationalistic universe of cause and effect, a pragmatical universe of organic drive and utilitarian function. It exemplifies the personal achievement of abstraction, of transcendent self-containment. In its idealization of the body it strips away all necessity for practical accomplishment, turning certain of its conformations to use more harmonious than the functional processes that have shaped them, and superseding where possible even structural elements which have been bred by utilitarian demands alone. ([1939] 1965: 212)

By devoting itself to a glorification of the body for itself, rather than as a unit of labor, ballet freed itself from cause-and-effect rationalization.

Martin's defense of ballet is startling, considering his insistence on the notion that an authentic dance communicated essential life experience. Ballet, as a spectacular form, had no interest in penetrating to experiential roots. Martin based his defense on the notion of balletic abstraction, that although ballet was concerned with form, it was essential form. Thus, the dancer's body achieved an abstraction that was greater or more harmonious than the rational processes that had fashioned it. Martin also maintained that dance always contained implied meaning because its medium was the body and, consequently, it could not be completely separated from life. This idea considerably weakened his argument against formalism, which Martin implicitly linked to ballet and which he claimed severed the ties between art and life. However, it gave to ballet some possibility of meaning. Yet ballet, since it was dedicated to form alone, made only a kind of accidental use of corporeal meaning. It lacked the power to embody, as Joseph Campbell had said, "the invisible pattern of the psyche reflected in time and space" (1944b: 66). Since an autonomous ballet could only circumvent cause-and-effect logic through its corporeal idealization, it would continue to have little or no power to change society. This enabled Martin to maintain modern dance's superiority, as it was dedicated to functional form.

Martin's argument for an authentic ballet may have been strained, but in 1939 that was not of crucial importance because, in any case, he saw no indication of ballet's moving toward modernist autonomy. He looked sympathetically on the work of Michel Fokine as a choreographer who had attempted to reform ballet through a synthesis of "realistic life impulses" and classical means. However, Martin felt that Fokine had led ballet as far in the direction of synthesis as possible; the next step would have been to abandon the classical vocabulary altogether ([1939] 1965: 210). As for Diaghilev, Martin considered his modernism faulty because it was not based on dance but developments in painting and music. Nor was he impressed with Balanchine, whose aesthetics, as noted earlier, he labeled anemic and whose work he considered part of a decadent Franco-Russian tradition.

By 1952, when he published *The World Book of Modern Ballet*, Martin had radically changed his view of ballet's likelihood of becoming an independent form. He had also become convinced that Balanchine was the choreographer to lead ballet toward that goal. Now he argued that Fokine's experiments, though admirable, had been useless. To locate the correct trajectory for ballet, one had to go back to Marius Petipa, the great classicist of the nineteenth century, who realized that ballet could not tell stories and attempted to solve the problem by alternating dance with pantomime, thus separating the two. In the mid-twentieth century it was Balanchine who, in his development of the plotless ballet, had assumed the mantle of Petipa. It was he who had most consistently purged ballet of the unnecessary elements of narrative and pantomimed illustration to become a neoclassicist and a true reformer.

As Martin's enthusiasm for Balanchine grew, certain elements of his interwar theory fell by the wayside. Among them were his attacks on formalism and his frequent, thinly veiled conflation of formalism and ballet. In his postwar writing Martin spoke little of formalism as a corrupter of authentic dance. He rarely mentioned the notion that formalism promoted an elite form that robbed dance of its social function and that robbed the public of dance by making it impossible for all but a small group of cognoscenti to understand. Now he spoke instead of Balanchine and Kirstein's refusal to surrender to market interests (1952: 14, 125–158). Balanchine's work was difficult; it did not court audiences, which indicated that it was more than easy entertainment. The difficulty of his work also put Balanchine on the side of innovation and experiment. According to Martin, Balanchine had replaced the flair of the old Russian ballet with substance. Significantly for the United States and its postwar policies of cultural domination, Balanchine, according to Martin, had also made New York the capital of the dance world (1952: 14).

It is worth noting that Martin's defense of Balanchine was written in the early 1950s, while *Introduction to the Dance* was published at the end of the 1930s. In those dozen years not only had the political landscape shifted as markedly as Martin's opinions, modern dance was facing problems that had not yet surfaced in the late 1930s. Martin's support of Balanchine went hand in hand with his critique of postwar modern dance, which reflected the genre's travails at the time. Martin continued to support Graham and Limón, but now he depicted them as the last standard-bearers of a true modern dance. He contrasted their authenticity with the younger generation's lack of ability to embody emotional essences. He also ignored the fact that Graham's and Limón's postwar choreography owed far more to dramatic form and characterization than had dances of the 1930s. Yet, this position allowed Martin to support what he claimed to be an authentic modern dance while faulting the younger generation of modern dancers and defending the neoclassicism of Balanchine.

Edwin Denby (1903–1983) had none of Martin's difficulties reconciling ballet with social function because his ideas about the purpose of dance and how it fulfilled that purpose were quite different. At the same time, however, Denby's thinking was similar to Martin's in a number of ways.

A poet as well as a critic, Denby was an eloquent spokesman for an American ballet during the crucial years of the 1940s. His upbringing could not have differed more from Martin's (MacKay 1986: 11–34). Born into a family of diplomats, Denby was raised in Asia, Europe, and the United States. He was a brilliant student, entering Harvard at sixteen. Halfway through his second year he left, confused and unsure of what he wanted to do except in some way to write. In 1923, he traveled with a friend to Vienna where he eventually discovered the Hellerau-Laxenburg School, devoted to the teaching of Emile Jaques-Dalcroze, the father of eurythmics, and also a center of *Ausdruckstanz*. Denby studied *Körperbildung* (physical development) at the school, graduating three years later. He then worked as a dancer-choreographer based in Germany and Switzerland. He also visited the Soviet Union where he saw much of the vanguard theater that was taking place there in the 1920s, as well as the Bolshoi Ballet. And in Paris he saw Balanchine's short-lived Ballets 1933, which made as profound an impact on him as it did on Lincoln Kirstein.

Returning to the United States in 1935, Denby settled in New York where he soon began writing dance reviews for *Modern Music*. He also rekindled old friendships with artists he had known in Europe such as Aaron Copland, Virgil Thomson, and Paul Bowles, and he made new friends with the abstract expressionist painters Arshile Gorky and Elaine and Willem de Kooning, poet Frank O'Hara, actor Orson Welles, and a host of other New York artists and intellectuals. From 1943 to 1945, he replaced Walter Terry as dance critic for the *New York Herald Tribune*. Most of the rest of his life was devoted to writing poetry, with occasional essays and reviews on dance. His criticism was collected in *Looking at the Dance* (1949) and in *Dancers, Buildings and People in the Streets* (1965). Much of Denby's theory is summarized in five essays written in the late 1940s and early 1950s: "Ballet: The American Position" (1947), "A Briefing in American Ballet" (1948), "Against Meaning in Ballet" (1949), "A Letter on New York City's Ballet" (1952), and "Some Thoughts about Classicism and George Balanchine" (1953). However, he elaborated his position in numerous reviews and in comments throughout his writing in the 1940s and '50s.

Denby's focus in his writing and his standard in dance was ballet, as Martin's was modern dance. Denby would not have differed greatly

Edwin Denby. *Photo: Jerome Robbins. Courtesy of the Robbins Rights Trust and Jerome Robbins Dance Division, The New York Public Library for the Performing Arts, Astor, Lenox and Tilden Foundations.*

from Martin in his assessment of ballet as an art that emphasized form and spectacle, nor would he have disagreed with Martin on the need for ballet to return to its classical roots in order to become autonomous. Classicism for Denby consisted, above all, of a dance in which movement was the driving force ([1953] 1986: 438). Classical ballets might have stories, he said, but they were unimportant; audiences went to see the dancing, not to witness fascinating plots unfold. As its means, classical ballet employed the vocabulary, comportment, and placement of the *danse d'école*, a virtuosic technique that allowed the body to be seen with the greatest possible clarity. It was this orientation toward movement in combination with the *danse d'école* that characterized the classic dance. Where Denby differed from Martin was that, for him, a ballet stripped of associations with literature and painting was not only enough to give it autonomy, it was all that was needed in dance. Modern dance's attempt to communicate essential experience was simply adding literary elements to an art that did not need it. Denby also decided, long before Martin, that Balanchine was the choreographer who was most completely dedicated to returning ballet to the classical values lost after Petipa. But Denby went further, defining the quintessential American balletic style as virtually synonymous with his idea of Balanchine's neo-classicism. Denby's theory and position become clear when we examine the ways in which he contrasted the old European with the new American ballet, classicism with other ballet styles, and ballet with modern dance.

Denby was writing when native ballet companies and dancers were only recently established. Ballet Theatre, the first major American company, was founded in 1940. The Ballet Russe de Monte Carlo settled in the United States during the war and gradually replaced its European personnel with Americans, becoming in essence an American company. From 1944 to 1946, Balanchine served as informal artistic director of the Ballet Russe before taking command of New York City Ballet when it emerged out of Ballet Society in 1948. Within this context of recently arrived American ballet, Denby defined an American ballet style in a way that served to differentiate it from the older Franco-Russian style typified by the Ballet Russe companies of the 1930s.[6] Speaking of the Ballet Russe style at its height, Denby described it as "more hot-and-bothered, its rhythm in dance scenes made more sweeping climaxes, its techniques looked more casual and undefined, and its temperament was more exotically fiery" ([1947] 1986: 510). In contrast, American dancing, he wrote, was large, clear, accurate, and unaffected. It was not very personal or emotional. The Europeans were better at "effects of imaginative impersonation, of imaginative atmosphere or stage presence" (ibid.). In other words, the Europeans excelled at those elements that were less dependent on movement than on acting and personality. They were less technically accurate, more affected, perhaps less honest and straightforward than the Americans, who depended on movement alone to create their effects. The problem with this argument was that there were many Europeans in American companies. Balanchine was living and working in New York; Ballet Theatre had European stars, such as Alicia Markova and Anton Dolin, both of whom had danced with Diaghilev's company in the 1920s. Denby's answer was that these artists had been transformed in the United States, absorbing American characteristics. European artists who could not change, failed ([1948] 1986: 518–521).

Once Denby had placed American ballet at the center of the dance field, he bisected the field again by identifying two branches of a distinctively American kind of ballet choreography. One was the neoclassicism of Balanchine; the other, the psychological ballet of Antony Tudor and the American folk ballet of Agnes de Mille and Jerome Robbins ([1947] 1986: 512–513).[7] Denby's argument was that the dance of de Mille and Robbins was dependent on literary means rather than movement for its full effect. Contrasting the two kinds of ballet, he said that Balanchine's work was more difficult to discuss because it was based on "dance qualities" rather than literary ones: "It is easier to talk about the novelty of our gay local-color Americanism in ballet or about the gloom-steeped psychological aspects of Tudor's gripping large-scale dramas of frustration. These pieces make a good deal of their appeal through their literary content, and from a literary point of view the value of them in nationalizing our ballet or in modernizing it has been properly stressed by many reporters" (ibid.: 512).

In other analyses, Denby pointed out that the American local-color ballets were derived from pantomime and character-dance elements. He found Tudor's works more ambitious and complex than those of de Mille and Robbins, but equally dependent on literary elements. Tudor's ballets were "full of passion, of originality, of dramatic strokes, of observation, of brilliant pantomime ideas and fastidiously polished detail" ([1948] 1986: 524). Denby further commented on the weak formal aspects of Tudor's works: "Their shock value, thrilling at first, does not last; their shaping force is discontinuous; they have a weak and fragmentary dance impetus; they peter out at the end. They can find no repose and no spring because balance is no element of structure in them" (ibid.). Although Martin was more sympathetic to Tudor's ballets than Denby, Martin also found them disturbing when he felt they moved too far outside the limitations of academic dance (Martin 1952: 71).

Denby's analyses of the works of Tudor, de Mille, and Robbins did not easily fit his description of the new American style that, he said, was characterized by a dependence on movement alone to make its effects. On the other hand, his descriptions of Balanchine's style emphasized just that element: "Not the story, but the dance rhythm, the surprising dance figures, the witty solutions, the clarity, and above all the musicality of the action seem to carry the piece" ([1947] 1986: 512). And speaking of Balanchine's classicism, he noted: "He has made our dancers look natural in classicism. His pieces carry onstage when they dance them classically clear and large, without nervousness or self-conscious glamour;

he has shown how fascinating their buoyant rhythm can be in all sorts of variations of forthright impetus" (ibid.: 511). Balanchine's neoclassical style, which Denby stressed here as definitively American, closely resembled what Martin had called for in an authentic ballet and that Martin himself came to see in Balanchine by the end of the 1940s.

The case Denby made against modern dance was similar to the one he had made against ballet that did not conform to a classical model. Of Graham, he wrote:

> I cannot omit mentioning Martha Graham, the greatest dance celebrity in the United States. Now past fifty, she is an actress of magnificent power, a dancer of astonishing skill; her choreographies abound in extraordinary plastic images of great originality. They are expressionist in rhetoric, violent, distorted, oppressive, and obscure; there is rarely a perceptible rhythmic unit or any dance architecture. But the ardor of her imagination, the scope of her conceptions, the intensity of her presence make her a dance artist of the first rank. ([1948] 1986: 525–526)

As with Tudor, Denby faulted Graham's choreography for its lack of dance qualities. It had, he said, no rhythmic structure, nor dance architecture. Instead, it was built on plastic images (an element of painting) and on Graham's personality and acting skills (elements of literature). Graham's dance, like Tudor's, owed what power it had to pantomime and personality, rather than movement. It was only in Balanchine's neoclassicism that dance became truly independent.

John Cage's critique of modern dance was not based on the genre's fatal attraction to literature but on its lack of dance structure and an impossible desire to communicate. Cage (1912–1992) was one of the best known and most influential American composers of the twentieth century. The son of an inventor, he was raised primarily in Los Angeles, where he studied with Arnold Schönberg (Cage 1973; Revill 1992). Cage became involved with dance in 1938, when he worked at the Cornish School in Seattle, accompanying and composing for the classes of former Graham dancer Bonnie Bird. There he met Merce Cunningham and five years later, when they had both settled in New York, their lives and work became connected in an association that lasted until Cage's death.

John Cage with prepared piano.
Courtesy of the Cunningham Dance Foundation.

Among the occasional articles on dance that Cage wrote was a piece from 1944 entitled "Grace and Clarity." Published in *Dance Observer*, it called for new thinking in modern dance (1944: 108–109). Like Denby and Lincoln Kirstein, Cage complained that modern dance had been too dependent on personalities. The first-generation modern dancers had developed practices based on their own interests, dispositions, and bodies. These practices were treated as sacrosanct; they could only be altered by the dancer who had developed them. Then, Cage said, the first-generation dancers had gradually deserted their own teachings, often adopting ballet elements, particularly ballet vocabulary, which had caused confusion among their students. The next generation of dancers had either copied their elders and remained shadows of them, or had, themselves, sought to incorporate into their own dance aspects of other established idioms such as folk and Asian dance and ballet, or had capitulated to Broadway and the commercial theater. Cage, then, echoed much of the criticism that modern dancers were leveling at themselves during the 1940s.

Cage had an answer, but it wasn't one that most modern dancers were considering. Modern dance, Cage contended, needed to establish stable, impersonal art practices. He cited ballet, singling out Balanchine's "exceptional" *Danses Concertantes*, as a form that achieved this objective and that flourished despite being "devoid of interesting personalities and certainly without the contribution of any individual's message or attitude toward life" (1944: 108). It was not ballet's vocabulary, style, patterns, or set and costume designs that was the secret, Cage declared, but its clear rhythmic structure. What made it completely legible to a viewer was the way in which the length of time the dance took was divided into large parts and then phrases. Whether one was speaking of a dance, a poem, or a piece of music, Cage said, this was a time art's life structure.[8] The pleasure in watching dance, as in any of the time arts, was to see the interplay between rhythmic structure and what Cage called "grace," "the play with and against the clarity of the rhythmic structure." Modern dance, with rare exceptions, had no understanding of this concept. In order for it to become a mature art form and to serve a useful social purpose it was necessary for it to "get itself a theory, the common, universal one about what is beautiful in time art" (1944: 109). Cage thus advocated the use of more impersonal methods in modern dance, not through vocabulary, which is where many dancers were focused, but through the rhythmic structure of dances.

In his 1944 article, Cage acknowledged that modern dance should have contemporary relevance, although he did not specify how. It was not, though, to be through purposeful communication, which he had abandoned in his own music by the mid-1940s. Cage came to believe that art could not communicate artistic intent. "I could not," he said, "accept the academic idea that the purpose of music was communication" (Revill 1992: 88). Citing his own experience as evidence, he went on to say that whenever he tried to communicate particular emotions through music, he failed. In addition, he felt that "all artists must be speaking a different language, and thus speaking only for themselves. The whole musical situation struck me more and more as a Tower of Babel" (Tomkins 1976: 97).

However, if dance was not to communicate, what was it to do? In an article taken from notes for a talk before a joint concert with Cunningham in 1956, Cage expanded on his ideas: "We are not, in these dances and music, saying something. We are simple-minded enough to think that if we were saying something we would use words. We are rather doing something. The meaning of what we do is determined by each one who sees and hears it" (1957: 10). Cage went on to point out that there were no symbols in the dance, no stories, no psychological problems. "There is simply an activity of movement, sound and light." This did not mean that the dance was not expressive. "The activity of movement, sound, and light, we believe, is expressive, but what it expresses is determined by each one of you" (ibid.). Unlike Martin, Cage did not believe the dancer could purposefully transmit emotional experience to the spectator. What, then, was the function of art? Cage found it in the spiritual. Quoting the teacher of an Indian friend, he wrote, the purpose of music is to "sober and quiet the mind, thus rendering it susceptible to divine influences" (Tomkins 1976: 99; Cage 1973: 158).

Part of Cage's means of quieting the mind was to make his work more impersonal, ridding it of what he called likes and dislikes. Cage employed a number of strategies for eliminating preferences and judgments in his music, the best known being chance operations. Beginning in 1951, he used the *I Ching* (*Book of Changes*) to introduce unpredictability into his work (Cage 1973: 57–61, 67–76; Tomkins 1976: 111–112; Revill 1992: 128–139). This ancient Chinese book had been employed to obtain oracular knowledge; Cage used its procedures, governed by tossing coins, to take decision making out of his hands. The dada and surrealist artists had also employed chance procedures to escape means-ends rationality (Richter 1965; Nadeau 1989; Bürger 1984: 64–66), and Cage, with his many surrealist contacts (he had camped out at the home of Peggy Guggenheim and Max Ernst upon arriving in New York) may well have discovered the notion through surrealism. Cage also had by this time discovered Zen Buddhism, which greatly influenced his theory and which fit well with anticausal ideas behind the use of chance procedures. The specific impact of Zen will be discussed in greater detail in chapter 7 within the context of Cunningham's choreography.

In addition to eliminating intentional communication and preferences in dance, Cage, and through him, Cunningham, also changed the relationship between dance and music, making music separate but equal to the dance. The two existed in a cooperative arrangement, but independent of each other. In a sense, Cage's idea of a modern dance was a more extreme version of the dance that Denby and Martin had outlined for an autonomous ballet. That is, it favored movement that excluded an attempt to communicate meaning. However, it was more self-sufficient than an abstract ballet, which remained dependent on music. Modern dancers had long attempted to sever ties to music, usually by settling on a score after having choreographed a work. This strategy, though, made music subservient to the dance. Cage, being a musician, sought a more equal, but nonetheless independent relationship between the two. Although separating music and dance was an important difference between modern dance and ballet, the crucial difference between Cage's conception of a new modern dance and modern dance as it heretofore had existed was that Cage sought the genre's basis in rhythmic structure rather than in movement that emerged out of feeling, and in doing so he pushed communication off the stage.

Yet as different as Cage was from Martin, and even from Denby, all three men shared views and assumptions that kept them firmly within the bounds of modernism. To begin with, they all attempted to shear away from dance those elements that were dependent on other art forms, particularly literature. A dance became authentic when it made movement its central focus. The difference among them was their notion of when extraneous elements intruded. For Denby and Cage, modern dance's attempt to communicate produced a dance dependent on acting and pantomime, while for Martin such elements appeared only when a dance dealt with characterization and plot. Where Martin saw embodiment, Denby and Cage saw representation.

In addition to an insistence on artistic authenticity through autonomy, all three theorists took a position against rationalization. At its most obvious this showed in a common dedication to anticommercialism. Martin did not wish to see modern dance enlarge its audience at the expense of compromising its vanguard principles; he deplored the use of elements such as balletic virtuosity and what he called "theatrical effects" as part of his critique of postwar modern dance. Martin also approvingly ascribed an anticommercial stance to Balanchine and Kirstein, and Denby likewise applauded what he considered Balanchine's lack of interest in the market. Cage and Cunningham's work was so arcane that there was no question of their being interested in commercial aims. Audiences walked out of their concerts for years without any noticeable change in their approach.

For Martin, an authentic dance defied a culture that was increasingly defined by industry and technology. Art's inability to represent nature with the perfection of the machine made it clear that the artist's strength lay in the power to abstract from nature. Armed with this advantage, the artist was able to give experience more value than nature itself ([1939]

1965: 122–123). It was in this unique human ability to find and explore the roots of experience and to expose essential truths that the artist defied the power of a culture ever more oppressed by means-ends calculation.

For Denby, classicism embodied the civilizing virtues of grace, courtesy and harmony, especially needed as a weapon against the violence and destruction of the modern age (Denby, [1947] 1986: 507–508; [1948] 1986: 518; [1953] 1986: 433–440). Denby compared Balanchine's attention to stylistic details to speaking a language with "purity of vocabulary and cleanness of accent, qualities that belong to good manners and handsome behavior" ([1953] 1986: 435). Denby used these terms in what Raymond Williams calls their traditional sense, as standing against barbarism (1983: 57–60). Civility was part of art's arsenal against the encroachments of the brutality of twentieth-century war, made possible by the rationalized processes of modern technology. For Denby, freedom from market forces also came down on the side of civilization. Commenting on Ballet Society in 1947 he wrote, "At the moment it [lack of commercial interest] is the most effective way of keeping it [ballet] civilized, though the method is obviously a lot of trouble. But unless it stays civilized, ballet is no fun. Staying civilized is always everybody's trouble, so why not ballet's?" ([1947] 1986: 516–17).

Cage broke up means-ends rationality through chance procedures, and through the 1950s he developed additional methods to guarantee unforeseen results in his compositions and performances. He mentions using collage, and he also experimented with other means employed by the dada and surrealist artists, including the *cadavre exquis*, in which a group of artists sequentially made part of a composition with only the knowledge of a small fraction of the preceding artist's effort (Revill 1992: 103). Such processes disrupted rational patterns of control that Cage felt prevented sounds or movements from becoming themselves. He noted that the devices he used were familiar from modern art and architecture, and he said he shared the philosophic principles of these modernists.

Perhaps the most important aspect of the three theorists' antirationalization was that they all had faith in the ability of the dancing body to mitigate the power of means-ends logic. They did this by claiming it was possible to "understand" dance, no matter how unfamiliar it might be, if only the viewer disconnected intellectual analysis. Dance was based on human movement, which everyone performed and understood intuitively no matter how transformed that movement might be. For Martin, dance was assimilated through such physiological mechanisms as muscular sympathy and inner mimicry. When dance was not absorbed, it was because spectators brought to it learned mental obstructions, including theories aimed at mystification, that inhibited their motor responses ([1939] 1965: 54–55). Although Martin did not separate psychic from physical processes, he made a sharp distinction between conscious and unconscious ones. For him responding to dance was quite a different process from intellectual contemplation: "It is useless to approach any work of art with the notion that it must be understood before it can be responded to. Understanding is a process of rationalization after the experience; first there must be the experience or there is nothing to rationalize about" (ibid.: 51). For Martin, the process of communication from dancer to viewer was a transference of experience that was different from any rational analysis that necessarily took place after the fact.

Denby and Cage also viewed dance reception as being outside the grasp of intellectual mediation. Denby argued that ballet, like poetry, was first responded to in a "spontaneously sensual" way, and he advised viewers not to think about what they were seeing but to simply enjoy it ([1949a] 1986: 530). Like Martin, he believed that intellectual endeavor ruined a viewer's ability to be receptive to dance. This is not to say that ballet could not be analyzed; rather, it was that its expressive qualities had little to do with rational thinking. Denby wrote: "Anyone who cannot bear to contemplate human behavior except from a rationalistic point of view had better not try to "understand" the exhilarating excitement of ballet; its finest images of our fate are no easier to face than those of poetry itself, though they are no less beautiful" (ibid.: 531).

Denby also alluded to an idea of bodily intelligence, which he called dancers' intelligence. Pierre Bourdieu has described bodily intelligence as a kind of understanding that occurs "only with our bodies, outside conscious awareness, without being able to put our understanding into words" (1990a: 166). According to Denby, dancers make the dance expressive through this kind of intelligence. He remarked that, "it is an error to suppose that dance intelligence is the same as other sorts of intelligence which involve, on the contrary, words only and no physical movement whatever" ([1944a] 1986: 204). Dance intelligence allowed the dancer to heighten the viewer's perception of her in line or silhouette and in mass:

A dancer can emphasize a passage in the dance by emphasizing the shape her body takes in the air. When she does this she does not call attention merely to the limb that moves, she defines her presence all around in every direction. At such moments she looks large, important, like a figure of imagination, like an ideal human being moving through the air at will. . . .

These are some of the physical characteristics of dance expression, and the brilliant use of them to arouse our interest, to thrill and to satisfy us, is proof of an artist's exceptional dance intelligence. (ibid.: 204–205)

For Denby, the body had agency. It could, as Susan Foster has argued, theorize in the moment through practice rather than after action in contemplation (Foster 1995: 15–16). Foster sees this agency coming into play especially in the rehearsal process, but as Denby noted, it also occurs on the stage in the act of dancing. For Denby, then, intelligent and articulate bodily practices could produce an entire world of expression that lay outside the control of conscious thought and language.

Cage, too, believed that dance could best be understood without the interference of any sort of intellectual contemplation. Sounding much like Denby, he commented in 1957, "At a recent performance of ours at Cornell College in Iowa, a student turned to a teacher and said, 'What does it mean?' The teacher's reply was, 'Relax, there are no symbols here to confuse you. Enjoy yourself!'" (1957: 10). Cage credited this ability to respond to dance to Martin's concepts of inner mimicry and muscular sympathy, which he called "kinesthetic sympathy," and which took place between the body of the spectator and dancer (ibid.). Audiences had only to look and allow themselves to respond to the movement without any intellectual blockage, and the dance would make its effects. What Martin, Denby, and Cage were all saying in different ways was that an authentic dance could only be absorbed, at least initially, on a corporeal level between bodies and free from the tyranny of causal logic. In this sense, to come to a corporeal "understanding" of dance was to experience freedom.

Since rationalization was considered a social problem, dance's ability to deal with it would have been enough to give it a social function. However, for all three men, dance was socially relevant in other ways, as well. To begin with, Denby and Cage would have agreed with Martin that dance could not be separated from life because it embodied movement, which was common to everyone. For Martin, the social function of an authentic dance was to challenge the status quo by demonstrating truth as society changed through time ([1939] 1965: 15–16). An authentic dance aimed at closing the fissure between art and society that a modern division of labor and market economy had opened. For Denby, dance could offer society practices for a civilized and peaceful world after two brutal wars, while for Cage dance provided a means of bringing a healing peace to the troubled human mind. In all, then, despite their differences, Martin, Denby, and Cage shared a theoretical view based in modernist tenets and assumptions. They also attempted to solve one of the central problems of modernity, finding in the dancing body a means of escaping the stranglehold of rationalization. But for all three, dance was more than simply an escape; in its truth it held the possibility of a better world, however utopian such an idea might have been.

Embodying Community

In *The End of Ideology*, Daniel Bell wrote of a "rough consensus" that dominated Western society. He argued that the ideological revolutions of the years preceding the mid-twentieth century had died due to a number of causes. These included, on the one hand, disillusionment after the rise of fascism in Germany and Stalinism in Russia and, on the other, modifications in capitalism that took social welfare into consideration. Now, he said there was general agreement on political and economic issues: "the acceptance of a Welfare State; the desirability of decentralized power, a system of mixed economy and of political pluralism" (Bell [1960] 1988: 402–403). The consensus that Bell invoked with such complacency was not unusual during the Cold War. As historian Alan Brinkley has noted, many observers saw American society as one in which divisions were disappearing, a society that "reflected an essential unity of interests and values widely shared by Americans of all classes, regions, races, and creeds" (Brinkley 2001: 62). Although Cold War rhetoric had much to do with such thinking, another factor was the astonishing growth of the American economy during the 1950s, which led to the conclusion that the United States could grow its way out of any internal tensions (Chafe 1999; O'Neill 1986; Diggins 1988; Pells 1989; Brinkley 2001). Yet the "illusion of unity," to use Brinkley's term, hid a good deal of dissent, much of it from disaffected minorities as disparate as artists and intellectuals, women, African Americans, and the young. What made the illusion successful was that dissent tended to be hidden or disguised. Bell maintained that most dissent was social rather than political. Critique, he said, was aimed at such areas as mass culture or an increasing sense of anxiety and alienation in American society. He was right to a degree, but he failed to understand the necessary political aspect of social issues. Bell also ignored the fact that during the Cold War years it wasn't always safe to overtly criticize political institutions and policies. If dance was any measure, social critique had political implications that Bell and others of his generation did not see or did not wish to acknowledge.

Although postwar high-art dance included its share of consensus thinking, there were choreographers who engaged with social concerns that veiled political issues. In some instances these choreographers focused on ideas relating to community. Examples that come to mind include the numerous works depicting the Salem witch hunts, which presented communities rent by betrayal. Anna Sokolow, whose work will figure prominently in this chapter, showed how anxiety and alienation characterized a society in which collective life no longer held.

Concepts of community formulated in the Progressive era of the late nineteenth and early twentieth centuries posited difference as a given, with consensus being hammered out through argument and compromise (Wiebe 1990; Chambers 1992; Cooper 1992). Consensus ideology replaced this idea with an aggregate of supposed commonly held attitudes and beliefs. Instead of accepting difference as part of a collective whole, consensus thinking advocated accommodation to the group through such means as "togetherness" and "belonging" (Leuchtenburg 1973: 73–74; May 1988). Regulation was imposed through rules of normalcy that suppressed difference. Consensus thought admitted few racial, class, or ethnic differences to disturb the flow of postwar American life (Skolnick 1991: 68–69; Lears 1989; Pells 1989: 116–261). Furthermore, as we will see, the rules of modernism could be invoked to suppress difference through modernism's demand for universal meaning. Among those who sought to account for difference while struggling to obey the rules of the game they played were African Americans (whose work will be discussed in the next two chapters) and dancers who interested themselves in Jewish ethnicity.

In the wake of the holocaust and the emergence of the state of Israel, a number of Jewish dancers turned their attention to their ethnic roots. Others, who had long dealt with Jewish themes, found their work given new impetus by current events. Among the dancers who treated Jewish subjects were Hadassah, Pearl Lang, Sophie Maslow, Fred Berk, and Anna Sokolow. Naomi Jackson, in her study of Jewish dance at the 92nd Street Y, argues that Jewish modern dancers who treated Jewish subject matter were not trying to depict realistic representations of Jewish life but rather sought to embody an essential Jewish identity (Jackson 2000).

Yet one has to ask how possible it was within the bounds of modernism to capture those sought-after essences, given that modernism demanded "universal" essences that were inevitably defined from the point of view of a dominant social order. One of the questions to be discussed here is how an idea of Jewish identity, as distinct from any other, could be fit into a modernist framework. Sophie Maslow's *The Village I Knew* (1950) and Anna Sokolow's *Kaddish* (1945) are cases in point.

Maslow was born in 1911 on New York's Lower East Side, the daughter of Jewish immigrant parents from Russia. She took her first dance classes at a socialist school, followed by studies at the Neighborhood Playhouse with Graham and Horst. She danced with Martha Graham's company for twelve years beginning in 1931. At the same time, she was involved in protest dance, often in her capacity as a member of the New Dance Group. The group was the only one of the revolutionary dance associations to survive through the postwar years. It had been founded in 1932 as a means of educating dancers in order to participate in the class struggle. After the war the group continued to provide a variety of dance classes to amateurs and professionals at nominal fees, and it supported a performing branch (Korff 1993; Graff 1997). In keeping with its goals, the New Dance Group company specialized in socially conscious works. Maslow taught classes at the school and performed and choreographed for the company. She was also part of a trio that included Jane Dudley and William Bales. The trio, started in 1942, made its debut under the aegis of *Dance Observer*, which was trying to help keep modern dance afloat during the lean war years. After the war, Maslow, Dudley, and Bales continued to appear together under the banner of Jane Dudley, Sophie Maslow, William Bales and Company, drawing on dancers from the New Dance Group for their supporting artists.

In the 1930s, Maslow had created such protest pieces as *Two Songs about Lenin* (1935) and *Ragged, Hungry Blues* (1937). She had also been interested in folk idioms, including Russian folk dance and themes. By the end of the 1930s, she became concerned with the plight of itinerant American farmers, which she treated in *Dust Bowl Ballads* (1941) and *Folksay* (1942), both set to music by Woody Guthrie. *The Village I Knew* was related to Maslow's earlier work in that it dealt with folk material, now focused on her Jewish roots. It was the most ambitious piece Maslow created in which she tried to come to grips with the issue of Jewish communal identity.[1] Based on Yiddish stories by Sholem Aleichem, it was danced to traditional songs and music set by Gregory Tucker and

Samuel Matlowsky. The work was premiered on 18 August 1950 at the American Dance Festival in New London, Connecticut. I want to describe *The Village I Knew* in some detail in order to make clear its various dance elements, as well as the degree of mimetic gesture found in it compared with less literal movement.

Most of the seven sections deal with the small pleasures and dramas of shtetl life in nineteenth-century Eastern Europe. However, the last dance, "Exodus," radically changes the mood of the work by depicting a pogrom. The first dance, "Sabbath," has men on one side of the stage, women on the other, each going about Sabbath prayers. The women form a circle, then break into two groups, three women holding candles, the other three praying, alternately holding their hands out to the candles and covering their eyes in the traditional Sabbath blessing. Meanwhile, the men place prayer shawls over their heads and shoulders, swaying in what is also part of orthodox prayer. The praying gestures and positions are integrated into repeated dance patterns that serve to emphasize the ritual aspect of their movement. The women and men remain separate on each side of the stage, as they would in an orthodox setting. The women dance in closely knit circles and parallel lines, while the men spread out more, their movement and gestures larger and freer as they arc their arms up and out in prayer, their bodies boldly arching as they sway.

"It's Good to Be an Orphan" is essentially a pantomime. A girl skips, stretches, and kicks her heels in happiness as she inspects two apples she has apparently stolen. An older woman enters, scolds her, and extracts one of the apples from the girl's pocket. The woman then softens, shrugs, and hugs the girl. Finally she takes off her boots and gives them to the child. The next dance, "A Point of Doctrine," is also a pantomime vignette in which a housewife drives a rabbi to distraction with her incessant talking and complaints.

"Festival" consists of a group dance that is less mimetic and plot-driven than the previous sequences. It was clearly inspired by folk dances, especially evident in the line that snakes through the scene from time to time like a leitmotif. However, the movement also includes numerous modern dance steps, such as sweeping extensions and floor work. And although folk elements like flexed feet and stamping runs are used, the dancers' comportment tends to be upright and straight in the modern dance style rather than less formally held-up, as it is in many folk forms.

"The Fiddler" section again includes a great deal of mime to convey

Jane Dudley, Sophie Maslow, and Ronne Aul in "The Fiddler," from Maslow's *The Village I Knew* (1950). *Photo: Walter E. Owen. Courtesy of Jerome Robbins Dance Division, The New York Public Library for the Performing Arts, Astor, Lenox and Tilden Foundations.*

a mother's argument with her daughter who wishes to marry a poor violinist rather than, presumably, someone with more financial security. "Why Is It Thus?" follows. It is a dance for three men, who are called students in the program, and who appear to be meditating on a Talmudic question. A bench is used as a prop for sitting and reclining as the men take up various positions of meditation and prayer. As in the first scene, there are the sways and sweeping gestures of the arms outstretched in prayer.

Finally, in "Exodus," Maslow shifted the mood of the work from one of affectionate humor to fear and panic. Chaos reigns as the characters we have just seen in previous sections rush across the stage waving their arms in terror, embracing each other, and running off. Women in stiff, angular poses of pain are carried off amid the melee. Meanwhile, a group of dancers acts as a chorus, commenting on the action through their movement. They cross in a line at the back of the stage, their bodies bent as if bearing a heavy load. The work ends with this scene of destruction.

As Naomi Jackson notes, Maslow did not attempt to replicate Jewish religious practices or shtetl life in *The Village I Knew*, rather she reimagined them through mimetic gesture and dance. Her view of the past, a past she had never experienced, was painted in primitivist forms and colors, like the illustrations in a children's book. The movement throughout the work is made up of simple ballet steps like *pas de basques* and *pas de bourrées* along with modern dance movement, including the Graham contraction (the latter particularly present in "Exodus"). These are combined with folk elements and that amalgam, in turn, is attached to pantomime that tells the individual stories of each vignette.

The Village I Knew became one of Maslow's most successful works. John Martin called it "warm and tender and funny and distinctly a credit to Miss Maslow" (1950: 8). Walter Terry commented, "Its glimpses (sharply focused and knowingly selective) of Jewish community life in czarist Russia are amusing, touching, colorful and intensely human" (1951a: 7). The only complaint concerned the last scene, which nearly every critic, including Martin and Terry, commented upon. Nik Krevitsky's objection was typical. He wrote in *Dance Observer:*

> Only one point, which we have made previously, and which still applies, seems to detract from the perfection which it is possible for this dance to achieve. That is its sad, though realistic, ending. The Exodus, though relevant to the type of community which this work portrays, is alien in spirit to the attitude of life which Aleichem emphasizes; the notion of hope is gone and with it much of the zestful dancing that precedes this sad closing. (1951c: 43)

Krevitsky was correct in saying that Maslow's conclusion was not in the spirit of Aleichem, but from a modernist standpoint that was the least of the work's problems. The modernist issue lay in Maslow's specificity of time, place, and character and in her extensive use of pantomime, which constituted, in modernist terms, a representation of Jewish identity rather than its embodiment. Yet none of the critics objected to the work on those grounds. What they did object to was the intrusion of realistic tragedy into the dance, implying they viewed the rest of the piece as fantasy. It would appear that as long as Maslow's vision of Jewish identity lay in the realm of the picturesque, of quaint villages and amusing peasants, it wasn't necessary to come to grips with issues of abstraction and essential truth. *The Village I Knew* could be specific because it was not really modern, and commentators could therefore excuse Maslow's work from the rigors of an authentic dance. Massacres were something else, though. "Exodus" was a jarring reminder of life experience, which modern dance was supposed to essentialize. It imposed harsh reality on fantasy, and it remained alarmingly specific. As such, it had no place in the exotic folktale world Maslow had depicted.

Another element of *The Village I Knew* that obliquely touched on its modernist problem had to do with Maslow's inclusion of African Americans in the cast. Ronne Aul and Donald McKayle were members of the New Dance Group, which Maslow drew on for dancers.[2] According to McKayle, John Martin did not understand why there were, in McKayle's words, "black boys" in a Russian Jewish village (McKayle 1993; 1966: 73).[3] McKayle said he wrote to Martin advising him to ask himself why the fact that there were no Russian Jews in the ballet didn't bother him. Martin replied that by including black dancers the work lacked theatrical verisimilitude and that it was as incomprehensible as Shirley Temple playing Hamlet or John Barrymore playing Juliet. It is notable that Martin's comparisons were to drama, not to dance, and his belief that characters who were supposed to be of a specific race or gender could not cross those boundaries. As Martin made clear in his own theory, drama was far more literal than dance, and the more drama a dance included, the less it was concerned with essential life experience. Martin's comments, leaving aside the issue of racism, indirectly addressed the problem of modernism in *The Village I Knew*; that is, the work's specificity of time, place, and character kept it from coming to grips with abstraction. Maslow's effort, although a dance work that pleased many, was unable to bridge the gulf between communities that sought identity outside the dominant order and the rules of modernism.

In her solo, *Kaddish*, Anna Sokolow tried a more strictly modernist approach to Jewish identity than did Maslow in *The Village I Knew*. However, this only served to demonstrate the limits of modernism in other ways. Sokolow (1912–2000), like Maslow, had been involved in social protest dance in the 1930s. Also like Maslow, she was the daughter of Jewish immigrants from Eastern Europe who became interested in her own Jewish roots. In 1939, she choreographed *The Exile*, in which she contrasted an idyllic Jewish culture before the war ("I had a garden . . .") with the horror of Nazism ("The Beast is in the garden . . ."). The solo was set to a poem by Sol Funaroff and had music by Alex North. In 1943, she created *Revelations* made up of *The Exile* and dances devoted to the biblical women Ruth, Naomi, Miriam, and Deborah. As was her habit, she combined older pieces with new ones, sometimes retitling them. *Songs of a Semite* of 1943 was essentially *Revelations* with the addition of a dance entitled "March of the Semite Women." Sokolow premiered *Kaddish* in Mexico in 1945, then performed it for the first time in New York on 12 May 1946 as part of a solo concert at the 92nd Street Y. In that concert she also offered two other works with Jewish themes: *Images from the Old Testament* (which included the "Miriam" solo) and *The Bride*.[4]

In the mid-1940s, Sokolow was working primarily in Mexico and so performed infrequently in New York. In general, her dances of these years were not considered to be her strongest, but *The Exile* and *Kaddish* were exceptions. Although *The Exile* has disappeared, *Kaddish* has survived and exists in a video danced by Deborah Zall. I want to compare it here to Graham's solo *Lamentation* (1930), long accepted as a model of modern dance.[5] *Kaddish*, listed in the program as a "prayer for the dead," was inspired by a Jewish mourning prayer. It is set to Ravel's meditation on the Kaddish. For the dance, Sokolow wound a tefillin, an Orthodox prayer box, around her head and arm, something only men do in the Orthodox faith and which they use for daily prayers, not for the Kaddish. Deborah Zall eliminated the prayer box in her reconstruction.

The solo begins with the dancer standing erect on a darkened stage, her hands folded into fists at her breast. It is this tight, narrow vertical that is the central position in the dance, the one repeatedly returned to. The dancer slowly unfolds her hands, palms up, and looks up as if questioning heaven. She moves forward haltingly, her movement tense and bound as if constrained by pain. She places her fist against her opposing shoulder, bends forward, her hand to her head, and stands swaying. She kneels and does a back bend, then falls forward. Gradually her movement enlarges. She swings her arms outward as she turns from side to side, then runs with her arms outstretched. She plunges to the ground, rises, plunges again. As she rises a second time, her movement once more

Anna Sokolow in *Kaddish* (1945). *Photo courtesy of the Sokolow Dance Foundation.*

becomes constrained. The dance ends as she haltingly steps backward, lightly tapping her breast.

If one compares this dance to Graham's solo of grief, the differences and similarities are instructive. Graham's celebrated solo is done primarily while seated on a bench, and she is wrapped in a flexible jersey tube. Her movement is literally contained, consisting mostly of sways forward and back and from side to side accompanied by arm gestures that sweep to the side or plunge downward between her legs, the latter open in a wide second position. At one moment she touches each side of her face in a ritualized wiping of a tear.

Martha Graham in *Lamentation* (1930). *Soichi Sunami, photographer. Courtesy of the Sunami estate.*

Both Sokolow and Graham's solos have a sense of containment, but Sokolow's movement breaks out of the vertical in periodic explosions that carry her to the side or down onto the floor. Whereas Graham's gestures have no clear mimetic associations except the ritualized touching of her face, Sokolow included gestures that could be associated with Judaism but that are also part of a general lexicon of lamentation, like the beating of the breast and the questioning gesture of the arms. The title of the dance and Sokolow's use of the prayer box would have tied her solo to Judaism, but the movement itself is, as a whole, generalized. Yet despite their similarities, the two dances differ markedly in mood. Graham's containment is so complete it is tempting to call it puritanical while Sokolow's is broken, the emotion more exposed and more antique in its gestural associations, however abstracted they may be. In this sense the dance's references can be viewed as biblical and hence by extension Jewish. Yet both dances are highly abstracted treatments of the pain of grief, and the less specifically "Jewish" Sokolow's dance was, the more it spoke of a generalized pain and the less of something essentially Jewish. *Kaddish* therefore points up the problem of encompassing difference within the rules of modernism. Created to confront a dominant culture from within, modernism was not a flexible instrument for dealing with issues of difference. Jewish dancers attempted to expand modernist boundaries to include constituencies outside the dominant social order. In doing so they also challenged notions of consensus culture where difference was muted. In this instance, the rules of modernism aligned with consensus ideology to emphasize unity, as illusionary as that idea may have been.

In addition to grappling with problems of how to reconcile modernism to an idea of essentialized Jewish identity, Sokolow took on another issue of modernism and community. Here she did not approach community from outside the mainstream; rather she attacked it from within, focusing on the dysfunction that occurs in a society where community has come apart. Sokolow explored this theme in two ways: through the concept of alienation and through rebellious youth.

Alienation had always been closely connected with modernity, but the concept took on particular force in the 1950s. Writers of every stripe considered it until, by the end of the decade, it had worked its way into the general vocabulary of the country. Alienation was tied to notions of rationalized society in ways that I would like to consider by comparing two nearly contemporaneous works: Erich Fromm's sociological study, *The Sane Society* (1955), and Sokolow's *Rooms* (1955). This is not to imply that Fromm and Sokolow influenced each other, but rather that they treated alienation in often parallel ways.

Like many intellectuals in the United States during these years, Fromm had begun his career as a Marxist and ended, by the 1950s, a liberal in the consensus vein (Jay 1996). He had been a member of the Frankfurt School in Germany, emigrating to the United States in 1934 and soon after breaking his ties with the Institute of Social Research. A psychiatrist, Fromm had been particularly interested in merging Marxism with Freudian theories; then after the war he rejected Freud's view of society as too pessimistic. He is of interest here because he treated the subject of alienation at length, and his ideas had much in common with other intellectual thought of the day.

Sokolow had long been associated with leftist causes. Like Maslow, she danced with Martha Graham's company during the 1930s. She also managed her own group, the Dance Unit, which appeared at union halls and working-class social organizations. During the 1930s and '40s Sokolow lived with Alex North, a composer and leftist whose brother, Joseph, was a founder of *New Masses*. Sokolow spent three months in Russia with North in 1934. Although North considered Sokolow naive in her political views and she was apparently never a member of the Communist Party, she retained her critical viewpoint of capitalist society throughout her life (Warren 1998: 29–30). When Sokolow returned to New York from Moscow, she renewed her association with Graham, as well as continuing her own choreographic career. During the 1940s, as noted, she worked extensively in Mexico City, returning from time to time to New York. The 1950s found her again working with her own company in New York, as well as taking assignments abroad in Israel and Mexico. She premiered *Rooms* at a concert at the 92nd Street Y on 24 February 1955.

Rooms is a suite of dances that depicts various types of men and women who are out of touch with themselves and cannot make contact with others.[6] It has a jazz score by Kenyon Hopkins. Sokolow once remarked that *Rooms* dealt with the loneliness of the city; however, as one critic noted, it was not about loneliness but aloneness (Terry 1955: 12). Fromm defined alienation as "self-estrangement" and related it to social rationalization, or as he awkwardly called it "quantification and

The Juilliard Dance Ensemble in the opening dance from a 1977 production of Anna Sokolow's *Rooms* (1955). *Photo: © Peter Schaaf.*

abstractification" (1955: 110–152). His explanation, largely based on early Marxist theory, found the source of alienation in the development of capitalism. As the division of labor took hold, exchange value took precedence over use value, and people were separated from the making of a whole product, which they had previously controlled. They could no longer see or understand the whole with the result that the power they unleashed through their labor, primarily through science and technology, came to rule over them. Men and women thus lost themselves as the center of their own experience. In a quantified and abstracted society, people viewed themselves as salable commodities rather than as active agents and bearers of power. Consequently, they measured success by what others thought of them rather than by their true identity. (Fromm, like most of his contemporaries, assumed that each person had an essential human identity that was authentic but corruptible.) In a society in which the division of labor was so complete, community was separated from the individual, as was public from private life. Individuals could no longer understand their own interest as part of a greater community, so selfish interest prevailed. By the 1950s, Fromm said, society had become almost completely alienated.

It is in the notion of fragmentation and a resulting sense of loss, particularly in terms of community, that Sokolow's works most closely resemble Fromm's idea of alienation. *Rooms* begins with a section entitled "Alone," in which eight men and women are seated on chairs, all facing front. As a plaintive trumpet solo begins, one, then another dancer, rises and is seated again. Sokolow equated the chairs with cell-like rooms, which each individual inhabits. Seated, the dancers alternate between tense and twisted clutches and stretches and awkward flops that leave them prostrate across their chairs. From time to time one of the dancers looks up and then collapses again. Each individual moves independently of the others with no apparent relationship to the whole. This initial dance introduces several solos, the first of which is entitled "Dream." Here a young man rolls away from his chair and across the floor. He does slow cartwheels and back bends, lies on the floor, feeling forward with his fingers, then grips and claws his way along before struggling to rise. He takes large steps forward in slow motion runs in circles, lies on his back, then suddenly sits up. Finally he walks slowly back to his chair, his head bowed. Many years after creating *Rooms*, Sokolow described how she had thought about each of the solos. The first, she said, characterized the actions of a man who "dreams contrary to what he is in life" (Sokolow 1974). Fromm might have said the man dreams because his real work is unsatisfying. He dreams of a life in which he controls his actions and is a bearer of power instead of being merely a small part of a whole he does not understand or control.

The next solo, "Escape," is set for a woman. Her movement is sometimes languid as she shakes out her long hair, sways to the jazz rhythms and slowly stretches out her body. At other moments, however, her actions become frantic; she rushes from one empty chair to another, she dances madly, tossing her hair obsessively from side to side, then suddenly flings herself down, all her energy drained away. At the end of the dance we find her walking aimlessly, then she stands behind her chair gazing off into space. She appears strangely narcissistic, resembling Fromm's individual who views herself from a distance as an object, a salable commodity. Certainly such objectification has long been the plight of women, but in an age of alienation it becomes a general condition.

The other dances in *Rooms* further demonstrate the loss of self that characterize alienation. "Going" is a solo for a male dancer who acts as if he is on amphetamines. This dance is the only one in which Sokolow used jazz movement. The young man snaps his fingers to the beat, his body bent forward as he prances in tight steps, hep-cat fashion. He switches suddenly to a manic kind of boxing, punching and dodging invisible blows, then he hammers out the beat with silent, clapping hands. He runs, he slides, he falls, he hammers the beat, he punches, he snaps his fingers until finally, seated on the stage he slowly raises and lowers his outstretched arms, his whole body straining upward as if attempting to fly. The dance ends with the man seemingly nailed to the floor and straining to escape.

The next dance, "Desire," is for six men and women who remain sealed in their own worlds as they crawl, curl, and stretch within the precincts of their limited space. Their movement is full of both yearning and sexual tension as they reach, then twist and hunch in on themselves. The dance is dominated by a step in which the dancers rhythmically rub their feet forward and back on the floor in a way that suggests a masturbatory soothing of frustrations. They remain in their hermetic worlds, close to each other but unseeing, mirroring each other's movement but never connecting. "Panic," another male solo, contains a recurring image: that of a man bent from the waist who reaches out blindly in front of him. He staggers as he moves this way and that. He covers his eyes and shakes his head as if in the grip of migraine. He rushes forward, retreats, and finally crouches behind his chair as the dance comes to an end.

"Daydream," is for three girls and perhaps was meant as a lyrical moment in an otherwise wholly bleak work. The music is sweet and the girls dance, supported by their chairs. Although they face the audience they appear to be regarding themselves in a mirror. At the end they stand behind their chairs, sling a leg over the back and lean forward, elbows on knee, as if contemplating their faces. Since, as Fromm said, community is separated from the individual in an alienated society, individuals no longer perceive themselves as part of a community and self-interest takes over. The narcissism of the characters in *Rooms*, speaks of that aspect of alienation. The penultimate dance is entitled "The End?" and is a female solo, very percussive, that Sokolow associated with madness (Sokolow 1974). Among the woman's gestures is a tense wriggling of the fingers of her outstretched arms. This solo is followed by a return of all the dancers, who bring on their chairs and seat themselves. The work ends with them sitting, staring blankly ahead.

In his discussion of alienation Fromm mentioned that early psychiatrists were called alienists because they dealt with people who were both lost to themselves and unable to make contact with others. That sense of loss permeates *Rooms*. The characters have little idea where they are or who they are, as they alternately embrace and attempt to escape their fragment of real estate. There is also about them an obsessiveness and yet aimlessness that is neurotic and in some cases pathologic. Above all, there is the dancers' gaze, which is never allowed to connect the performers with their fellows. This hermetic disconnect from others through the device of the gaze is ironically what most binds the work together. For Sokolow, this was the world that modernity had wrought.

As close as Sokolow and Fromm were in their views of alienation, they parted company on the solution to the dismal condition that was the lot of modern men and women. Fromm sought an answer not in revolution or organized communal pressure but in individualism, the courage to be different, to become in his words, "productive." Fromm looked to changes of life practice to bring about this productive individual who must learn how to handle continuing conflict, to be aware of suffering, and to act on his or her own initiative. The sane society would be one that attacked the problems of rationalization and attendant alienation from all standpoints—economic, political, spiritual, and philosophical, as well as through character and culture (1955: 270–363; see also 1947, 1950). Fromm's optimistic turn and his emphasis on production brought him into conflict with some of his peers, notably Herbert Marcuse, while linking him to consensus liberals like Seymour Lipset, Daniel Bell, and Arthur Schlesinger Jr. (Marcuse 1955: 248–274; see also Jay 1996; Pells 1989). Sokolow saw no such happy solution to modern ills. For her, the world was as it was. In her pessimism, she was closer to Adorno, Horkheimer, and Marcuse than to Fromm. For Sokolow there did not seem to be a way to regain communal power or for the individual to be at once herself and part of an integrated whole.

Yet if Sokolow was relentlessly pessimistic in her critique of modern society, she nonetheless found effective ways to embody its pain. She did this through the structure and form of her dance. She began by creating the piece in suite form, which allowed her to dispense with any sort of story line. Her theme made its effect through accumulation, one segment added to another to reinforce a point, rather than through a series of causal events. Sokolow was careful to avoid narrative vignettes, staying within broad thematic boundaries.

Rooms also showed that it was possible to treat contemporary social problems in a highly metaphorical manner. Although it seems contradictory, Sokolow may have developed her successful strategy through her work with actors. Sokolow had taught movement to actors at the Group Theatre in the 1930s. When Elia Kazan, Cheryl Crawford, and Robert Lewis, who had been associated with the Group Theatre, started Actors Studio in 1947, they asked her to teach movement classes for them (Warren 1998: 89–94). Actors Studio specialized in a training method that was loosely based on that of Constantin Stanislavski, which taught actors to search deeply within their own experience to discover the feelings and actions for their characters. Sokolow became interested enough in the workshop's approach to participate in some of its acting classes. She also worked with the actors on specific projects of her own.

Sokolow actually started to make *Rooms* at Actors Studio but was disappointed in the results and decided instead to make a dance piece (Warren 1998: 115). However, she may have found the basis of the movement she wanted for *Rooms* by working with the actors to locate movement and gestures of people under mental and emotional stress. Sokolow had studied with Louis Horst in the 1930s, and it appears she returned to his idea of modern dance's beginnings in vernacular movement. In his book *Modern Dance Forms*, Horst wrote: "Both [German and American modern dance] built up the art form by abstracting familiar everyday movement. The realistic gesture or posture is taken as a point of departure on which to construct a poetic metaphor" (Horst and Russell [1961] 1987: 18). Sokolow returned to the roots of modern dance to find powerful new metaphors for an alienated age.

Sokolow said she discovered her mature movement vocabulary while choreographing *Lyric Suite* of 1954. Although certainly *Lyric Suite* contains the seeds of much of the vocabulary for *Rooms*, it also employs a great deal of conventional modern dance movement. In contrast, *Rooms* is a more radical work. It contains hardly a recognizable step from the standard modern dance vocabulary that by 1950 had coalesced from the techniques of the pioneers. Rather, Sokolow started fresh from non-dance movement, which she then heightened through exaggeration, accumulation, and especially, repetition. She also made use of what is called in Laban Movement Analysis, "bound flow," in which bodily energy is put in tension with itself to hinder the flow of movement. She then alternated this with a total depletion of energy. The constant wrenching of the body from one extreme energy level to another helped to produce an effect of abnormality. Finally, there was the gaze, which Sokolow began to develop in *Lyric Suite*. In that work, the dancers tend

The Juilliard Dance Ensemble in a 1977 production of Anna Sokolow's *Rooms* (1955). *Photo: © Peter Schaaf.*

to stay focused into the distance rather than on each other, but it isn't consistent throughout. Particularly in the central duet, the man and woman frequently make eye contact. In *Rooms*, however, Sokolow made the separation complete.

Rooms was premiered on 24 February 1955 at the 92nd Street Y, and critics had the chance to assess it at various performances over the course of the next few months. The work was immediately recognized as important, but also disturbing and unpleasant. Several reviewers called it a theater piece, saying that it was realistic. Doris Hering, however, noted that, "though her [Sokolow's] viewpoint was philosophical, it did not fall into the trap of being literary." What impressed Hering "was the great complexity of dance material woven into what seemed like the most simple of dance surfaces" (Hering 1955: 75). One would tend to side with Hering in this assessment. For although the movement in *Rooms* is gestural, Sokolow's treatment of it is anything but realistic. Gestures are danced, that is, they are conceived as rhythmic pattern rather than as mimetic elements that interrupt the dance flow. If she sought the basis of her vocabulary in the non-dance movement described by Horst, Sokolow was also prompted to use that vocabulary in dance terms, imbuing it, in Denby's words, with dance qualities. This is not to say that *Rooms* is objectivist. It is expressional; that is, it is formally abstracted from life experience to perform a social function. The work may have done this a little too well for John Martin, who found it objectionable on several points, particularly in its unrelentingly dismal tone. But he also conceded that it was impressive. "The explanation," he said, "probably lies in the extreme concentration of movement, of its music and especially of its performance" (1955a: 26).

Most critics viewed *Rooms* as psychological, as pertaining to individuals who are cut off from society. Only George Beiswanger, in a thoughtful piece written after seeing the work at the American Dance Festival in 1956, commented on it in sociological terms (Beiswanger 1957: 21–23). To view *Rooms* as psychological was to keep it at a distance, to consider it involving simply individual cases at odds with the world. To view capitalist society as a whole in such bleak terms was far more damning. If alienation were an inevitable result of capitalism, therapy would be of little help. However, whether psychological or sociological, part of the reason *Rooms* impressed even if it did not please, was surely due to the fact that it could pass for universal truth. Audiences perceived in its alienation an essential element of modernity. As such, *Rooms* proved to be one of the rare instances in the 1950s when a dance of devastating critique was acknowledged as successful, even if its full implications were deflected.

In 1958, Sokolow began a project of related works that continued her exploration of social critique and that occupied her for a decade. All were set to jazz scores by Teo Macero, with whom Sokolow often worked beginning in the 1950s, and all concerned disaffected youth, or so the works were interpreted by critics at the time. Sokolow herself did not speak of any particular age group in these dances, but perhaps because she used contemporary social dance in them it was assumed the works dealt with young people. In the 1950s, youth was also very much on the minds of Americans; the rise of a postwar youth culture riveted public attention.

Although rebellious youth is probably as old as human relationships, the flappers were the first generation in the twentieth century to become celebrated for flaunting society's rules in often self-destructive behavior. Rebellion had little place in a country in deep economic depression and then world war, but the 1950s ushered in an era of prosperity accompanied by the baby boom, both of which accelerated consumerism. This provided a climate for developing a specific culture of white middle-class youth in conflict with adult society (Lipsitz 1981, 1989; Gilbert 1986; Diggins 1988; Goodman 1960). At the same time, politicians, law enforcement professionals, social scientists, and the media became focused on what was perceived as an increase in juvenile crime. This occurred even though the statistics on whether or not there was an actual crime wave were far from conclusive (Gilbert 1986: 63–78). The disparity between reality and perception appears to have been the result of experts and the media finding it difficult to separate youth culture from delinquency. The concern with juvenile crime resonated with parents who could barely recognize their children in the adolescents living in their homes.

In the 1940s, mainstream America had listened to the same pop music whether the listener was sixteen or sixty. Singers like Frank Sinatra, Perry Como, and Rosemary Clooney dominated the Top 40 charts. Ten years later the situation was vastly different, as teenagers danced to the aggressive sounds of rock music and imitated the provocative gyrations of Elvis Presley. By the mid-1950s, teenagers not only listened to their own music, danced their own dances, wore their own clothes and hair styles, they seemed to be more influenced by their peers and the mass media than by their parents. In addition, as increasing numbers of working-class adolescents began attending high school after the war, middle-class parents worried about influences from these unfamiliar, and possibly dangerous, sources. Many adults feared they could no longer impress their own values on their children. This translated into the specter of rampant juvenile crime, which was cast in the media, both by social scientists and journalists, as nothing less than a breakdown of society. The focus on adolescent misbehavior was further fueled by congressional hearings on juvenile delinquency throughout the 1950s and by an outpouring of magazine and newspaper articles on both adolescent crime and life styles. Films such as *The Wild One* (1953), *Blackboard Jungle* (1955), and *Rebel without a Cause* (1955) fanned the flames of concern as they romanticized adolescents acting-out to the horror of adults.

Sokolow had dealt with youthful rebellion long before the 1950s in *Case History No. ——* (1937). In this solo she treated juvenile delinquency from the standpoint of how social inequality led to crime. Her program note read: "A study of a majority of case histories shows that petty criminals usually emerge from a background which begins with unemployment and follows its course from street corner to pool room, from mischief to crime."[7] Margaret Lloyd described the dance as "a study in juvenile delinquency by the poverty route, showing a youth, bored and restless in his grim environment, releasing stifled energies in the petty offenses that lead to felony, and culminating in a tense crouch of fear against the backdrop" (1949: 217). Sokolow's new series of works did not portray youth as a victim of society but rather as representative of it. Here she was not dealing with juvenile delinquency among the lower classes, as she had in *Case History No. ———*, but instead with a more generalized and ambiguous group that was seen by observers as contemporary youth.

Sokolow also had used social dance in several earlier works, among them a jitterbug duet in the Kurt Weill–Langston Hughes musical, *Street Scene*, of 1947 (Lloyd 1949: 214, 217). Nor was Sokolow the only choreographer to be interested in youth culture in the 1950s. The most celebrated of them was Jerome Robbins, whose *West Side Story* (1957) and *N.Y. Export: Opus Jazz* (1958) were far better known than Sokolow's works. Sokolow and Robbins were friends and respected each other's choreography, but Sokolow, typically, took the vanguard high road. Her studies did not glamorize youthful bad behavior, but once again showed the bleak alienation of capitalist society. To reinforce her vision Sokolow eschewed the kind of quasi-commercial music by Leonard Bernstein and Robert Prince that Robbins favored, choosing instead the complex, often harsh sounds created by Macero.

Sokolow began her series with *Session for Six*, which premiered in February 1958 in New York. She continued it with *Session '58*, which had its first performance in April 1958 at Juilliard, where Sokolow was teaching. That same year she presented *Opus '58* in Amsterdam, *Session for Eight* at Juilliard, and *Opus Jazz 1958* in Israel. Then came *Opus '60* in Mexico, *Opus '62* in Israel, *Opus '63* at Juilliard, and finally *Opus '65*, which she made for the Joffrey Ballet. Speaking of *Opus '58*, Sokolow said, "I used jazz for an over-all aura of the sounds and rhythms of today. I wanted the feeling of a new era, one where life is violent and precarious, and the individual seems unimportant" (Sokolow 1965: 39). Although the works in this series differed over the years, a sense of violence, aggressiveness, and boredom endured.

Filmed versions exist of *Session for Six*, *Opus '63*, and *Opus '65*. From these and accounts of some of the other works it is possible to assemble at least a partial idea of how the series developed. Viewed in conjunction with the later pieces, *Session for Six* looks related to, but nonetheless quite different from, the later dances, which are closer to each other in structure and movement. However, although *Session for Six* is not an earlier version of the *Opus* works, it is nonetheless a clear precursor.

Session for Six, which premiered at the 92nd Street Y, begins with a man and woman alone on stage, who do a combination of *coupé jeté* steps, leave, then quickly reemerge with the group.[8] Teo Macero's score resembles a baroque trumpet motif as the couple begin to move, then quickly segues into jazz variations as the group of dancers replaces the initial couple. It's as if the music tells us what will happen. This first dance is dominated by *coupé jeté*, *grand plié*, and *petit échappé*, all seen in continuously changing combinations of steps and dancers. While executing these movements, the dancers maintain clearly arranged patterns of lines and groups so that the structure is always emphasized. Their comportment for the most part is held-up and academic. Yet within all the strict patterns and steps there are small ruptures—a handshake, alternating clenched and open hands, a hand to the head, or undulating hips in a *plié*. A man executes one twist—it's a harbinger. The first dance ends with the performers executing *grands jetés*, first crisscrossing the stage, then in a circle. The hand-to-head gesture is increasingly seen until it becomes a motif in its own right.

The second dance begins with the performers entering the stage as if at random. Now instead of maintaining upright, academic comportment, they bend their torsos forward slightly and execute small swing and jitterbug steps. They become couples, join hands as if doing a fast arm-wrestle that then turns into full body twists. They are doing twisting social dance steps, but the dancers still stay in the same structured patterns as earlier. They change patterns in jazzy prances with their hands held in front of them in the pawlike gesture borrowed from social and jazz dance.

In the third and final dance, the three girls take center stage and do *grands battements* and *pliés* interspersed with jazzy steps. Halting in deep *plié*, they look around for the boys, who enter and lift them, still in a *plié* position into the air. They separate and all exit, except one boy and girl who look intensely at each other for a split second before running into the wings. Everyone returns, and the dance ends with the group doing fast jump turns in fifth position, their arms outstretched, their bodies erect and their heads bent forward, their gaze on the floor.

Doris Hering wrote of *Session for Six* that it had a note of "bitter hunger." Yet despite its emotionality, the work "was etched in spare outlines colored by a bold use of spatial and rhythmic counterpoint. Structurally it was the most disciplined work Miss Sokolow has created to date" (1958: 27). Hering mentioned the emotionality of the piece, but other critics were less clear about that aspect. Louis Horst, for example, found it "bright, gay and perky and was definitely contemporary with its suggestions of jazz." He also noted "an explosive nuclear ending" (1958a: 55), while P. W. Manchester at *Dance News* called it an abstract work that was over before it had a chance to solidify into "what promised to be an exciting exposition of male and female dance" (1958: 9).

Looking at *Session for Six* today, one can see how all these ideas might be found in it, depending on the viewpoint. It is certainly short, lasting barely eight minutes, which may account for some of the tentativeness Manchester felt. Sokolow also placed more emphasis on formal elements than she usually did. Yet at the same time she included certain gestures and movements that suggested an emotional texture. Hering, who found the work bitter, may also have been responding to the dancers' gaze, which tended to be focused inward and which gave the performers the look of cool hipsters. On the rare occasions when the dancers made eye contact, it was like an exclamation point.

In *Session for Six*, Sokolow seems to have been trying to combine elements of different genres and styles to see what kinds of moods and movement qualities she could achieve. Her goal was not simply to start in academic dance and end in jazz, but to see how different combinations of movement could work together. Judging from the critical response, it was uncertain at that point what she had achieved. But *Session for Six* was only the beginning, in a sense the material she would be dealing with when she came to make a more definitive statement. Certainly, Sokolow's own comment about her goals in *Opus '58* indicate that after nearly a year she had a clear idea of what she wanted to accomplish. Reviewing *Session '58*, which Sokolow made for Juilliard students and premiered in April, Horst spoke as if Sokolow had already found a more emphatic emotional tone. He wrote: "This work, in a jazz vein, seemed to reflect the negative, almost existentualist [*sic*], state of mind as evidenced by the young of today. As such the choreography projected some telling and bitter comments" (1958b: 86). In a later review of *Session '58*, Manchester noted a "remarkable solo for Patricia Christopher reclining in a veil of black hair with all the mystery of a sphinx and rising to move like a goddess" (1959a: 7). Horst also remarked on the same dance (1959: 39). This solo may have been a forerunner of a dance in the later *Opus* works, in which a woman maintains a sphinxlike calm amid her frenzied male companions. By *Session for Eight*, which Sokolow made for her company and which premiered in December 1958, ten months after *Session for Six*, Hering noted that the work achieved "an impact of frenzied emotionality" (1959: 28). She added that it was a variation of *Session for Six*. It appears that after nearly a year Sokolow was well on her way to producing the work that would become *Opus '63*.

By 1963, the relatively simple *Session for Six* had developed into a twenty-minute piece of five movements. The work contained echoes of *Session for Six*, particularly in the use of the jive and twist steps and in certain recurring gestures such as the hand to the head.[9] Sokolow also used a strong formal structure, although it was far more complex than *Session for Six*, and she maintained some of the alternating academic and jazz comportment found in the earlier piece. However, now both the choreography and Macero's score were far more violent than the relatively sedate *Session for Six*.

Opus '63 starts with a girl running toward two men who grab her and slide her forward on her back.[10] She turns as she slides and ends sprawled face-down on the stage. The other dancers enter, and two other trios repeat the slide. The boys straddle the girls' prostrate bodies, looking down at them. Couples form, they crouch and clutch each other. Then a group dances while a boy and two girls stare out at the audience. Their posture is tough and aggressive; they slouch, but their arms are tense, as if ready to act. Next the boys hold the girls upside down and move forward looking like multilimbed creatures.

The second dance is a twist for a girl and four boys. Macero's score sounds like an extended train crash, with a fast driving rhythm behind it. The movement is coldly orgasmic. The twisting is very tight, rapid, and obsessive. A boy moves on the floor between the legs of the other dancers, writhing wildly; no one appears to notice. The dancers remain locked into their own sexual worlds. The girl, here much taller than the boys, remains especially untouched by the violent movement. At one moment the boys hold her aloft; she sits upright on their outstretched arms staring out at the audience; she runs her hands through her luxurious hair and opens her mouth wide in a silent cry—or a yawn. After holding the girl horizontally over their heads, the boys repeatedly

Lynne Fippinger and men of the Juilliard Dance Ensemble in Anna Sokolow's *Opus '63* (1963). *Photo: Radford Bascome. Courtesy of The Juilliard School.*

throw her in the air. She then slides down their bodies, and the dance ends with all of them on the floor. They give their heads one staccato shake.

The third movement looks as if it had developed from the second dance of *Session for Six*. The dancers take couple positions, as they did in the earlier dance. But although they are in couple formations, they actually dance alone, ignoring their potential partners and moving about the stage in frantic but introverted motion. They collapse, pick themselves up, then move on seemingly at random. They plod or wildly execute a few mambo steps. Everyone exits except one girl, who repeatedly flings her arms and body in fierce, jagged fits. The others enter, and a couple moves to the center, dancing tightly together. As they move, they gaze into each others' eyes with rapt attention, then quickly part. The dance ends with the performers in two lines along the sides of the stage, making weakly threatening gestures at each other.

The fourth dance includes numerous moves for couples that involve bending and lifting. Sometimes the boys press themselves tightly over the girls' limp bodies, sometimes they lift the girls, whose bodies seem leaden. The boys carry the girls while attempting to execute simple jazzy steps, but they are hampered by their oppressive burdens. The couples separate and face off, then repeat the lifts. Finally the boys place a hand over the girls' eyes and they all blindly stamp, their heads raised as if trying to see the light.

The last dance begins with couples linking elbows at the front of the stage. They move in synchronous steps backward and forward. They lie on the floor, arms outstretched. They stare out at the audience. They rise, and for the first time, the music softens. They raise their arms alternately with the palms upward. They take a *retiré* position and rest there. Finally they join arms again and move forward as the curtain drops.

Although Sokolow's view of contemporary society in *Opus '63* is similar to that of *Rooms* in its narcissism, aimlessness, and disconnection, the alienation is less complete. There are a few brief moments of connection, and at the end there is a softening, perhaps a hint of change. But if optimism is what Sokolow had in mind, she made no attempt to clarify her position. When she created *Opus '65* for the Joffrey, which was similar in a number of ways to *Opus '63*, she ended the work with the dancers moving ominously to the front of the stage and then leaping into the audience as if on the attack. It is difficult to see this aggressive action as a sign of hope rather than as an example of a ruling class turning on itself. In any case, Sokolow's stance on this issue remained, at best, ambiguous.

Much of the movement Sokolow used in her youth works drew on the vocabulary she had begun to develop in *Lyric Suite* and greatly expanded in *Rooms*. It was here she found the gestures, steps, rhythms, and comportment of stress and neurosis. To these she added social dance movement that imbued the pieces with the suggestion of youth. As in *Rooms*, there was no story and little use of mimetic gesture to depict specific meaning so that the modernist formula was generally adhered to. And while one might point out that the social dance, in its specificity, moved the work away from a notion of essential experience, it nevertheless read as universal in its focus on dominant-class concerns. So once again, Sokolow was able to critique the ruling order from the inside. She did it by finding ways to put pressure on modernist rules without reaching the breaking point. Still, Sokolow's works were rarely greeted with enthusiasm. Rather, they were recognized as worthy, and they were tolerated. Her vision was too dark and uncompromising. Jill Johnston succinctly summed up the dance field's view when she dismissed Sokolow as "an excellent choreographer with a death-rattle message" (1968: 32).

Yet Sokolow had her followers, and over the next decade they made a considerable impact on what would be called postmodern dance. Two of her dancers, Jeff Duncan and Jack Moore, founded Dance Theater Workshop in 1965. Many of her company members were part of DTW, and Sokolow worked there as well, in addition to offering advice and encouragement. Others of her company also distinguished themselves. Martha Clarke went on to join Pilobolus in the early 1970s before starting an independent career. Paul Sanasardo created works in the late 1950s and 1960s that owed much to Sokolow's preoccupation with alienation and that used some of the techniques that she employed, such as repetition and accumulation. Pina Bausch was part of Sanasardo's Studio for Dance group, and, through him, she also absorbed some of Sokolow's approach before returning to work in her native Germany. However, that was later. In the 1950s, Sokolow was a respected choreographer but one who was little known outside the dance world. Her leftist past and her critical stance would have worked against her in a time of consensus. It is hardly surprising she was not chosen to be one of America's "cultural ambassadors," when the State Department began to fund dance companies on foreign tours in the 1950s. One cannot imagine government officials wanting Sokolow, with her vision of capitalist society, to represent the United States abroad.

AFRICAN-AMERICAN VANGUARDISM: 1940S

Like so much having to do with race in America, black dancers' position in the postwar modernist vanguard was particularly complicated. In order to gain acceptance within a modern dance that was defined and dominated by whites, black artists needed to be able to obtain
access to the vocabularies and techniques of the genre as well as avenues
to patronage. But equally important, they had to learn the unspoken
norms of modern dance and, more broadly, of modernist aims, whether
to absorb or challenge them. This began to take place in the 1930s and
accelerated in the 1940s. However, the process was hardly straightforward, considering the problematic nature of race in America. White
critics struggled in the 1940s to define a "Negro" high-art dance that
was distinct from other forms, and then struggled again to decide how
a black person might be a modern dancer rather than a "Negro" one.
By the 1950s, these convolutions eased as more black dancers made
their way into the modern genre and found acceptance there. Yet problems of discrimination and stereotyping persisted, just as they did in the
United States at large.

The difficulties that black dancers and choreographers faced in the
1930s, '40s, and '50s have been well documented.[1] My intention is not
to contest these findings but to add to the discourse on African Americans in modern dance through an examination of black artists' relationship to modernism. I will focus attention on two intertwining issues that
have attracted little notice but that affected black vanguardism in the
postwar years. The first is a critique that arose in the 1940s that served
to distinguish and separate black concert dancers from white. This critique centered upon the black body and on Africanist elements in black
movement vocabularies. Sporadic but persistent, it tied black modern
dancers to commercialism, specifically to the exploiting of a high-art

form through sexual and virtuosic exhibition. The critique is important because it reflects modernist concerns regarding commerce and at the same time points to ways in which such concerns were used to differentiate and control black dancers within a white-dominated form.

The second point, which will be dealt with in chapter 6, has to do with the universalizing of black experience in modern dance that occurred during the 1950s. While this signified a new acceptance of black choreographers and their dances within the modern genre, it also made it more difficult for dancers to deal with racial issues. As was seen in works concerning Jewish identity, modernism's demand for universality tended to put limits on objectives that fell outside dominant (white) standards, values, and interests.

One of the important legacies of the 1930s revolutionary dance movement and New Deal programs was that they helped open the doors of modern dance to black artists (Graff 1997; Perpener 2001: 189–190). Although, as Susan Manning has pointed out (2004), leftist organizations were more given to lip service than to action on the issue of racial equality, inroads were made through greater access to ballet and modern dance training and in some cases through performing opportunities under the aegis of both leftist groups and New Deal programs. Katherine Dunham, for example, produced her dance-drama *L'Ag'Ya* (1938) under the sponsorship of the Federal Theatre Project in Chicago, and in 1939 she was invited to New York to choreograph some of the dances for the Labor Stage's production of the musical revue *Pins and Needles*. The Labor Stage was affiliated with the International Ladies Garment Workers' Union. When Dunham presented her first company concerts in New York in 1940, it was at the Labor Stage's home, the Windsor Theatre, and with the help of its producer, Louis Schaeffer. The New Dance Group also did much to nurture black dancers. Artists such as Ronne Aul, Pearl Primus, and Donald McKayle, all of whom began their careers in the 1940s, studied, taught, and/or performed with the New Dance Group.

Black dancers' access to a white-dominated modern dance paralleled to a degree the gathering momentum of the civil rights movement. More than a million black soldiers fought in World War II, and when they returned to the United States, they wanted more equality (Dalfiume 1968; Lawson 1976; Chafe 1982; Sitkoff 1993). Veterans took part in many of the early civil rights battles and some even succeeded in registering to vote in the South in 1946 and '47. In addition, a million blacks moved north to jobs in the 1940s. They created a significant voting block, and in response to this new constituency President Truman created a Committee on Civil Rights in 1946 that recommended antilynching legislation, protection of voters' rights, desegregation of the armed forces, and other antisegregation legislation. Few of these recommendations were acted upon, but they were the beginning of the wedge that would eventually lead to laws passed and enforced in the coming decades. In the meantime, violence continued in the South, often in conjunction with blacks trying to register to vote.

Like the small advances made in civil rights while discrimination continued, African Americans made headway into modern dance while in many ways continuing to be excluded. White critics didn't fault black dancers for being on white stages; in fact by the 1940s the dance press in general welcomed black dancers. The criticism was more subtle. Although diffuse and often vague, it primarily hinged on an idea that black dancers were commercializing a vanguard form. In this case commercialism was perceived primarily in two ways: as an excess of sexuality and of virtuosity. This excess appeared to be natural to the black body and, according to contemporary critique, was something that needed curbing. The critique of commercialism in African-American dance will be examined here through the work of Katherine Dunham, Pearl Primus, and Talley Beatty, all of whom rose to prominence in the 1940s.

Katherine Dunham was the most famous black high-art dancer of the 1940s. However, Dunham's relationship to modern dance was ambivalent, and although most black dancers of these years held similar positions, hers was particularly uneasy. Born in Glen Ellyn, Illinois, in 1910, Dunham followed her older brother to the University of Chicago where she studied with Robert Redfield, one of that generation's most important anthropologists. In 1935, Dunham was awarded a Rosenwald Foundation grant, which allowed her to do fieldwork in the Caribbean for eighteen months. It also made it possible for her to do her field research under another eminent anthropologist, Melville Herskovits, who was head of the African studies department at Northwestern University.[2] Dunham's work with two of the most gifted social scientists of the interwar years not only aided her in forming her own dance theory and philosophy, it was vital in giving her a grasp of modernist aims.

This knowledge, coupled with her fieldwork and her training in western dance forms, provided her with an unusually sophisticated foundation on which to develop her own dance.

While Dunham was pursuing her university education, she was also deeply involved in dance practice. She had become interested in dancing in high school, where she learned what appears to have been a Dalcrozian and Laban-influenced free dance. When she arrived in Chicago, she added ballet to her studies, working with Mark Turbyfill, a leading dancer with the Chicago Opera Ballet. In 1929–1930, she and Turbyfill attempted to start a black ballet company called Ballet Nègre, but the project foundered for a variety of reasons, many having to do with the racism of the times (Barzel 1983). Dunham also worked with Ludmilla Speranzeva, who had been trained in ballet in Russia and in modern dance with Mary Wigman in Germany. Speranzeva was a friend and mentor who allowed Dunham to use her studio to teach classes. She also rented a studio for Dunham in her own name after the latter's return from the Caribbean. With Speranzeva's urging, Dunham formed the Negro Dance Group, which was primarily devoted to modern dance. In 1933, Ruth Page, ballet director of the Chicago Grand Opera, invited her to dance in her ballet *La Guiablesse*, set in Martinique, which helped to make Dunham better known in the community. After her Caribbean journey Dunham added Afro-Caribbean movement to the classes she taught and began to choreograph works in the fusion vocabulary she was developing. In 1937, her group was invited to perform in New York as part of the Negro Dance Evening at the 92nd Street Y. In 1939, Dunham returned to New York with some of her company for the *Pins and Needles* revue.

Dunham premiered her first full concert in New York on 18 February 1940 at the Windsor Theatre. The production was at first billed simply as Katherine Dunham and Dance Group, but after its initial success the title was changed to *Tropics and Le Jazz "Hot": From Haiti to Harlem*. The first part of the title was drawn from two suites of dances that were part of Dunham's program; the last indicated the breadth of dances presented. The production met with such demand that it ran for thirteen consecutive Sundays at the Windsor. The Dunham company program consisted of three segments. The first included *Primitive Rhythms*, which was comprised of *Rara-Tonga*, *Tempo-Son* (a Cuban slave song and dance of possession), and *Tempo-Bolero;* this was followed by two rumbas. After the first intermission there was *Peruvienne*, which

Katherine Dunham as the Woman with the Cigar in *Tropics—Shore Excursion* (1940). *Courtesy of Jerome Robbins Dance Division, The New York Public Library for the Performing Arts, Astor, Lenox and Tilden Foundations.*

consisted of two dance-drama vignettes; *Island Songs,* which included a Haitian carnival meringue and a Martinique folk dance; another drum interlude; and *Tropics—Shore Excursion,* which featured Dunham as the Woman with the Cigar. After the second intermission the company performed *Le Jazz "Hot,"* which included a boogie-woogie, *Barrelhouse,* and *Honky-Tonk.* The program ended with another narrative piece, *Bre'r Rabbit an' de Tah Baby.*[3]

Dunham's program demonstrated objectives she often expressed through articles and interviews. Foremost among these was to show white audiences the contributions blacks had made to American culture and, at the same time, the cross-influences between black and white forms. She told an interviewer in 1947, "I was determined to have a group of dancers who would be able to show the people of the U.S. what others have contributed to our culture" (Pierre 1947: 13). One of the key elements in her statement are the words "our culture" and the inclusiveness they assume. For Dunham, American culture was a mix of black and white, not two separate entities. She expanded on this idea in an article published in 1941 ([1941a] 1978). After documenting African retentions in Caribbean and American religious and secular dances of the past, she spoke of European influences, particularly through English square dance and the French quadrille, on plantation dances. Out of these dances emerged minstrelsy, which Dunham said was important because for the first time it was possible to see the influence of black culture on American white culture. What Dunham called "this instrument of fusion between the two cultures" gave recognition to black cultural expressions. The result in the United States was twentieth-century dances that drew on black tradition and grew out of black inspiration. Such cross-fertilization gave African tradition "a place in a large cultural body which it enjoys nowhere else" (ibid.: 73). The concert program that Dunham brought to New York made her thesis clear, from the African retentions in the Caribbean dances, to European influences in the plantation and minstrel dances, to the cross-fertilization in the social dances of the twentieth century.

Dunham not only attempted to make cross-fertilization of cultural expression evident in her programming and selection of material, she also demonstrated it in her choreography. This was shown first by the fact that she choreographed her dances to fit the standard forms and practices of the Western theater. She did not try to reproduce authentic African and Afro-Caribbean rituals and practices. Although an anthropologist, Dunham never transferred dances directly from the field to the stage.

Dunham also incorporated techniques dominated by whites into her choreography. Ballet and modern dance were the major techniques she knew before going to the Caribbean, and after her return she continued to employ them as a part of her choreographic vocabulary. Two films made in the 1940s of extracts from a number of Dunham's dance works show how often she used elements of ballet vocabulary. For example, in the duet from *L'Ag'Ya* (1938) such steps as *saut de basque*, poses in front attitude, and hops in arabesque are to be found.[4] In many of the dances she created for the men of the company, which tended to be more virtuosic than the dances for the women, she also frequently employed steps such as *grand jeté, cabriole,* and pirouettes in a variety of positions including *en dehors, à la seconde,* and *attitude.* These can be seen in the film excerpts of *Choros #1* (1944) and *L'Ag'Ya.* In addition, she sometimes used balletic lifts, which are shown in the film of *Rhumba Jive* (1941) where a man lifts a woman onto one shoulder.[5]

Dunham didn't end her ideas of racial cross-fertilization with her choreography; she started early to develop and codify a technique that incorporated ballet, modern dance, and Afro-Caribbean movement. She said that among her goals was "to develop a technique that will be as important to the white man as to the Negro" (Orme 1938: 46). To a large extent, she accomplished that goal. In the late 1970s, Millicent Hodson was able to write that Dunham had contributed to modern dance a liberation of the pelvis and knees as well as a new movement vocabulary of the lower body (Hodson 1978: 187). She might have mentioned a liberation of the shoulders, neck, and spine, as well. In looking at the films of the Dunham company from the 1940s, it is notable how the shoulders, in particular, are given pronounced articulation. Also emphasized is the use of body-part isolation, fundamental in Dunham technique, which allows the body to work in countermovements and thus to create complex dynamic rhythms. Today many of the movement elements Dunham codified have become an integral part of American high-art dance as a whole.

When Katherine Dunham and Dance Group opened at the Windsor Theatre, the critics were generally enthusiastic. They treated the production as a high-art recital, and they understood that it was likely to mark a turning point in black high-art dance. However, they showed less understanding of Dunham's specific intentions. Walter Terry wrote that "last night at the Windsor Theatre Katherine Dunham broke the bonds that have chained the dancing Negro to the alien techniques of the white race and introduced us to a dance that was worthy of her own people" (1940a: 13). In a lengthy Sunday piece John Martin noted: "Miss Dunham has apparently based her theory on the obvious fact so often overlooked that if the Negro is to develop an art of his own he can begin only with the seeds of that art that lies within him" (1940b: 114).

Dunham was assumed to want to distinguish her dance from white dance and maintain its separation. Terry and Martin thought this a laudable endeavor and wrote as if it were the central issue for Dunham. When they noticed white-dominated techniques in her work, they generally did not approve, as witnessed by Martin's comment: "There is among certain of the male dancers, including Talley Beatty, a distressing tendency to introduce the technique of the academic ballet. What is there in the human mind that is so eager to reduce the rare and genuine to the standard and foreign!" (1940b: 114; see also 1940a: 23). In some cases, however, the absorption of "white" elements was considered commendable. Terry wrote that although Dunham's dances appeared spontaneous (a quality considered typical of black dance), they obviously were not, "for the works are beautifully constructed with an eye to stage pattern, movement, development and compactness" (1940a: 13). In other words, Dunham had overcome black spontaneity for white discipline and restraint. Although such comments reveal cultural assumptions that have long been discredited, Terry and Martin were, in fact, excited by the possibilities of Dunham's work and were writing extremely positive reviews. They saw her dance as an important breakthrough, even if they did not fully appreciate her goals.

Dance Observer did not review the Dunham company until it opened the Dance Theatre Series at the 92nd Street Y on 10 November. This venue placed Dunham more fully within a modern dance context than Broadway, and it reinforced her high-art aims. However, there were aspects of the production and company that were not typical of modern dance recitals and that made Dunham harder to categorize. To a degree these differences may have set the stage for future criticism. Dunham's vision was always ambitious. Her company was large by modern dance standards, consisting of fourteen dancers plus two pianists and two drummers. Also, thanks to her designer husband, John Pratt, the company had elaborate sets and costumes. Few modern dance companies short of Martha Graham's could mount such a sophisticated production. Mary P. O'Donnell, who reviewed the 92nd Street Y performance for *Dance Observer*, seemed to sense these differences. She compared the concert to the productions of Argentina in that "authentic folk ideas and movements were molded by formal aesthetic standards," and she noted that the company presented its material with "extraordinary showmanship and a real sense of the theatre." She ended her review by saying that Dunham warranted "appreciation as a dancer, as a choreographer and as an arresting personality" (O'Donnell 1940: 148).

Critics from the black press were as positive as white commentators about Dunham. However, they were far less concerned with how she fit into high-art dance than that she had gained success with white audiences. Dan Burley wrote in the *Amsterdam News* that "some day a careful chronicler will set down on paper in detail the story of how Katherine Dunham conquered Broadway" (Burley 1940: 21), while Edgar T. Rouzeau in the *Norfolk Journal and Guide* wrote "Catherine [*sic*] Dunham's art takes her into the very best circles. When it comes to hobnobbing with the Astors, the Morgans, the Vanderbilts and the Rockefellers, she is away head of us" (Rouzeau 1940: 17).

For all the positive response to Dunham's first New York season, there were also hints of the negative criticism to come. Terry noted that while the dances in *Tropics* "possessed a veneer of cheap sophistication," those qualities were essential to the street and bar dances they portrayed. Similarly, the jitterbug and shimmy dances of *Le Jazz "Hot,"* although full of "unrestrained cavortings resolve themselves into healthy, yet extremely lusty, folk dances" (Terry 1940a: 13). He concluded that if such dances appeared cheap, it was undoubtedly owing to white performers who had cheapened them. Rouzeau of the *Norfolk Journal and Guide* echoed Terry in saying that the "cheap sophistication" of *Island Songs* and *Tropics* was necessary to convey the style and feeling of the dances. He felt that Dunham was at her best in *Peruvienne*, because the graceful movements showed "her subtle technique at its best." (Rouzeau 1940: 17). Margery Dana of the *Daily Worker* was positive overall; however, she felt the second half of the program "was too influenced by musical comedy," by "gaudy costumes, cheap sensuality and, of course, 'Uncle Tom'" (Dana 1940: 7).[6] Dana appears to have misunderstood Dunham's intentions in depicting minstrelsy in the section entitled *Bre'r Rabbit an' de Tah Baby*. As noted, Dunham felt that minstrelsy was the first theatrical form to show the influence of black culture on white and wanted to make that point, whereas Dana saw the depiction of minstrelsy as succumbing to stereotypes.

By 1943, when Dunham presented her next set of concerts in New York, the uneasiness hinted at in earlier comments about the theatricality and sexuality of her dances began to coalesce into more overt accusations of commercialism. Dunham had starred in *Cabin in the Sky* on Broadway in 1940, then toured with the show. When it closed in California, Dunham and the company stayed on, performing in several Hollywood films and in nightclubs. Sol Hurok, one of the most powerful impresarios in the United States, then invited Dunham to appear under his management. Hurok added a singer and a Dixieland jazz ensemble to the piano and percussion Dunham had previously employed. He also gave her production the title *Tropical Revue*, although Hurok himself described the production as "somewhere between revue and recital" (1953: 59; see also 1947: 267). However, the categorizing of Dunham's dances as a revue changed audience expectations, despite the fact that with one exception the 1943 program did not differ markedly from that of 1940. This exception, though, was important and may have influenced critics, although for the most part they did not acknowledge it. The major addition to the repertory was an ambitious work entitled *Rites de Passage*. It replaced *Peruvienne* and *Island Songs* from the 1940 production, with the rest of the program similar to that of *Tropics and Le Jazz "Hot."*

Rites de Passage was composed of three sections: "Fertility Ritual," "Male Puberty Ritual," and "Death Ritual." The fertility ritual centered on a man and woman who in their duet advanced, retreated, and circled each other while executing a rhythm of backward and forward pelvic movement. The ritual aspect of the dance was emphasized through the repetition of movement; through the dancers' gazes, which did not meet; and through their faces, which remained neutral throughout. The male puberty ritual depicted an adolescent boy who dreamed or underwent trance, then faced ordeals before being welcomed as an adult into the community. The last segment dealt with the death of a chief, the society's mourning, the crowning of a new king, and his marriage to the queen.

In the original program note Dunham described *Rites de Passage* "as a set of rituals surrounding the transition of an individual or group of individuals from one life crisis to another. The ritual period, often at

Lucille Ellis and James Alexander in the "Fertility Ritual" section of Katherine Dunham's *Rites de Passage* (1943). The photograph was taken during the company's London season in 1948. *Photo: Roger Wood. Courtesy of Jerome Robbins Dance Division, The New York Public Library for the Performing Arts, Astor, Lenox and Tilden Foundations.*

once both sacred and dangerous, is under the guidance of the elders of the community: the entire community joins in this critical transition so that the individual may, in a changed status, have a complete rejoining with the society."[7] The program note went on to say that the work did not represent any particular culture but was an abstraction meant to capture the "emotional body of any primitive community and to project this intense, even fearful personal experience." The costumes by John Pratt reinforced the idea of nonspecificity in fantastic garments that recalled no definite source. The women wore earth-colored bandeau tops and short skirts, braided to resemble natural fiber. Their hair was hidden beneath high, crownlike wigs of braids. The men wore briefs and over them loincloths. Like the women, they also wore braided wigs.

As Ramsay Burt has pointed out (1998: 166–179), Dunham was concerned not just with understanding the technical aspects and overt social function of the dances of so-called primitive people but also the deep psychological needs and desires that motivated them.[8] There is ample evidence that Dunham saw in these psychological motivations particularly powerful examples of universal experience that both the artist and anthropologist sought to tap into. As such, Dunham placed herself on the side of modernism. She wrote in an article in 1941 that the artist "seeks to recreate and present an impression of universal human experience—to fulfill either human needs or wants. The instrument is the specific art form which may have been chosen; the effectiveness depends upon skill in handling the form and upon the originality of the individual imagination. But the experience which is given expression cannot be either too individual or too specific; it must be universal" ([1941b] 1978: 55). She then went on to explain the value of anthropological study: "In such a survey, the student of anthropology gradually comes to recognize universal emotional experiences, common alike to both the primitive Bushman and the sophisticated cosmopolitan" (ibid.).

At the time, however, commentators did not make a connection between modernist goals and the universal emotion Dunham tried to embody through an abstraction of primitive ritual. When *Tropical Revue* opened on 19 September 1943 at the Martin Beck Theatre, Louis Horst and John Martin agreed that *Rites de Passage* was the best and most serious work of the evening, but they didn't say why and made no attempt to analyze it (Martin 1943b: 24; Horst 1943: 90). Roberta Lowe, critic for the *Amsterdam News*, felt that *Rites de Passage*, which she called "Haitian inspired," was not authentic in the sense that it did not portray a specific culture convincingly (1943: 9). John Meldon of the *Daily Worker* also saw *Rites de Passage* in specific cultural terms, saying that it was based on an authentic Haitian folk dance (1943: 7), although he disagreed with the *Amsterdam News* in that he felt the work was the highlight of the evening.

Rather than focus on the modernism of *Rites de Passage*, commentators turned their attention to what they considered the commercial nature of Dunham's production, showing greater ambivalence about her work than they had earlier. This was undoubtedly aided by the fact that the fertility section of *Rites de Passage* caused a flurry of publicity as the

company toured the United States. Descriptions of the Dunham repertory as "hot" and "sizzling" abounded. When the group reached New
York, John Martin mentioned that Dunham now called her production
a revue, although he said it was in truth "part recital, part nightclub"
(1943b: 24). Anatole Chujoy, writing of Dunham for the first time in
Dance News, thought she presented "an excellent show," but treated it
as light entertainment, refusing to intellectualize her dances or to try
"to find a justification for what she is doing and for the way she is doing
it" (1943: 3). Louis Horst gave *Tropical Revue* only cursory treatment
in *Dance Observer*, saying its material was "frankly of revue and nightclub caliber" and so needed only brief comment (1943: 90).

Martin's remarks in 1943 reflected a shifting attitude toward Dunham's work that would become more emphatic as time went on. He
wrote: "As an anthropologist the gist of Miss Dunham's report seems to
be that sex in the Caribbean is doing all right. She even seems to have
remembered certain testimony along this line that eluded her when last
she appeared here-abouts, and which no doubt Hollywood has brought
to her mind" (1943b: 24). Martin's suggestion was that Dunham had
made her dances sexier after being in the Hollywood marketplace and
that because of it they were anthropologically less authentic. Martin
overlooked the fact, which he had noted in his 1940 reviews, that Dunham's works were never meant as anthropological reconstructions. Yet
Martin praised the dances of the first part of the program, "dealing with
primitive rituals and the like" which, he said, "fell well within the recital
category" (ibid.).

Soon, the Dunham company left on another national tour during
which *Rites de Passage* was dropped in Boston after complaints led to a
visit by the censor (Perpener 2001: 152–153). When John Martin saw
Tropical Revue again the next year on its return to New York, his opinion
had taken a much harder edge. He found it to be "from anthropology
à la Minsky to the frankest kind of honky-tonk. There are rumbas and
rituals, barrel-house boleros and blues, and the characteristic accent of
all of them is pelvic" (1944a: 15). Martin's indiscriminate grouping of
rituals with folk and bar dances as all somehow distastefully sexual was
an idea that had not appeared in his earlier reviews, and his comparison
of *Tropical Revue* with the burlesque shows at Minsky's theater suggests
moral outrage more than reasoned argument. But although his reaction
was more extreme than most, a thread ran through several other reviews tying Dunham's production to commerce. Writing in *New Masses*

under the name Francis Steuben, Edna Ocko linked Dunham's work to Broadway: "Miss Dunham's recitals several years ago set an enviable standard for authenticity and impeccable taste. It is no news that Broadway is not exacting on either score" (Steuben 1943: 26). However, both John Meldon in the *Daily Worker* and Henry Simon in *PM* praised the company, Meldon calling the group one of the brightest and most entertaining on Broadway (Meldon 1943: 7; Simon 1943: 22).

Significantly, Roberta Lowe of the *Amsterdam News* defended Dunham's use of sexuality. In doing so she was perhaps responding to criticism of the production. Lowe contrasted the sophisticates who would see the beauty and vitality of *Tropical Revue* with the barbarians who would be attracted to the "hip-swinging" that she noted was a hallmark of the show. Her reference to barbarians may well have been a swipe at prurient white interest. She commented more than once on what she called "hip" rather than "pelvic" movement, but said that it was relegated to its proper place in the street and bar dances (1943: 9).

Edwin Denby, in a *New York Herald Tribune* review, did not conflate sexuality with commercialism in *Tropical Revue*. He didn't care for *Rites de Passage*, but he faulted it on formal grounds, saying that Dunham had not been able to fit African expressive method to that of the Western stage. " The movement," he said, "is based on African dance elements but the choreographic plan is that of the American modern school" ([1943a] 1986: 143). He noted that the latter, like all Western dance, made its effects through contrasts of weight, volume, speed, and dynamics, whereas African methods favored reiteration. Yet contrasts were not absent from African art, he argued, citing African sculpture as a form that showed "distinctness of contrasts and their surprising reconciliation" (ibid.). Denby preferred Dunham's bar and street dances. He singled out the three different "hot" styles of Dunham's Brazilian *Bahiana*, Cuban *Shore Excursion*, and American *Barrelhouse:* "She has observed these fashions of tropical entertainment intelligently, she knows what they are each after. Better still, she knows there is nothing arch about a hot style, that its expression is serious and sometimes even angry" (Denby [1943a] 1986: 142). He thought Dunham's gestures "provocative and yet discreet and she can even keep a private modesty of her own. As a dance entertainer, she is a serious artist." Denby linked art, entertainment, and sexuality in positive terms that a number of other critics found impossible to do.

Sociologist St. Clair Drake wrote in 1981 that "the deep strain of

Puritanism in American life that tended to turn sexuality into prurient interest was a constraint that serious black performers had to break through" (Drake 1981: xii). He went on to say that Dunham showed her audiences that "sexuality as expressed in some aspects of African and New World black tradition has symbolic meanings relevant to utility as well as to sexual satisfaction, and that ostensibly erotic dancing can be cherished for the sheer joy of the bodily movement and display of dancing skill" (ibid.).

Dunham's accentuation of pelvic movement accurately reflected the African retentions she wished to show, but such movement also related to an element of form and function that was important to her. In an article written in 1941, Dunham made the point that in Caribbean peasant societies social and sacred dances with pelvic movement were directly associated with sexual activities; that is to say, form and function were closely linked (Dunham [1941c] 1978: 192–196). She described the banda dance of Haiti, which was performed at funerals and had a sexual character, "in keeping with the African philosophy which closely associates procreation with death, perhaps as a compensatory effort" (ibid.: 193). She mentioned, too, the *danses grouillière*, which included both sacred and secular dances and which featured the grinding of the hips. Dunham was extremely interested in the links between form and function as part of her general choreographic strategy. She took her cue from that connection in making her fertility duet in *Rites de Passage*. The movements she chose were ones she had seen in the Caribbean, and they reinforced the purpose of the dance.

However, for some American observers form could only follow function under certain conditions, at least if the result was to be considered art. Commentators who willingly accepted sexuality as art when it was depicted as neurotic or pathological, for example in the works of Graham or Tudor where the use of the pelvis was also in evidence, were far less eager to give sexuality a place in art when it was portrayed as a universal and often joyous part of life. This was particularly the case when sexuality was being expressed by black bodies. Then the tendency was to tie sexuality to commerce and to the exploitation of a high-art form. Dunham's dances, clouded by Puritanism and racism, lent themselves to the fear of commercialism that modern dance commentators were already feeling.

However, it must be said, too, that Dunham fed the fire of sexual controversy. The public attention it brought her helped ensure the sur-

vival of her company while allowing her to demonstrate some of the contradictions of racial assumptions. Among her tactics was, in interviews,
to encourage the image of herself as the sexualized primitive then put it
in tension with the educated sophisticate. Margaret Lloyd described
her this way in an interview: "Lithe and slender in her tight, leopard-
cloth slacks, gentle of voice and manner, she was poised and charming,
and very keen in her observations. It was difficult to realize that not many
generations ago her ancestors had left Africa in slave ships" (1949: 247).

Lloyd's patronizing tone is a little amusing considering how thoroughly Dunham controlled the interview. Certainly Dunham was aware
of what she was doing. She promoted the dichotomy in her publicity
materials, spoke about it often, and wrote at least one article on the subject. In "Thesis Turned Broadway" ([1941b] 1978: 55–57) she explained
that she saw synthesis rather than conflict in the two aspects. As an
anthropologist she had no interest, she said, in presenting the exotic on
stage. She wanted to investigate the cultural and psychological framework of why people danced. She sought the common patterns that
bound them together as human beings. Sexuality was part of a universal human totality that was no more to be denied than birth and death.
Dunham, in emphasizing the compatibility of sexuality and serious
artistic intent in her dances and her person, chose to disrupt stereotypes
both on the stage and off.

There was another element to the issue of sexuality in Dunham's
dances that was not openly discussed but that she understood and dis-
turbed. This was the stereotype of blacks as primitive, in the sense of
uncivilized, and sexually uninhibited. As Sander Gilman has pointed
out in his study of racial stereotypes and pathology, black women in the
nineteenth century came to be associated with unbridled sexual appetite
in contrast to white women. This was part of a broader agenda of differentiating the races, with blacks portrayed as antithetical to whites.
Both art and science in the nineteenth century depicted black women
as inherently immoral and uncontrollable due to their primitive sexual
makeup. That is to say, they were not only primitive in spirit but in the
physical construction of their sexual organs. It was a small step to link
the image of the black woman to that of the prostitute in nineteenth-
century iconography (Gilman 1985: 76–108; Giddings 1992). Other
scholars have shown that black men were similarly cast as sexually in-
satiable and for similar reasons (Fanon 1967; Mercer 1994: 131–220;
Collins 2004: 149–180).

Although any scientific basis for such stereotypes had long been dismissed by midtwentieth century, the stereotypes themselves persisted, as Gilman shows in his analysis of modernist literature (1985: 109–127). Dunham unsettled these stereotypes in her dances by seeming to conform to them through her movement vocabulary and then countering them with anthropological insights. As is evident in her interview with Lloyd, she could also conjure similar tensions through her own persona, dressing to suggest sexuality and the jungle while speaking with "civilized" charm and intelligence. Denby said there was provocation in Dunham's dances, and it is likely he was correct. When Dunham returned to New York in 1944, Denby reiterated many of the ideas he had expressed earlier, concluding that "Miss Dunham's wit and charm and complete knowingness are the key" (1944d: 10). Thus, Dunham used sexuality to make a number of points about race in America, but in the 1940s few commentators understood her intent.

Dunham was not alone in being criticized for the sexuality of her dances. Pearl Primus, Talley Beatty, and others were also faulted, particularly for pelvic movement, which offended white sensibilities and was linked to the exploitation of modern dance. Dunham, however, was seldom condemned for emotional or virtuosic excess, other elements linked to commercialism in black dance. Here Primus and Beatty were especially singled out.

Primus's career was different from Dunham's in that her training placed her firmly within the New York modern dance scene. Born in Trinidad in 1919, Primus's family moved to New York when she was three (Green 2002; Barber 1992). She attended Hunter College High School and then Hunter College, where she studied biology and pre-medicine with the idea of becoming a physician. After deciding that medicine was not for her, she entered Columbia University for a master's degree in anthropology. In the meantime she had started dance classes at the New Dance Group and also studied with Martha Graham and Louis Horst. Primus's association with the New Dance Group, under whose auspices she often appeared, gave her legitimacy as a modern dancer. Also, her performances fit the concert format, being mostly solos and small group works with modest costumes, music, and scenic effects. Such details were important, as they allowed a dancer to be categorized and judged according to the norms of the genre.

Dance Observer followed Primus's early career avidly. When five young dancers presented a concert at the 92nd Street Y on 14 January 1943, Primus earned the best reviews. Gervase Butler wrote: "Pearl Primus is not a "Negro" dancer in the conventional sense of the term. Trained in the New Dance Group and now studying with Martha Graham, her aptitude and feeling for racial rhythms is secondary to a direct and unusually ample response to the modern idiom. Pearl Primus is about the most exciting evidence this reviewer has seen that there are no inherent confines to the dance capacities of her race" (1943: 27). Butler defined a "Negro" dancer as one who used "racial rhythms," that is, African and diasporic sources of movement. He felt that for Primus these were secondary to the movement vocabularies of modern dance. The fact that Primus gave primary importance to the modern idiom meant that her race would not limit her to specificity; she could communicate universal emotion and in this way become truly a modern dancer. Butler suggested that it was Primus's training and vocabulary that made the difference, rather than her subject matter. This was an important distinction, for Primus's dances were in many instances specifically about black experience. Her program included *A Man Has Just Been Lynched*, later called *Strange Fruit*, and *Hard Times Blues*, which dealt with the plight of tenant farmers. These social protest themes were welcomed during the war when modern dancers were expected to deal with problems of modern life. In addition, her concerts included African and diasporian-inspired suites, spirituals, and jazz-based abstract dances.

John Martin was also impressed with Primus, saying "it would be hard to think of a Negro dancer in the field who can match her for technical capacity, compositional skill and something to say in terms that are altogether true to herself both racially and as an individual artist" (1943a: 5). Martin particularly pointed out the originality of Primus's choreography and its strength of composition. In *African Ceremonial*, he said she employed "genuine primitive movement and shapes it precisely and authoritatively into artistic theatre form," while in *Hard Times Blues* she explored the music's rhythmic possibilities to achieve original choreography that had great impact. In *A Man Has Just Been Lynched*, she captured the passion and terror of the onlooker's experience in extraordinary movement.

Leftist and black critics greeted Primus with as much enthusiasm as Martin and Butler but with a different emphasis. Edith Anderson announced in her headline in the *Daily Worker* that Primus was the first

Negro to make her debut at the Y, thus breaking the color barrier. She spoke of Primus's "terrific power, exuberance, ease and control" and that she "tore the house down" in her debut (1943: 7). Peter Suskind of the *Norfolk Journal* said Primus embodied the spirit of the dance and had something new and original to say. He also noted that Primus had appeared with four other dancers who were white, and she was the only one who was cheered for a curtain call after each dance (1943: 14).

In October 1944, less than two years after her first appearance at the 92nd Street Y and several months after her first solo concert, also at the Y, Primus made her Broadway debut. As Hurok had done with Dunham, Max Jelin, Primus's impresario, arranged her material in the shape of a revue, with musical numbers by Frankie Newton's band and solos by Josh White placed between her dances. Although some critics, including John Martin, were still highly laudatory, the general response to her work was less positive than it had been earlier. Some blamed the introduction of elements unrelated to the dance, in particular the band numbers, which they thought intrusive.[9] But others found something amiss with Primus's choreography and presentation.

Edna Ocko, writing under the name Francis Steuben in *New Masses*, summed up the problems. She found Primus's dances to be deeply felt but lacking in structural coherence: "These very social and artistic convictions demand imaginative and connotative movement of a creative caliber not always achieved by Miss Primus" (Steuben 1944: 28). Ocko went on to say that often the only element that bound the dances together was their emotional intensity. "The stuff and substance of the craft itself—its inner connectives, its patterns of developing movement, its structural continuity—basic dance elements which cannot be conjured out of thin air—are resolved by Miss Primus in what seems too easy and too unoriginal a manner" (ibid.).

Edwin Denby also found the production only partially successful, although he still thought Primus "a thrilling dancer." He felt the protest dances, which included the recently choreographed *The Negro Speaks of Rivers*, were less compelling than the playful jazz pieces, in which Primus's choreography was inventive and the dances well-made. He said the protest works were less successful because when the audience agreed beforehand with the artist, the protest no longer became the center of attention. Instead viewers focused on the elegance of the dance execution, and Primus occasionally "hammed" her protest pieces ([1944c] 1986: 247–248). N. S. Wollf of *Dance News* agreed that it was in the

Pearl Primus in *Hard Times Blues* (1943). *Photo: Gjon Mili/Time Life Pictures/Getty Images.*

social protest dances where Primus failed. Wollf found them too literal (1944: 7).

The most extensive analysis of Primus's work in the wake of her Broadway debut was Lois Balcom's two articles in *Dance Observer* (1944a, 1944b). Balcom couched her analysis in terms of three different types of audience. The first was the least demanding. It consisted of spectators who came with certain preconceptions about "Negro" dance, all of which Primus fulfilled. This audience liked the dances inspired by African tribal sources (stereotypes of the primitive), the jazz dances (stereotypes of minstrelsy), and the modern protest pieces, because they all seemed to reinforce preconceived ideas of race. The second audience was more sophisticated and less easily pleased. It believed that the Negro dancer could not be modern because she could not overcome her race. This audience declined to like the "primitives" because they were interpretations rather than recreations. Nor did it appreciate the modern protest dances because they did not reflect the style of Graham or other established moderns. The preference here was for the jazz dances because Primus was performing them best at that moment.

The last audience believed that modern dance and the Negro race were not mutually exclusive. Clearly Balcom considered herself among this group and as such sought to give Primus advice. She began by quoting John Martin's concept of modern dance as he expressed it in 1933 in *The Modern Dance:* "From the desire to externalize personal, authentic experience, it is evident that the scheme of modern dancing is all in the direction of individualism and away from standardization" (Balcom 1944a: 111). Balcom did not consider such a modern dance to be in conflict with race. Being modern was a matter of being oneself in the deepest sense, and if one were Negro, then racial heritage would be included in being modern. The problem for Balcom was that she did not believe Primus was offering authentic experience in her modern dances. She located the trouble in a lack of discipline. Using *Strange Fruit* as an example, Balcom said it was the most effective of Primus's modern dances, but it was "formless, undisciplined, unconcentrated" (1944b: 123). She noted that "it is not enough to say that 'discipline' is not notably a Negro characteristic" (ibid.). The artist must discipline herself in order to be able to use her medium to express her intention. In flinging herself about the stage, doing spectacular leaps, stamping her feet, and beating her thighs, Primus was not showing discipline. Balcom enlarged on her theme: "Economy, tautness, like 'discipline,' may seem not to be characteristic of the Negro temperament, but the Negro artist has no choice but to master the seeming paradox of expressing with economy and tautness the emotional prodigality of her race!" (1944b: 124). If Primus did not get herself under control, Balcom said, she would remain little more than a talented and popular entertainer.

Certainly in these articles Balcom showed her concern for nurturing a black modern dancer. She appared to want Primus to succeed but was worried she would fall into the arms of easy entertainment where she would never become modern. One could argue that as a talented individual Primus had moved too quickly from unknown to star, a view that was reflected in several reviews of her Broadway debut. But there is in Balcom's criticism a shift from the problems of a young dancer to an issue of race. In her view, blacks were by nature undisciplined and emotionally profligate, and Primus's dances, in which she flung herself about and made spectacular leaps, were examples of it. Balcom's comment resonates with criticism of Dunham as sexually extravagant, and in both cases this excess was tied to exhibitionism and commerce.

Although Balcom's articles constituted only one opinion, *Dance Observer* was a highly influential voice in the dance field and devoting two lengthy articles to a single dancer's performance was extremely unusual for the magazine. In addition, once Balcom set the critical tack, the other *Dance Observer* critics followed her direction. Besides finding fault with the undisciplined character of Primus's modern dances, they began to link sexuality, exhibition, and commerce in them. Horton Foote spoke of the "pelvic dullness" of Primus's "primitive" dances, while the spirituals and songs of protest "emerged thin and superficial" (1945a: 44–45). In 1946, Mary Phelps was not altogether clear about what she objected to in Primus's work, although she harshly criticized the choreographer for insulting her own dance, a paean to the Watusi people, which Phelps found undignified (1946a: 24). Several months later another *Dance Observer* critic, Eleanor Anne Goff, again connected pelvic movement to exhibitionism. Speaking of the "primitive" dances she said: "As for the rest, what could be beautiful savagery descends to the blow by blow repetition of uninspired torso and hip flexions, play-dances, reminiscent of, but not as successful as, some of Katharine [*sic*] Dunham's works, and tinged with a theatricalism and exhibitionism which rightly do not belong in sincere works of this nature" (1946: 76). Goff, in what can only reflect her own rather fevered imagination, looked for "beautiful savagery" from a black dancer, but then criticized the dancer for a use of repetition and pelvic movement, which were Africanist elements, though hardly "savage." The jazz and play-dances, Goff said, were theatricalized and exhibitionist.

The charge of exhibitionism in Primus's dance extended beyond sexuality and emotional excess to technical virtuosity. Margaret Lloyd, writing in her 1949 book on modern dance, exemplified the suspicion that surrounded Primus's remarkable elevation, something that Balcom also mentioned. She commented:

> *Hard Time Blues* [*sic*], to a record by Josh White, is phenomenal for its excursions into space and stopovers on top of it. Pearl takes a running jump, lands in an upper corner and sits there, unconcernedly paddling the air with her legs. She does it repeatedly, from one side of the stage, then the other, apparently unaware of the involuntary gasps from the audience. The feat looks something like the broad jump of the athlete, but the take-off is different, she tells me, and the legs are kicked out less horizontally. The dance is a protest against sharecropping. For me it was exultant with mastery over the law of gravitation, and the poor sharecroppers were forgotten. "Going up in the air does not always express joy," she explained. "It can mean sorrow, anger, anything; it all depends on the shape the body takes in the air." So what appeared to be a triumphant assault was evidently a projection of defiance or desperation. (1949: 271–272)

Lloyd was skeptical about Primus's intentions in her jump, feeling it was out of keeping with the themes of her dance. However, for Primus it was a means of expressing a number of different emotions, depending on its form. It was part of her means of expression, and to have suppressed it would have been like asking Graham to suppress her signature contractions. It is important to note that, according to Primus, she did not simply stage protest through subject matter. *Hard Times Blues*, *The Negro Speaks of Rivers*, and other dances may have expressed protest in their themes, but they also embodied it in movement. In this she fulfilled John Martin's notion of a modern dance as one that abstracted from life experience through individual means, a quality he, himself, saw in her dances. Yet for Lloyd and others the virtuosic nature of Primus's dance was a means of exhibiting herself rather than calling forth authentic emotion.

In 1948, Primus, who eventually earned a Ph.D. in anthropology from New York University, won a fellowship from the Rosenwald Foundation to study dances in Africa. She spent nine months there, and it was only with her return that she was once again wholeheartedly welcomed into the high-art dance fold, this time as an anthropologist and expert in African dance as much, if not more, than as a choreographer of modern dance. She returned to Africa often after her first trip, and her appearances in the United States included numerous lecture-demonstrations of African dances and culture as well as dance concerts. In this way, her virtuosity was folded into broader interests and was given anthropological legitimation.

Although critics may have faulted Primus, they also treated her as one of their own. Talley Beatty, on the other hand, came from the Dunham company and was frequently condemned for his early choreography, as well as criticized for his dancing. Like Dunham and Primus, he was charged with exhibitionism. Born in 1923 in Chicago, Beatty began his career as a youngster with Dunham in the 1930s (Beatty 1990, 1993; Nash 1992). He had been studying for only a few months before he began appearing with her group. At that time Dunham had not yet been to the Caribbean and was teaching primarily ballet and modern dance. When she left for her fieldwork, she suggested Beatty study with other teachers. He took modern classes with Kurt and Grace Graff, but he was not allowed to mix with white students, so he went early in the morning and took a class alone in the dressing room. Edna McCrae, a well-known Chicago ballet teacher, also agreed to have him as a student, but again he could not take classes with her white pupils. He therefore followed what was happening in the studio from an office that had a small window looking out on the classroom. This kind of discrimination was common in Beatty's early career and made a lasting impression on him. He later commented: "That was part of our lives then in the South Side. I mean it was really quite a hard role. We were very aware of it and I think that perhaps, I was kind of a rough character. I mean I was rather frank so I'm sure I must have said something about it. But there was nothing. . . . It was either doing it that way or not doing it at all" (Beatty 1990).

When Dunham's company began appearing in New York in the late 1930s, Beatty was often singled out for the brilliance of his dancing. However, he was also one of the men John Martin castigated for having an inappropriate balletic virtuosity. Martin seems not to have understood

Talley Beatty as a young dancer in New York. *Courtesy of Jerome Robbins Dance Division, The New York Public Library for the Performing Arts, Astor, Lenox and Tilden Foundations.*

that Beatty had been trained as a ballet dancer and therefore bore the marks of that training on his body. This must have been particularly visible in Dunham's choreography, which utilized ballet along with Afro-Caribbean and modern dance techniques. That Beatty was an accomplished ballet dancer is supported by the fact that Lincoln Kirstein asked him to appear in Lew Christensen's *Blackface* (1947) with Ballet Society and to choreograph a work for the company.[10] Although at that time Martin was expressing a commonly held opinion in saying that ballet was inappropriate for black bodies, Beatty himself could not have disagreed more. He later commented, "I think that [ballet] is part of our culture, a part of the American culture. . . . It's just as close to blacks as it is to whites. This is a part of us" (Beatty 1990). Like Dunham, he saw ballet as a legitimate source for all Americans, and like her, he used ballet technique and vocabulary in his own choreography.

Beatty began his choreographic career on 3 November 1946 with two dances for the inaugural concert of Choreographers' Workshop. He made a duet for himself and Lavinia Williams entitled *Blues*, and another duet for himself and Tommy Gomez called *Southern Landscape*. The only publication to cover the concert was *Dance Observer*, and Louis Horst said of Beatty's offerings simply that they showed him to be a better dancer than choreographer (1946: 124). Two months later, Beatty had enlarged *Southern Landscape* to three scenes, which he again presented under the aegis of Choreographers' Workshop. Again Horst reviewed. He wrote that the scenes, which were listed as "Defeat," "The Mourner's Bench," and "The New Courage" had exciting and beautiful passages, "but one longs for more restrained choreography and less display of obvious technical stunts by Mr. Beatty himself" (1947: 20).

On 11 May 1947, the Workshop presented the five best pieces of more than twenty given that season, and *Southern Landscape* was one of them. By this time Beatty had completed the entire work, which was set to a score by Elie Siegmeister. The inspiration for *Southern Landscape* was Howard Fast's novel, *Freedom Road* (1946), which in part dealt with blacks being forced off the land they had been given after the Civil War. Beatty choreographed a series of dances that focused on the grief and loss that African Americans felt at being dispossessed.

We are fortunate that *Southern Landscape* survives today in a video recording of a reconstruction overseen by Beatty in 1992. There is also a film made in 1948 of Beatty himself in the work's central solo.[11] The first section, "The Defeat in the Fields," shows men and women working the land and then being terrorized there. It is the closest thing to dramatic action in the work. Next is "Mourner's Bench," which Beatty later said he imagined as a solo for a man who had just returned from a nighttime burial.[12] The third section, "My Hair Was Wet with the Midnight Dew" is a dance of sorrow performed by two couples. A program note from 1948 states that the "survivors of the attack wandered at night through their ravaged fields."[13] "Up, Ring Shout" follows. Historically the ring shout was a slave dance of religious release in which the participants moved counterclockwise in shuffling steps to the accompaniment of spirituals. The dance went on for long periods of time during which possession sometimes took hold of one or more of the members (Emery 1988: 120–126; Stuckey 2002: 44–47). Beatty did not attempt an authentic recreation of the dance but rather used it as the basis for his own choreography to signify the release of communal grief. The dance begins with shuffling steps, which gradually lead to more varied movement. The movement becomes increasingly fast and more densely packed, creating a sense of building intensity. The last scene of *Southern Landscape*, entitled "Settin' Up," was described in the program as a dance of mourning for the dead. According to dancer/ historian Joe Nash, who saw early performances of the work, Beatty changed the choreography of the last section when he revived the piece in the 1990s.[14]

The early reviews of *Southern Landscape* were generally encouraging. When *Dance Observer* critic Mary Phelps saw the finished work at the Choreographers' Workshop concert, she did not mention stunts, as Horst had done earlier (1947: 65). She called *Southern Landscape* "a straight impassioned cry of suffering and determination." She said it only needed increased contrast in the overall design to make it entirely effective. In *Dance Magazine*, Doris Hering described *Southern Landscape* as a thunderstorm and Beatty as the lightning in it. He was, she said, "an exciting, inventive, intuitive, virtuosic dancer," and his choreography, like his style, was "wild, undisciplined, and pixy-like" (1947: 20–21). *Southern Landscape* itself was over-long and diffuse, and contained "much that is merely stagey and spectacular." She singled out "Mourner's Bench" as an example. The work also contained "much that is sincere and shows real talent and theatrical sense."

In 1948, Beatty formed a company that presented its first full concert on 24 October 1948 at the 92nd Street Y. It was at this point that criticism of Beatty's virtuosity began to harden. The concert program

Kim Bears-Bailey and members of the Philadelphia Dance Company in Talley Beatty's *Southern Landscape* (1948), which Beatty revived for the company in 1992. *Photo: Patented Photos. Courtesy of the Philadelphia Dance Company.*

consisted of *Rural Dances of Cuba, Southern Landscape, Saudades do Brazil, Blues,* and *Kanzo.* Of these, *Kanzo,* which depicted Haitian vodun initiation rites, and *Rural Dances of Cuba* were new. The *New York Times* and the *Herald Tribune* ran announcements of the concert, but neither paper covered the debut. The concert was also ignored by *Dance News* and by the black press. Doris Hering, giving *Southern Landscape* another viewing, was not impressed. She wrote that it was ambitious but naive. "Even Mr. Beatty's solo, 'Mourner's Bench,' while visually arresting, does not grow from the deep roots that make sincere concert dance. There is a feeling of movement chosen merely for its eye appeal" (1948: 35).

In her brief review for *Dance Observer,* Harriet Johnson said the Afro-Caribbean dances were too closely aligned to Dunham and advised Beatty to pursue work more on the order of *Southern Landscape* (1948: 122). This was mild criticism considering that a number of the *Dance Observer* writers had begun to focus attacks on Beatty's virtuosity. Earlier in 1948, Martha Coleman had written that "Mr. Beatty's technical skill continues to express only his virtuosity, and to confuse exhibition with expression" (1948: 7). By 1950, Robert Sabin was speaking of the need to pare down "attempts at virtuosity" in Beatty's *Vieux Carré,* a work that survives only in Sabin's description of it as imitative of Massine's *Gaîté Parisienne* (1950: 71). That same year, Joan Brodie wrote a particularly harsh review of a concert that was similar in content to the 92nd Street Y performance of 1948. She was incensed by what she called Beatty's "cheap sensationalism," which she blamed on both the sexuality she perceived in some of his material and on his technical skill (1950: 138–139). "It is," she wrote, "upsetting to see a group of well-trained, hard-working dancers . . . performing in such trash" (1950: 139). Even *Southern Landscape* did not escape her censure. Conceding that it was a serious work, outstanding for its dignity and attempt at real communication, she wrote that "Mourner's Bench," while affecting, needed more conviction "so that a more genuine emotion might come through the brilliant movement" (1950: 138–139).

One has to turn to Cecil Smith, editor of *Musical America,* to find a more thorough and balanced analysis of Beatty's work. Writing of the 92nd Street Y concert in 1948, Smith commented:

His YMHA program was consistently brilliant, and at times as breathtaking as any dancing to be encountered on the American stage today. But it offered hardly more than a suggestion of Mr. Beatty's potential in-

vention and scope as a choreographer. Three of the four longer compositions were opportunistic, in the sense that they were derived lock,
stock, and barrel from the style of Miss Dunham's folk ballet, though
they are better composed, for the most part. It was only when Mr. Beatty
turned from Cuba, Brazil and Haiti to a highly individual and heartfelt
modern-dance work, *Southern Landscape*, that a new dimension of depth
appeared. Drawing its inspiration from Howard Fast's chapters on the
Reconstruction period, *Southern Landscape* seeks to express the defeat,
the grief, and the religious release of a people who had briefly tasted
freedom and had seen it taken away from them again. The second and
third of the five movements, in particular, capture the essence of this grief
in genuinely moving form, and Mr. Beatty's solo dance is remarkable for
the way in which his superb virtuosity remains constantly meaningful.
(1948: 10)

Smith's review gives a clearer idea than most of the content of Beatty's
concert and the relative merits of the works. He found the dancing brilliant rather than tasteless and exhibitionist, as had other critics. He took
no particular offense at the Afro-Caribbean dances, although he found
them derivative, while *Southern Landscape* impressed him for its sincerity and emotional force, especially Beatty's solo. Undoubtedly referring
to *Southern Landscape*, he said the concert suggested Beatty's potential
and scope as a choreographer.[15] Yet what appeared to Smith as both virtuosic and "constantly meaningful," was for the critics of *Dance Observer*
and *Dance Magazine* excessive. For Brodie, Beatty's works lacked "form,
meaning, unity, and good taste" (1950: 138).

In order to try to come to grips with the radically different views
Beatty's work elicited and the recurring critique of his virtuosity, I
would like to compare "Mourner's Bench" with two solos by Jean Erdman of about the same year. In the late 1940s, Erdman was considered
one of the most promising of the new generation of modern dancers. I
have chosen to use her dances for comparison rather than a solo by another male dancer because the great majority of modern dance choreographers and performers in the late 1940s were women. For example,
eight out of the eleven dance performances reviewed in *Dance Observer*
in January 1948, when *Southern Landscape* was also reviewed, were by
women. What I want to emphasize here are differences in the approach
to choreography and performance that race, class, and gender might
have made during these years.

The extant film of Beatty in "Mourner's Bench" shows him performing a technically demanding solo that depicts the spiritual anguish of a grieving man. But not only is the dance demanding, it is choreographically innovative, that innovation made possible in part by the technical abilities of the choreographer-dancer. Beatty used the bench as a partner and support on which to balance in a wide variety of ways. He stands while moving into high extensions, he braces his legs beneath the bench and cantilevers his body out into space like the bowsprit of a ship, he rolls off onto the floor in a controlled extension to the side, and more. The dance is a technical tour-de-force, but it is also a metaphor for pain as the body struggles against the gravity that pins it down.

Joan Erdman's *Ophelia* was called "probably Miss Erdman's finest solo," notable, in particular for its dynamic quality (Larkey 1949: 152). This dance can be seen on video in a reconstruction Erdman oversaw in the early 1990s.[16] Looked at solely in terms of the movement, it consists primarily of walking steps, now slow, now fast, sometimes coming to rest in the hitched hip pose of medieval sculpture and paintings.[17] The walking steps are most often combined with turns, sometimes stepping turns, sometimes larger circles made while doing walking steps. It also includes occasional high-swinging leg kicks that swirl the dancer's long skirt in an arc above her head, high side extensions, and shallow lunges to the side. The Graham contraction is also in evidence from time to time. There is much use of arm movements, which tend to be nonspecific gestures. For example, at certain points the dancer extends her arms overhead, or holds her arms close to the body and moves her lower arms from side to side in unison. None of this movement extends the general modern dance vocabulary, and according to Erdman, as noted earlier, she had little interest in creating a vocabulary of her own. Like many other young dancers of the time, she was more concerned with using existing dance vocabularies in an impersonal way, rather than developing new personal forms.

In contrast, Beatty extended a ballet and conventionalized modern dance vocabulary in "Mourner's Bench." He did this first by abstracting movement and gestures derived from African and diasporic movement. For example, he used torso articulation in which shoulders and torso move forward and back, adding this to modern dance contractions. In addition, he extended modern dance movement through his experimental use of the bench, in which he found a number of steps that could work in concert with the prop he had chosen. For instance, at one point in the film Beatty lies across the bench perpendicular to its length and rolls his body slowly from one side to the other, turning each time into a high arabesque. At another moment he *pliés* into a crouching fourth position that he uses as a springboard into a series of quick turns that take him behind the bench, his back to the audience, from which he assumes a wide second position bending back over the bench toward the spectators.

In contrast to Erdman's dance, Beatty also stretched and filled out the movement to the maximum reach of his body, making the dance image appear large and forceful. The steps flow from one to the other, rarely coming to a halt in a pose, giving the impression of dynamism and a stretched tension. The movement in Erdman's dance often stops before being fully developed, as if held back and made small. Rather than powerful, the dance image is one of neatness and control. The many halts between steps also continually stop the flow of movement. Of course this may have something to do with the mood she was trying to convey in the dance. In the video, she speaks of wanting to communicate a sense of "psychic dismemberment" in the piece. But here one might also point to another of Erdman's dances of the same period, which had quite a different aim, but nevertheless still employed movement in a similar way. *Hamadryad* (1948) is a dance that Erdman said was meant to convey the "sheer enjoyment of movement, a voluptuous, joyous outdoors feeling. . . . There was nothing civilized about it."[18]

This dance contains more varied and energetic action than *Ophelia*, but it, too, constantly freezes the flow and stretch of the steps. Although one must always consider the fact that we are not seeing Erdman, herself, but another dancer of a later period performing, nonetheless, I think it is fair to say that the arrangements of the steps make the movement appear highly controlled, despite the sense of abandon Erdman wanted to convey. The steps move from pose to pose. In fact the dance begins with a pose, head looking up, torso twisted, legs bent in a *demi-plié*, arms low and open. From this position the dancer moves into a profile pose in a deep contraction out of which she reaches upward, then faces front repeating the first pose; her arms undulate in a quick waving motion; she resumes the first pose; and then repeats the phrase. This start-and-stop construction constantly breaks the force of the action. Each pose is clear, but there is little sense of a powerful thrust of movement.

Critics may well have found the control in dances by Erdman and other white performers reassuring. African Americans invaded this polite world and celebrated the power of the human body. Primus's jump, Beatty's pounces and balanced high extensions, and Dunham's undulating hips proved disturbing in their unabashed energy and forthrightness. Critics read these elements as uncontrolled and perhaps in a subliminal way, dangerous. And it can be argued that there was, indeed, danger to the status quo in these dancers' movement. Dunham's use of the pelvis and shoulders challenged American Puritanism, while Primus and Beatty's use of virtuosity called into question restrictions placed on blacks' physical means of expression, particularly means that were ruled alien to them. All three dancers threatened barriers constructed to control blacks and separate them from whites. Denby had commented that the injustice of slavery and its legacy was hardly protest, as it was generally agreed that slavery had caused egregious harm. Therefore, so-called protest dances could be celebrated with little disturbance to long-held beliefs and practices. But Dunham, Primus, and Beatty attacked discrimination and hypocrisy where it could sting, and they did it not so much with stories told but through a corporeal politics of danced movement. The resulting case made against them was that they trafficked in commerce, that virtuosity and sexuality were simply employed for display and as such could not contribute to authenticity. Accusations of commercialism lessened markedly as black artists made their way into modern dance in increasing numbers during the postwar years. In the 1940s, however, the sense that black dancers were exploiting a vanguard form played into white stereotypes of blacks as physically unrestrained and emotionally profligate while at the same time reflecting legitimate concerns within the field about the influence of the market on modern dance.

AFRICAN-AMERICAN VANGUARDISM: 1950S

In the 1940s, charges of commercialism and exploitation devalued the work of black modern dance choreographers even as black artists became increasingly visible in the field. What is surprising is how thoroughly these accusations disappeared in the 1950s. In fact, dance commentators' references to any aspect of race became far more muted.[1] There were several possible reasons for this shift. Certainly by the beginning of the 1950s, African-American dancers and choreographers were becoming more firmly established within modern dance than they had been earlier. Most modern dance and ballet teachers in New York accepted African Americans as students, and although ballet companies still resisted black dancers, African Americans found their way into a number of white modern dance companies, including those of Sophie Maslow, Anna Sokolow, Martha Graham, Jean Erdman, Alwin Nikolais, and Merce Cunningham (Greene 1997). At the same time, white dancers occasionally performed in black companies, as Remy Charlip, Louis Falco, and Esta and Eve Beck did in Donald McKayle's group. In addition to increased numbers of dancers, there was a gradual acceptance of Africanist movement in modern dance. During the 1950s, black popular culture, although generally diluted for white audiences, greatly expanded in the mainstream. When teenagers routinely shook their hips to rock-and-roll and Elvis ("the pelvis") Presley appeared on prime-time television, it was no longer shocking to see such movement in vanguard dance. As the works of black choreographers came to be viewed as modern rather than "Negro," their dances were universalized in keeping with modernist imperatives. While this helped integrate black choreographers into a white genre, it tended to erase concerns that were considered specific to black experience.

The muting of race also came at a moment when fears of the Soviet

Union and a communist takeover were at their height. In such an atmosphere few commentators wanted to call attention to America's problems for fear of seeming unpatriotic or of lending aid to the enemy. In her groundbreaking book, *Cold War Civil Rights*, Mary L. Dudziak documents the U.S. government's concern over international criticism of American racism and the vulnerable position in which it placed the country. Dudziak asks, "How could American democracy be a beacon during the Cold War, and a model for those struggling against Soviet oppression, if the United States itself practiced brutal discrimination against minorities within its own borders?" (2000: 3). The "Negro problem,"to use Gunnar Myrdal's term, caused foreign relations difficulties with countries in Asia, Africa, and Latin America, as well as the Soviet Union. Although international criticism of American racism was common during the postwar years, Dudziak notes that to criticize racial ills from within the United States was to risk being labeled subversive.

For commentators of the time, one way out of the predicament of dealing with racial problems was to avoid the subject altogether. For example, Daniel Bell, in his discussion of American society and its troubles in *The End of Ideology*, failed, except in the most cursory of references, to mention the existence of racial issues. Instead he spoke of alienation and fear of mass culture being major social concerns, along with the threat of communism. Other observers of the midcentury American scene from William H. Whyte Jr. to Arthur Schlesinger Jr. also ignored the subject. Like Bell, they talked of the fear and malaise they saw around them, focusing on middle-class angst.

The degree to which race was off the table in dance was most flagrantly illustrated by Katherine Dunham's *Southland*, which premiered in Chile in 1951 and dealt with a lynching. After the work was performed, Dunham met with increasing harassment from the State Department. This continued not only through the remainder of the South American tour but on subsequent appearances abroad. After performing *Southland* in Paris in January 1953 to mixed reviews and silence from the American Embassy, Dunham decided she didn't have the strength to try to perform it in the United States. But the ordeal wasn't over; throughout the 1950s, the U.S. government found numerous small ways to attack Dunham when her company was on tour outside the country. It comes as no surprise, then, that the State Department neglected to award Dunham one of the touring grants that were started in 1954 as part of the country's cultural diplomacy (Hill 1994; Dunham [1951]

1978). During the 1950s, the State Department also attempted to silence Josephine Baker for criticizing American racial discrimination while on tour in Latin America. Her passport could not be revoked because she had become a French citizen; however, Baker found it increasingly difficult to obtain engagements in Latin America and at one point was barred from landing in the United States on her way from France to Mexico City (Dudziak 2000: 67–76). Although Dunham and Baker's experiences were the exception rather than the rule, they suggest the climate that prevailed at the time regarding the discussion of racial issues.

The chilling effect engendered by the Cold War, coupled with modernist demands for universality and consensus culture's erasing of difference combined to make themselves felt in dance discourse in a number of ways. For example, a subtle shift occurred in the categorization of dance and dancers. In the 1940s, dances had been divided between "Negro" and modern with most black dances categorized as "Negro," because they were viewed as dealing with specific rather than universal experience. In the 1950s, as more black dancers came to be considered modern, the two categories shifted to a more generalized "ethnic" dance and modern dance. Ethnic dance occupied a lower position in the dance hierarchy than modern dance and the even more prestigious ballet. Dances that appeared to deal with the roots of black experience were categorized as ethnic, whereas dances that were viewed as universal were modern. So, for example, Geoffrey Holder, who was from Trinidad, frequently choreographed works that were inspired by aspects of Afro-Caribbean culture. Critics routinely used "ethnic" to describe his sources. Although such a categorization might have been to some degree understandable in Holder's case, at least one writer also used "ethnic" to describe Alvin Ailey's sources for his bitterly despairing *Blues Suite* (Bernstein 1958: 88). This work drew on Ailey's memories of the bars and brothels of the area in which he lived as a child in Texas. Nonetheless, the work, which depicted the effects of poverty and discrimination in rural America, was classified as ethnic in its source material.

In another example, Walter Terry categorized Dunham and Primus as ethnic dancers in his book *The Dance in America* ([1956] 1971), even though neither would have described herself in such terms. Terry did place Janet Collins and Ronne Aul in his section on modern dance and mentioned Primus there, although he said she had turned increasingly to ethnic dance after having traveled to Africa.

Gerald Myers, writing in the 1980s in an essay on ethnic and modern dance, addressed the issue of black dancers being designated as ethnic rather than modern. He defines ethnic dance as one that attempts to conserve tradition by replicating the past, whereas modern dance is characterized by originality and rebellion against the past; ". . . modern dancers are found rebelling against the tradition that begets, sustains, and to some degree entraps them" (Myers 1988: 24). However, he notes that even when it is acknowledged that black choreographers are simply referring to dances from, for example Africa or Haiti, those sources are considered so overwhelming that the new dances "represent a contemporary ethnic genre." He adds that "connotations of aesthetic rawness, of unsublimated primitivism, mingle in the mischievousness of the label 'ethnic'" (ibid.). At the least, the "ethnic" designation given to African-American dances in the 1950s indicates a move away from dealing directly with race, and at most, to the reduction of a potentially explosive issue into an innocuous matter of colorful folk and exotic cultures.

A more effective method than euphemism for avoiding the discussion of race was simply, like Daniel Bell, not to address it. Among the few articles in the dance press that met racial issues head-on in the 1950s was a *Dance Magazine* interview with Janet Collins that chronicled the difficulties she had experienced breaking the color barrier in ballet. Before migrating to New York, Collins had been a student of Carmelita Maracci in Los Angeles. Collins told Norma Gengal Stahl that while still living in California she had auditioned for Leonide Massine, at that time choreographer for Ballet Russe de Monte Carlo. Massine had complimented her on her dancing but said he could not accept her because the company did not have enough specialty roles for her, "and for the corps de ballet, he said he'd have to paint me white" (Stahl 1954: 28). Asked what her response had been, Collins said she "cried for an hour, and went back to the *barre*" (ibid.). Collins was finally accepted by the Metropolitan Opera Ballet, where she became *première danseuse* while also choreographing modern dance works for concerts of her own.

It is clear from Stahl's interview with Collins that the dance community was aware of the difficulties black dancers faced, and it may be assumed they were aware of racial issues on a broader level. However, in most instances, members of the dance press avoided speaking of race during the 1950s in much the same way they avoided decoding works that dealt indirectly with current troubles. There are many examples of writers failing to mention what would seem to be obvious racial references in works. A case in point is a review written by Lucy Wilder in 1952 that described Donald McKayle's early dance, *Saturday's Child*, as "a stunning solo piece . . . in which he delivers Countee Cullen's poem as the accompaniment for the dance." Wilder continued to speak at length about the dance, how the movement heightened the poem's effect, how the solo "was confined in space, physically taut and abrupt, emotionally direct and intense" (1952: 58). Yet she did not mention that Cullen had been a major figure in the Harlem Renaissance, or that the subject of the poem dealt with the anguish of grinding poverty, or how McKayle's dance, created and performed by an African-American choreographer, may have related to issues of race in the poem. The racial element of McKayle's *Saturday's Child* did not escape the notice of the black community, however. McKayle says in his autobiography that the solo, which he danced in several informal performances around New York, resulted in his being invited to join the Committee for the Negro in the Arts, an elite group that included such members of the Harlem Renaissance as Langston Hughes and Paul Robeson and younger rising black artists, writers, and performers including Sydney Poitier and Harry Belafonte (McKayle 2002: 35–36).

In another instance Doris Hering wrote exclusively in aesthetic terms of Louis Johnson's *Spiritual Suite*, presented in a concert at the 92nd Street Y on 27 November 1955. The opening section, she said, had to do primarily with design, while his solo to "Motherless Child" "was affecting because it was a free, spontaneous expression of emotion" (1956: 77). Similarly, Robert Sabin, reviewing a concert by Janet Collins at the 92nd Street Y on 3 December 1951, spoke of her works *Three Psalms of David* and *Spirituals* simply as dances of religious inspiration (1952: 10–11). Both, he said were derivative of Graham, but he made no reference to the fact that the former suite drew on Jewish sources and the latter on African-American ones, let alone how these two works might have been treated in company with each other. This was something John Martin had mentioned in his review of the spirituals when he had seen them in 1949, remarking that although Collins was "aware of racial backgrounds in the spirituals . . . they are in every sense dances rather than an exploitation of heritage" (1949). He went on to note that Collins was similarly interested in Hebraic dances and was working with composer Ernest Bloch on a series of them, which she would choreograph. Setting aside Martin's attempts to separate modern dance from "an exploitation of heritage," the point here is that he addressed the subject of race in dances that he viewed as related to it and tied the spirituals to the group of dances drawn from Jewish material as works that dealt with particular cultural and racial backgrounds. We might be led to believe that the lack of racial references in writing of the 1950s meant that race was simply no longer an issue in modern dance, were it not that it had figured so prominently a few years earlier and that its disappearance occurred when the social and political atmosphere in the United States discouraged discussions of difference. In order to explore what the muting of race in dance discourse meant for African-American choreographers, I want to turn to two important works from that decade: Donald McKayle's *Rainbow Round My Shoulder* and Talley Beatty's *The Road of the Phoebe Snow*, both choreographed in 1959.

McKayle, who was born in 1930, was the youngest child of a middle-class immigrant family from Jamaica who settled in Harlem (McKayle 2002). His father was a maintenance man for various theaters in New York until the war, when he started a career as an airplane mechanic. His mother worked in the garment district. McKayle went to the best public schools his parents could find and was an excellent student. A high school friend who was taking classes at the New Dance Group invited him to a Pearl Primus concert, which proved to be transformative. Although he had little dance experience, McKayle auditioned for a scholarship at the New Dance Group and won it. A year later he was performing with the New Dance Group and choreographing dances of his own. His first major work *Games* (1951) was a hit, and McKayle became a young choreographer to watch.

During the 1950s, McKayle not only made works for his own group, he danced with a number of other companies, including those of Anna Sokolow (he was part of the original cast of *Rooms*), Martha Graham, Jean Erdman, and Merce Cunningham. He also continued to dance with Maslow and appeared on television and in several Broadway shows, including *House of Flowers* (1954, Balanchine/Herbert Ross), *West Side Story* (1957, Robbins), and *Copper and Brass* (1957, Sokolow). By the time McKayle choreographed *Rainbow Round My Shoulder* he was a mature artist and dance maker.

McKayle conceived *Rainbow Round My Shoulder* almost by accident (McKayle 2002).[2] He had been hired at a summer resort in the Catskills as a weekend entertainer. There he met the great blues singer Leon

Bibb, who was also on the entertainment staff. They decided to do a number together, set to Bibb's singing of the chain gang song "Tol' My Captain." These songs were sung by prisoners in the South who were sent out to break rock for roads. The songs kept the rhythm of the prisoners' work as well as expressed their despair and hopes. In the number they worked out, Bibb sang while he pulled McKayle across the stage on a piece of chain that bound them together. As he sang, Bibb held rocks in his hands, which he pounded together for emphasis. McKayle gradually freed himself of the chain and danced unrestrained for a few moments before once again binding himself to the other man and collapsing to the floor. The number was enormously successful, and McKayle went on to create a full dance work from this idea.

McKayle gradually identified other chain gang songs he wanted to use, including "Rocks and Gravel," which opens *Rainbow Round My Shoulder* with the words:

> Well it's early in the morning, huh!
> Baby when I rise, oh-well-a, huh!
> Got the aches and pains, lordy mama, huh!
> Make a man wanna die, oh-well-a, huh!

As the song is heard, seven men enter in a line, their arms clasped.[3] The "huh!" at the end of each line reflects the rhythmic effort of the prisoners' work. McKayle's choreography embodies the same rhythmic effort, as the men's heads and torsos snap in harsh unison at the end of each line.

The next song, "I Had a Gal," introduces the sole woman in the piece. As the men lie collapsed on the stage, she conjures up fantasies of love and caring. The movement is balletic and lyrical. Her arm movements embrace and encircle. She disappears, and the men rise as the title song is heard:

> I got a rainbow, huh!
> Tied around my shoulder, huh!
> I'm goin' home, huh!
> My Lord, I'm goin' home

The men move to the song with sharp contractions as they embody the work being done. But the theme is soon interrupted by another brighter

An early cast of the men in Donald McKayle's *Rainbow Round My Shoulder* (1959): From back row left, William Louther, Tommy Johnson, Donald McKayle, Claude Thompson, Morton Winston, Charles Neal, and Don Martin. The photograph was taken at Jacob's Pillow. *Photo: John Lindquist ©, The Harvard Theatre Collection, Houghton Library. Courtesy of the Donald McKayle Papers, University of California, Irvine, Libraries.*

one that again introduces the girl, this time as a young woman with a bouncing flower in her hair. She flirtatiously shakes her shoulders and hips as she moves about the stage. One of the men tries to catch her, but she remains teasingly elusive. She disappears as "I Got a Rainbow" is heard once more. Then she is back, this time as a mother gently admonishing her neglectful child, then as a wife or lover helping up and encouraging a fallen man. The next song, "Take This Hammer," speaks of an escape:

> Take this hammer, carry it to the captain
> Tell him I'm gone
> I don't want no cold iron shackle
> Round my leg
> If he asks you was I laughing
> Tell him I'm crying

> If he asks you was I running
> Tell him I'm flying

The men gather in a crowd. Two run off. Shots are heard. One man somersaults on, and is picked up and carried off. The other man enters with the girl and they dance to "Another Man Done Gone":

> They killed another man
> He had a long chain on
> Another man done gone.

The man collapses, and the curtain falls.

McKayle's use of a socially conscious theme was not unusual for him; in addition to *Saturday's Child* he had created *Games* (1951), which dealt with childhood poverty and discrimination, and *Her Name Was Harriet* (1952) (later reworked as *Her Name Was Moses*), based on the life of Harriet Tubman of Freedom Train fame. This subject matter reflects the influence of the New Dance Group ethos and McKayle's work with Maslow and Sokolow. But although McKayle used pantomime in *Rainbow* in a way that sometimes recalls Maslow, he gave far more attention to metaphoric movement and to its relationship to the flow and pattern of the dance. For example, although there are suggestions of hammering as the men's arms reach over their heads with their hands locked together, the gesture is abstracted. The resulting metaphor is then interspersed with other movement so that it becomes part of the dance pattern. This may be why the men's dancing is so compelling at this moment; it is transformed into a poetic abstraction of physical labor rather than being an imitation of everyday activity.

McKayle also used the musical rhythm to suggest movement. The clearest example occurs in the work songs where the dancers' sharp contractions coincide with the "huh!" at the end of the musical phrase. The embodied sound reflects both the musical rhythm and the rhythm of the prisoners' work. McKayle has pointed out another way in which the relationship between movement and music is especially close.[4] When he rehearses *Rainbow*, he said he often sings the songs as the dancers move in order to encourage them to listen closely to the music rather than simply to count it. The phrases are uneven because of the mode of labor the men of the chain gang were doing. By singing the ragged musical phrases, he tries to instill in the dancers' bodies the rhythm that

Donald McKayle and Shelley Frankel in a 1962 photograph of McKayle's *Rainbow Round My Shoulder* (1959). *Photo: © Jack Mitchell. Courtesy of the Donald McKayle Papers, Univerisy of California, Irvine, Libraries.*

gives the timing to the movement and helps form the physical shape of the dancers' bodies in motion. In the original production, further connections between the dance and music were made through a male chorus that accompanied Leon Bibb and that was arranged in a pyramid on steps leading from the orchestra floor to the stage with Bibb at the top of the pyramid (McKayle 2002: 116). The chorus members swayed as they sang, which made them participants in the stage action. In this way the music and dance created a whole that is missing when the dance is done, as it often is today, with recorded music.

When *Rainbow Round My Shoulder* was premiered on 10 May 1959 at the 92nd Street Y, it was not greeted with the same level of enthusiasm that *Games* had been eight years earlier, although the work has since become a classic.[5] *Games* dealt with the street games children played when McKayle was growing up in East Harlem, a neighborhood of black, Puerto Rican, and Jewish immigrants. It depicted not just ways in which the neighborhood children entertained themselves but also the insecure and violent lives they led as a result of poverty and discrimination. The work revolved around an incident that happened to McKayle as a child when a friend was wrongly arrested for street fighting (McKayle 2002: 46–47). In the dance work, a child is violently beaten by a policeman. Although the policeman was originally performed by a white dancer, Remy Charlip, the children were played by an integrated cast, and it is understandable that reviews did not mention race as an element of the work.

Rainbow also referred to a situation that involved blacks and whites, but African-American references were more obvious in the later work because of the music and Africanist aspects of the movement. McKayle had studied briefly with Primus (who left the New Dance Group shortly after he arrived) and then with Haitian dancer Jean Léon Destiné, as well as having grown up in a household of Jamaican-born Americans. He was therefore familiar with various African diasporic forms. Although McKayle has said he was not aiming to create black characters in *Rainbow*, his use of pelvis and shoulder articulation, particularly in the flirtatious girl's dance, is based in Africanist movement. Certainly, too, McKayle was thinking of racial injustice when he created *Rainbow*. He wrote in 1965: "Then I became intrigued with the music of the Southern Negro chain gang. What first captured me were the pulsing, restless rhythms. They seemed wrapped in the chains that bound the suffering men together, and they seemed to explode in desperation and anger. The lyrics were sardonic and then, in turn, biting, sensual, and filled with protest" (1965: 59). In a more recent interview, McKayle told a story that linked *Rainbow Round My Shoulder* to the growing civil rights movement in the dance's focus on African-American dreams of freedom and equality. He said that shortly after the work's premiere he was invited to present it on CBS television. After the broadcast, a news program followed with Walter Cronkite reporting on the lunch counter sit-ins in the South. McKayle said it was an unforgettable moment for him because, "it was a time of great change and people putting their lives on the line to effect that change. I thought the dance was part of that in its own way" (McKayle 2000).

Race, though, made little appearance in reviews of *Rainbow Round My Shoulder.* Harry Bernstein of *Dance Observer* even neglected to mention that the theme involved a chain gang, saying simply that *"Rainbow Round My Shoulder,* the new choreography of Mr. McKayle to traditional music, produced, at its best, an exciting emotive response. But an over-literalness of the choreography and incompatible movement for Mary Hinkson, as the Woman, lessened the work generally and made of it one of narrow dimension" (1959: 93). In the limited space generally allocated for each review in *Dance Observer,* Bernstein had little opportunity to elaborate his comments, but he did manage to say that the work was set to traditional music (without specifying the source), that it was over-literal and its dimension narrow in part because of incompatible movement for the woman. One assumes that Bernstein objected to the narrative, mimetic aspect of the dance because of his use of the term "over-literal." Was it the last scene that put him off, where the men escape and one is killed? Certainly that is the most mimetic and the one that most specifically refers to the injustice of the men's situation. But Bernstein also wrote that the movement for the woman was incompatible, which with its literalness gave the work a narrow dimension. This sentence is far from transparent, but I don't think it is unreasonable to surmise that he meant the woman's use of hip and pelvic movement gave the work an Africanist character that made it less universal and more specific in character. Whatever the details of Bernstein's cautiously coded verdict, he did not refer directly to race while employing the epithet used routinely for any work that dealt too unambiguously with controversial subjects. He also couched his comments wholly in aesthetic terms without reference to social meaning.

In her review for *Dance Magazine,* Selma Jeanne Cohen did mention the theme of *Rainbow Round My Shoulder,* but she also spoke in much the same aesthetic language as Bernstein. She said that McKayle's ideas were built on characterization and so had functional integrity, while lacking adventurousness (1959: 17). Since Cohen was sympathetic to the experiments of Merce Cunningham and other objectivists, she was undoubtedly speaking of the expressional thrust of McKayle's work, which she found conservative. She added that only the last scene "lacked internal

motivation and seemed contrived." Cohen found Hinkson's performance stunning for its "remarkably fluid grace and dramatic sensitivity,"
while the dancing of the men "had a persistent forcefulness."

P. W. Manchester differed from her colleagues, finding the work "very
fine" in her *Dance News* review (1959b: 14). But except for noting that
it was based on "Negro prison songs" she did not mention race. Instead
she described the dance in terms of its emotion and form. McKayle, she
said, had encompassed in the dance "the despair, rage, terror and long-
ing of men from whom even hope has departed. Mary Hinkson, glori-
ously feminine, seductive yet gentle, is the image of all womanhood and
the subtle placing of her movements against the male background gives
the work its essential balance."

Several years later Walter Sorell wrote in *Dance Observer* that in *Rainbow Round My Shoulder* McKayle had "created haunting images and
conjured up many moods of despair and hope, of struggle and ultimate
defeat. In every phrase he pictured the stifled and strangled being in
man and his desire for freedom" (1962: 91). This review was more sympathetic than some of those of three years earlier, but Sorell couched his
comments in universal terms, not connecting the work in any way with
racial injustice.

The integrated character of McKayle's company contributed to his
work's being perceived as nonracial. So did his use of a predominately
modern dance vocabulary, which in viewers' eyes rendered the dance
more universal than specific. But while the response to *Rainbow Round
My Shoulder* demonstrated the degree to which black artists had been
absorbed into modern dance, it also meant that injustice was seen in
abstract terms. The rules of modernism made it difficult to deal with
problems that could not be viewed as universal from the standpoint of
a dominant white society, and this situation may not always have served
African-American interests.

Talley Beatty's *The Road of the Phoebe Snow* was a more immediate hit
than *Rainbow*, but it also was treated in generalized terms. In addition,
the work showed the degree to which Beatty's movement style and
vocabulary had been accepted in modern dance and how difficult it had
become to use these elements to political purpose. Beatty's virtuosic
amalgam of Africanist, modern dance, and ballet movement, which
critics had found deplorable ten years earlier, was now celebrated as

exhilarating, and Beatty himself was accorded a kind of success he had never known.

The Phoebe Snow was the name of a train that passed through an area of Chicago where Beatty's father, a house painter, had sometimes worked when Beatty was a boy. As Beatty explained it, in those days his father was not allowed to join the painters' union and so had to take work in the poorest neighborhoods (Beatty 1990). The ghetto beside the railroad tracks was one of these areas. The dance work centers on a group of disaffected youth. Like Sokolow's dances on the same theme, *Phoebe Snow* is set to a jazz score, here by Duke Ellington and Billy Strayhorn. Beatty's young people, however, are far more alienated than Sokolow's—angrier and more destructive.

When *The Road of the Phoebe Snow* was premiered on 28 November 1959 at the 92nd Street Y, the program mentioned no narrative. It listed only the names of the choreographer, composers, and dancers. However, the work does have an outline of a story: a couple is attacked by a group, and as the girl runs from her tormenters, she is killed by a passing train. The curtain goes up on a boy looking down at a girl, lying at his feet.[6] A crowd gathers, running on from various directions, during which the girl is carried off stage. This beginning action turns out to be nearly identical to the ending of the work so that, after the fact, the viewer realizes that the rest of the piece is a flashback of sorts. Treating the narrative in this way allows the work to be read as almost completely "pure" dance. Until those last moments, the focus remains on a driving, inexorable flow of movement, which finally becomes a metaphor for anger and disaffection.

The first dance begins with two men leaping sideways from the wings onto the empty stage. Three other men follow, dancing to a jangling, percussive musical score. They contrast long stretched pulls of the body and arms with snaking hips, snapping fingers, and then slow, drawn out poses. Fluidity is constantly set against hunched over hep-cat steps. Then the five girls come on with hard, unison movement. The men and women form into two independent groups dancing against each other in elegant, dense phrases. At the end the girls run and jump onto the boys.

The next dance starts in a circle, all the participants facing each other. They move out confidently, then as they go from the brightly lighted circle to the shadows beyond it, they seem to lose their nerve. They stumble back into the center then crouch and point into the dark. But what looks like the set-up for a dramatic scene never happens.

Rather, the dance takes over again in highly complex stage patterns in which the movement is set into a now contrasting, now synchronized clapping and finger snapping. Sometimes each dancer riffs independently, then the individuals coalesce into groups, the whole stage constantly on the move. Suddenly everyone leaves, and one boy remains. His short solo features big jumps and liquid transitions that shift to a series of kneeling poses. This dance segues into more ensemble movement, and this, in turn, is followed by a major duet. Here a boy and girl approach each other from across the stage in undulating steps. Their dance is like a deep, fast-moving river. Her movement is based on high extensions that interact in various ways with her partner's body. Throughout the dance there is a sense of tension, although the temperature remains cool. At the end, the other dancers move around them as the girl lies spread-eagled on the floor with the boy on top of her. The crowd moves back, and he rises, slapping her hand away as she reaches toward him.

A second couple enters, and they dance a tender duet that is highly balletic in its many arabesques and lifts. They stop from time to time and embrace. This dance leads to the last scene in which the second couple is attacked by the crowd, the boy is beaten, and the girl assaulted and taunted by the crowd. She runs and falls as lights flash and the sound of clanging signals is heard. The boy lifts the girl and lays her in the center of the stage as the other girls pose on their partners' shoulders.

The Road of the Phoebe Snow is unusual both for how Beatty reconciled thematic material with nonnarrative movement and how he used movement metaphorically. The work conveys some of Beatty's own anger at the discrimination he experienced as a student and dancer. This had not stopped in Chicago. When he reached New York, George Balanchine had been impressed with him in *Cabin in the Sky*, which Balanchine directed and which featured Dunham and her dancers. Balanchine gave Beatty a scholarship to the School of American Ballet, but when he appeared for class, Beatty said the receptionist refused to allow him to participate (Beatty 1990).

Beatty often gave his dances a driving use of technique that both emphasized the virtuosity of his dancers and at the same time spoke of his own anger at rejection. Beatty, like Primus, used virtuosity as a means of protest, but he went further than she did, not simply relating form to themes he wished to convey but using virtuosity to accuse a white society of discrimination and oppression. Speaking of the dancers in *Phoebe*

Enid Britten and Ulysses Dove as the central couple in an Alvin Ailey
American Dance Theater production from 1970 of Talley Beatty's *The
Road of the Phoebe Snow* (1959). *Photo: Alan Bergman. Courtesy of Alvin Ailey Dance
Foundation Archives.*

Snow, he commented: "In the opening dances of *Phoebe*, the dancers are
presenting themselves. They are saying look how beautiful I am, see
what I can do, do I get the job? You sure don't. I was making a statement
that no matter how good you are you will be pushed back. You see that
in the ballet" (Beatty 1993). At the time, however, critics saw nothing of
the kind, although they recognized an anger and violence in the work.
Doris Hering, for example, praised it extravagantly and spent a good

deal of her review speaking about the atmosphere it created: "And like the endless chains of freight trains from which it presumably draws its title, it is a dance with no special beginning, no defined ending. Just the miraculous capacity to alter the landscape as it passes" (1960: 80–81). Hering spoke, too, of the angry strut and reach of the men and of a lonely duet that was jazzy yet somehow contained and classical. She described the second duet as yearning and "tainted by the presence of an intruder. Then danger, separation, the group furiously closing in on them, and again the red and green lights."

A few months later, P. W. Manchester wrote in *Dance News:*

> If this [*The Road of the Phoebe Snow*] was exciting the first time (and it was) how much more so on this occasion! It has been shortened and this pulls the whole thing together. If we have thereby lost a little of the amazing dancing of Tommy Johnson we have gained a clearer pattern of the whole work which now has a rhythm driving clean through it from beginning to end. This rhythm pulses, quickens, slows but never relaxes and the spectators are caught up in it as surely as it has captured the dancers.
>
> There is a wonderful continuous series of short entries with various combinations of dancers sweeping in and out, and two miraculous dance duets—Georgia Collins of the gorgeous legs with Ernest Parham, languorous in their sensuality, and Candace Caldwell and Tommy Johnson, tender in the midst of passion until the casual brutality of the world breaks into their dream. (1960b: 10–11; see also 1960a)

And Jill Johnston, writing in *Dance Observer*, commented: "The jazz ballet, to a scintillating Duke Ellington–Billy Strayhorn score, with its frenetic rhythms born of ruthless city jungles, has all the searing excitement which may have been lacking in other productions. Georgia Collins and Ernest Parham's duet was easily the highlight of the program, arousing spontaneous cheers which were very well deserved" (1960: 89). Once again, race disappeared from discourse, absorbed into a generalized account of urban poverty and youthful alienation. Unfortunately, the black press did not cover Beatty's concerts during the 1940s and '50s, so we have no record of what African-American critics may have thought of the work.

Only John Martin mentioned race and only in passing. He also explained at more length than most how Beatty had subsumed narrative into abstraction in *Phoebe Snow:*

> To put a finger on any cut-and-dried program for the piece is difficult; its program is basically the projection of moods and states of mind and the formalized activities that grow out of them. In outline it seems to be virtually a suite of related dances, almost like some Negro folk "Sylphides," with its duets and trios and ensembles; until at the close we find ourselves suddenly in the midst of a highly dramatic situation, with anger and fear and violence in the air. Perhaps only then does it become clear that the numbers that have gone before may not have been quite so abstract as they have seemed to be. (1959: 18)

Martin also noted that to use ballet terms to describe the dances was not inappropriate "for the work, whatever its underlying human compulsions, ends by being essentially classic in form and texture" (ibid.). Martin's comment illustrates the extent to which opinion had changed regarding black bodies and "alien" techniques. There appears to have been no question in his mind that Beatty was a modern dance choreographer or that ballet technique was open to him.

Martin was one of the few critics who continued to speak about race through the postwar years. In his 1963 survey of high-art dance, entitled *John Martin's Book of the Dance*, he devoted a section to "Negro Dance" (in which he included Asadata Dafora, Dunham, Primus, Beatty, McKayle, and Ailey) and another to "Integrated" dance companies, which were white companies that accepted African Americans. As quixotic as these divisions seem today, they were a sign that race in the New York dance world was not a settled matter.

In all then, the acceptance of African-American choreographers into modern dance proved to be a two-edged sword. While it marked a new level of equality, it did so at the risk of blunting black choreographers' ability to use dance as a weapon of protest. It also pointed up the limitations of modernism to encompass difference. Like Jewish choreographers, African Americans were considered modernist only to the degree that they could be viewed as one with a dominant race and culture. When this was not the case, African Americans were pushed into a category of ethnic dance, which both demoted them in the dance hierarchy and once again positioned them as other. In addition, commentators' perception of Africanist movement and virtuosity as thrilling rather than dangerous raised the possibility of once more viewing black modern dance simply as display. In reviews of *The Road of the Phoebe Snow*, there was a sense of the sheer excitement of seeing highly skilled dancers in motion. Although this did not keep most critics from also noticing the anger and violence of the work, in the 1960s, black modern dance would come to be marked by the degree to which observers reduced it to beautiful bodies in virtuosic movement.[7]

The ways in which race, Cold War issues, and consensus ideology met and were refracted through modern dance's own needs and interests during the 1950s give some idea of the complex relationship between specific fields and the larger social field. African-American choreographers won a permanent place in a dominantly white form, but it was at the price of having racial issues minimized or ignored. At the same time, black choreographers' positions remained to a degree ambivalent, evident in the categorizing of some dancers and dances as ethnic rather than modern.

OBJECTIVISM'S CONSONANCE

In November 1957, *Dance Magazine* initiated a series of articles aimed at surveying the modern dance field. The reason for this unusual attention, according to editor Lydia Joel, was that sweeping changes over the last decade had brought modern dance to what she described as "an uncertain point." Modern dancers, she wrote, were no longer interested in opposing ballet, no longer concerned with social consciousness, or with psychological introspection. *Dance Magazine* "with its usual willingness to step into the hornet's nest," would try to discern some order in the field through articles to be published over a number of months under the general title, "Close-Up of Modern Dance Today" (Joel 1957: 20).

The series, however, did not so much attempt to discern order as impose it. Two of the six articles dealt with what Joel referred to as "the extremists," choreographers who demanded "the right of dancing to be its own subject matter." The first of these two articles included the written statements from a symposium that had been organized a few months earlier by David Vaughan, entitled "Four Dancers Speak and Dance." The dancers were Merce Cunningham, Merle Marsicano, Katherine Litz, and Shirley Broughton. The second article, written by Walter Sorell, concerned Alwin Nikolais and his work at the Henry Street Playhouse (Sorell 1958). Joel pointed out that these were not the only choreographers who focused on movement rather than the communication of emotion; there were a number of others, including Midi Garth, Marie Marchowsky, Erick Hawkins, Paul Taylor, and James Waring. She might have added Murray Louis, Phyllis Lamhut, and Gladys Bailin at the Henry Street Playhouse. With the exception of the Playhouse, these dancers did not constitute a coherent group but rather were tied only by their interest in making their subject the materials of dance.

The rest of the *Dance Magazine* series consisted of two articles on pedagogy published in December 1957 and February 1958 and two articles devoted to another symposium that included Doris Humphrey, May O'Donnell, Sybil Shearer, Carmelita Maracci, and others, which appeared in March and April 1958. Oddly, these were dancers who as a whole produced the kinds of works Joel said were no longer of interest.

Dance Magazine was not alone in its declaration of a new vanguard. In an article for *Dance Observer* in 1955, Jill Johnston had identified two trends in modern dance, one expansionist and one rebellious, but had not yet been able to articulate how the rebels were breaking with the old guard (Johnston 1955: 101–102). Two years later she was more successful in another article written for *Dance Observer* (Johnston 1957a: 55–56). Here, she again described two directions, one that expanded on the work of the dance pioneers and another that broke with it. Then she went on to characterize the first group as using a dramatic-realistic approach, exemplified by Limón, while the other was devoted to depersonalization and experimentation, exemplified by Cunningham, Nikolais, Shearer, and Litz. In still another article a few months later, Johnston continued her thoughts on the vanguard by tackling the question of the meaning of abstraction in dance (Johnston 1957b: 151–152). Abstraction, she stated, meant simply the absence of dramatic subject matter: "The basis of abstraction in dance is its proximity to or distance from *dramatic* subject matter, the carrier of which is *gesture*. And gesture is movement invested with meaning. . . . Representation in dance means more or less fidelity to dramatic character and situation" (1957b: 151). Although Johnston credited modern dance as a whole with making dance an abstract art, her division between abstraction and drama was one that objectivists commonly used to separate their work from expressional dance.

Why, one might ask, did *Dance Magazine* and *Dance Observer* find it advantageous to anoint objectivism as the new vanguard? What did objectivism do for modern dance? To begin to address these questions, I want to examine objectivism through the work of two of its most influential exponents, Merce Cunningham and Alwin Nikolais.[1] Cunningham and Nikolais were particularly important because they did not simply formulate an approach to modern dance that was antimimetic but articulated philosophies, embodied in their work, that put them in opposition to the dominant social order. However, the resistant aspects of their dance for the most part went unrecognized, with emphasis placed instead on the dances' lack of emotional basis, dehumanization, concern with form alone, and by extension their meaninglessness.

By 1945, Merce Cunningham (1919–) had been on the New York modern dance scene for more than fifteen years (Cunningham 1985; Vaughan 1997a). Born in Centralia, Washington, Cunningham attended the Cornish School (now the Cornish College of the Arts) in Seattle, where he met John Cage, who was accompanying the dance classes. Bonnie Bird, Cunningham's teacher at Cornish, encouraged him to attend a summer session with Martha Graham at Mills College in Oakland, California. Impressed by his technical skill, Graham invited Cunningham to New York, where he joined her company in 1939. There he quickly earned a reputation as a charismatic performer. Cage arrived in New York in 1942 and was soon urging the young dancer to strike out on his own. Cunningham and Cage gave their first joint recital in 1944, and Cunningham left the Graham Company permanently in 1945.

Over the next decade, Cunningham developed a dance that focused on movement and dance structure rather than on the communication of emotional essences. He has said that even during his years with Graham, he was most interested in how people moved and how dances could be assembled, and he worked long hours alone in the studio addressing these concerns (Cunningham 1985: 39–43). To begin with, Cunningham focused on dance technique, slowly building an approach to movement in which he clearly had ballet in mind. While studying at the School of American Ballet during his Graham years, he paid careful attention to Balanchine's attempts to give the dancing body a maximum of visual legibility. Cunningham developed a technique that incorporated a number of ballet steps as well as ballet turn-out (in addition to parallel positions) and that stressed high extensions of the legs and a comportment in which the weight was lifted off the legs to give the body a sense of lightness. However, he sought to engage the torso in a different way from ballet. He told Jacqueline Lesschaeve that in classical ballet he had noticed that the dancers moved the shoulders (*épaulement*) against the movement of the legs, but the torso did not move much. Consequently when the legs moved with great speed, as Balanchine demanded, the torso lost its clarity. Cunningham developed a more flexible back and torso that would make the entire body more legible when the legs moved with speed. "All of my work comes from the trunk,

Jo Anne Melsher, Merce Cunningham, Carolyn Brown (partially hidden), and Viola Farber rehearsing Cunningham's *Septet* (1953). *Photo: George Moffett. Courtesy of Jerome Robbins Dance Division, The New York Public Library for the Performing Arts, Astor, Lenox and Tilden Foundations.*

from the waist, nearest the hip," he said. "And you tilt it or you twist it in every direction. It doesn't come from the shoulders, but from much farther down. Further than that, I relate it to or against the leg" (1985: 62). At the same time, though, Cunningham's carefully constructed technique included a relaxation in the shoulders and arms that gave it a far more informal appearance than ballet. This sense of informality was reinforced in choreography that incorporated walking, standing, and other movement of everyday life.

Cunningham's early technique can readily be seen in a film of *Septet* (1953) made in 1964.[2] The work, choreographed in seven sections for six dancers, is set to Eric Satie's *Trois morceaux en forme de poire*. Cunningham has said it was one of the last works he made using "a wholly intuitive procedure" (Vaughan 1997a: 76). In the sixth section (an ada-gio danced by Cunningham, Carolyn Brown, Viola Farber, and Barbara Lloyd) the movement clearly shows Cunningham's indebtedness to ballet in the vocabulary of steps, which range from attitudes and arabesques to *developés*, *grands battements* and *pliés*. Important too is the degree of turn-out the dancers use in addition to parallel positions, and their use of weight, which is often held up off the legs. However, it is also clear that Cunningham has freed the torso to a far greater degree than occurs in ballet and, as mentioned, relaxes the shoulders and arms. As the dancers do their slow *developés* and *grands battements*, their upper bodies are canted in varied directions, and their arms do not appear to take set positions. The back remains engaged and the hips stable no matter how the torso bends. This stability is necessary when speed is added to the dancing. Cunningham's use of torso movement can be contrasted with Balanchine's in *The Four Temperaments*, where the trunk is allowed to shift from back to front or side to side, but is not given nearly the range that Cunningham gives it. In the parts of *Septet* that include faster movement, such as Cunningham's second-section solo and the dance for two couples at the beginning of the fourth section, it is possible to see the quick changes of direction Cunningham demanded at speed and the consequent necessity of a stable back and hips. It should be added that although lifting the weight off the legs also aids speed, Cunningham's technique does not call for abandoning a sense of weight altogether. This is clearest when the dancers take lunges; as they move forward or to the side, they emphatically push the weight of the descending foot into the floor.

The technique Cunningham developed opposed expressional mod-ern dance in several important ways. First, older modern dance tech-niques stressed weight and the floor; Cunningham's technique included weight, but counterbalanced it with lightness. In addition, he aban-doned the floor exercises that were so much a part of older techniques because, he said, humans mainly move while standing. He started his classes with standing exercises that warmed up the back. Although he retained the bare feet and flexible torso of traditional modern dance, as noted, he added a great deal more speed. Most important, Cunningham concerned himself with how movement worked and the shape it took rather than with communicating meaning.

Although Cunningham's dance was certainly rationally based, he de-veloped several strategies aimed at disrupting the cause-and-effect logic that resulted in what he called the sending of social messages. The first step was to treat dance as concrete, in the sense of being an activity. In a defining essay entitled "The Impermanent Art" written in 1955, Cunningham said that a new dance existed that did not yet have a name but did have ideas. "These ideas seem primarily concerned with something being exactly what it is in its time and place, and not its having actual or symbolic reference to other things. A thing is just that thing." ([1955] 1978: 310). Dance should not attempt to represent something else, but rather should be itself. "When I dance, it means: this is what I am doing" (ibid.). This focus on the concreteness of dance "eliminates the necessity to feel that the meaning of dancing lies in everything but the dancing, and further eliminates cause-and-effect worry as to what movement should follow what movement, frees one's feelings about continuity, and makes it clear that each act of life can be its own history" ([1955] 1978: 310–311).

Dance was not about emoting, Cunningham said. Rather, "in its essence, in the nakedness of its energy it is a source from which passion or anger may issue in a particular form" ([1955] 1978: 311). He added: "I am no more philosophical than my legs, but from them I sense this fact: that they are infused with energy that can be released in movement—that the shape the movement takes is beyond the fathoming of my mind's analysis but clear to my eyes and rich to my imagination" (ibid.: 312). A concrete dance, then, not only disrupted cause-and-effect meaning, it also escaped reasoned analysis and instead found a reality born of practice and bodily intelligence.[3]

Cunningham further allayed the temptation to impose meaning on his works by divorcing the choreographic process from music. In collaboration with Cage, Cunningham had by 1944 begun to base his dances on a structure of time units that allowed music and dance to be relatively independent of each other. This soon led to an arrangement in which composer and choreographer worked independently. Music and dance only came together at the moment of performance, where they coexisted in the way that pedestrians and the sounds of traffic coexist on city streets. Modern dancers had often separated music and dance but had done so by subjugating music. Cunningham made music and dance separate but equal. Cunningham also worked with designers in a way that was similar to his working methods with composers, giving them a minimum of information about a dance and then allowing them to develop ideas as they saw fit. For example, in 1958 Cunningham wrote to Robert Rauschenberg about a new dance that Rauschenberg was to design: "I have a feeling it's like looking at part of an enormous landscape and you can only see the action in this particular portion of it" (Vaughan 1997a: 110). For the dance, which was eventually titled *Summerspace* (1958), Rauschenberg devised an abstract pointillist backdrop and costumes in Day-Glo colors.

Although all the processes mentioned here helped to disrupt meaning in Cunningham's work, the most extreme element of anti-meaning was his use of chance procedures. In the early 1950s, Cage introduced chance into his music, and in 1951 Cunningham began to use it in his dances, as well. At first this was done simply, by letting sequences of movement or of individual dances be decided by a coin toss. Eventually, however, it became a complex system in which Cunningham constructed charts to indicate a variety of elements, including steps or movement sequences and their order, space and direction, and the duration of movement, then used chance procedures to determine how the various elements would be combined. Once the selections were made, the dance was set and rehearsed.

Suite by Chance (1953) with music for magnetic tape by Christian Wolff, was among Cunningham's early fully realized works using chance techniques. In this piece he made up charts that took him a few hours a day for several months to complete (Cunningham 1968: n.p.). The movements he had given the dance, Cunningham has written, were as flat and unadorned as he could make them (ibid.). Remy Charlip, one of the Cunningham dancers who participated in the piece, wrote a summary of the procedures Cunningham used for the work:

> For this dance, a large series of charts was made: a chart numbering body movements of various kinds (phrases and positions, in movement and in stillness); a chart numbering lengths of time (so that a phrase or position could be done in a long or short duration, or, in the case of the impossibility of lengthening the time of a movement, as for instance, a single step, it could be repeated for the length of time given); a chart numbering directions in space (floor plans).
>
> These charts, which defined the physical limits within which the continuity would take place, were not made by chance. But from them, with a method similar to one used in a lottery, the actual continuity was found. That is, a sequence of movements for a single dancer was determined by means of chance from the numbered movements in the chart; space, di-

rection and lengths of time were found in the other charts. At important structural points in the music, the number of dancers on stage, exits and entrances, unison or individual movements of dancers were all decided by tossing coins. In this way, a dancer may be standing still one moment, leaping or spinning the next. There are familiar and unfamiliar movements, but what is continuously unfamiliar is the continuity, freed as it is from usual cause and effect relations. Due to the chance method, some of the movements listed in the charts were used more than once in different space and directions and for different lengths of time, and, on the other hand, many movements, to be found in the charts, do not appear at all in the final choreography. (1954: 19)

Cunningham himself said of the dance:

> It was almost impossible to see a movement in the modern dance during that period not stiffened by literary or personal connection, and the simple, direct and unconnected look of this dance (which some thought abstract and dehumanized) disturbed. My own experience while working with the dancers was how strongly it let the individual quality of each of them appear, naked, powerful and unashamed. I feel this dance was classical—precise and severe—however unfamiliar the continuity, however unclassical the movements, in terms of tradition, and the stillnesses, that is, held positions by the dancers, may have been. It was unprompted by references other than to its own life. (Cunningham 1968: n.p.)

Both Cunningham and Charlip's use of language in these passages indicates the importance of certain ideas in Cunningham's experiments. Charlip commented on chance's disruption of cause-and-effect relations. Earlier in his article he mentioned that the surrealists and dadaists had also experimented with chance procedures. However, he did not say why they had done this, which was, according to Peter Bürger, to attempt to regain some of the freedom denied by rationality: "Starting from the experience that a society organized on the basis of a means-ends rationality increasingly restricts the individual's scope, the surrealists attempt[ed] to discover elements of the unpredictable in daily life" (Bürger 1984: 65). For Cunningham, applying chance procedures was a means of discovering the unpredictable in his own work. He has said chance was a "mode of freeing my imagination from its own clichés" ([1955] 1978: 312). He noted that this method of countering the dispositions that sent him along familiar pathways produced movement that was extremely difficult to perform (Cunningham 1985: 80; Vaughan 1997a: 59, 62–63, 72). The customary logic of dance movement was confused, sometimes to the point of being physically limiting. Cunningham said that there were several dances he created that he was never able to adequately perform. Nevertheless, it is important to note that although the procedures Cunningham developed disrupted familiar ways of structuring dances, they did not negate all rational processes or personal choice. Rather, they enlarged the possibilities of sequencing, shuffled continuity, interfered with norms. This in turn helped eliminate the imposition of narrative elements on the dance and gave it an openness that led to greater freedom of interpretation.

Freedom of interpretation empowered the spectator at a time when there was general social concern for decreasing individual freedom in America. A body of writing ranging from the work of the Frankfurt School to C. Wright Mills's *The Power Elite*, from William H. Whyte Jr.'s *The Organization Man* to David Riesman's *The Lonely Crowd*, attests to postwar anxiety over the individual's loss of freedom in an increasingly bureaucratized society. Cunningham's dance suggested that art was no longer an authoritarian given. Instead, each individual was free to find her or his own meaning in the dance.

If Cunningham's use of chance can be linked to dada, Marilyn Vaughan Drown (1997) has also connected his practices to Zen Buddhism. I would go further than Drown to argue that Zen permeated Cunningham's approach to his art, while at the same time being compatible with certain modernist precepts. Zen allowed Cunningham to offer, through his work, an alternative to Western, logically based systems. John Cage first encountered Zen while at the Cornish School, where he attended a lecture on Zen and dada by Nancy Wilson Ross (Cage 1973: xi; Revill 1992: 107–125). In the late 1940s, he began to sit in on lectures by D. J. Suzuki, who was teaching Zen philosophy at Columbia University. He also became acquainted with Alan Watts, who did much to popularize Zen in the English-speaking world through his numerous books. Although Cunningham's immersion in Zen may have been more limited than Cage's, he attended some of Suzuki's lectures, and he and Cage made a pilgrimage to visit Suzuki when the Cunningham company was in Japan in 1964 (Vaughan 1997a: 57, 145). Cage also undoubtedly introduced Zen ideas to Cunningham. Most important, though, Cunningham's working methods and his writings suggest that he had found concepts in Zen that paralleled and perhaps enlarged upon his own thinking.

Alan Watts wrote of Zen art:

> The art forms which Zen has created are not symbolic in the same way as other types of Buddhist art, or as is "religious" art as a whole. The favorite subjects of Zen artists . . . are what we should call natural, concrete, and secular things. . . . Furthermore, the arts of Zen are not merely or primarily representational. . . . Even in painting, the work of art is considered not only as representing nature but as being itself a work of nature. For the very technique involves the art of artlessness, or what Sabro Hasegawa has called the "controlled accident." (1957: 169)

As Drown notes, the controlled accident is an appropriate description of the relationship of dance, music, and design in Cunningham's work as well as his use of chance procedures. These elements are highly independent but come together in the same time and space. Within this time and space of performance they may coincide at certain moments in ways that reinforce each other, or that make unusual and interesting juxtapositions. One can expand on Drown's analysis to say also that these disparate elements, paradoxically, accord with each other. This is undoubtedly because the elements are not completely independent. The composer has an idea, within a few minutes, of how long the dance is to be and has to make his score flexible enough to accommodate the dance. Cunningham also might tell his collaborators something about his thinking for the piece, as he did with Rauschenberg in *Summerspace*. Most important, Cunningham chose his collaborators carefully and worked with them on a regular basis so that they were unlikely to produce something out of keeping with his own artistic aims. Cage, of course, helped form those aims and was Cunningham's partner in life as well as work. Earle Brown, who composed several of Cunningham's dances in the 1950s, was married to Carolyn Brown, Cunningham's principal dancer, and Morton Feldman was a close collaborator of Cage's. Rauschenberg, who designed virtually all Cunningham's sets and costumes during the 1950s, was a friend as well as a vanguard artist. Cunningham's circle of collaborators consisted of like-minded individuals who worked and played together for years.

If the controlled accident describes Cunningham's working relationship with his collaborators, it also describes his use of chance methods.

Watts writes that "there is no duality, no conflict between the natural element of chance and the human element of control. The constructive powers of the human mind are no more artificial than the formative actions of plants or bees, so that from the standpoint of Zen it is no contradiction to say that artistic technique is discipline in spontaneity and spontaneity in discipline" (1957: 169). Cunningham's use of chance methods allowed him to retain the control of a virtuosic technique and elements of organized movement, while achieving spontaneity through tossing coins to govern space, direction, time, and other aspects of the dance. Discipline is particularly important in Cunningham's work, not only the discipline it takes to acquire and perform his refined technique but the discipline of long hours of making charts and tossing the coins involved in the chance procedures of his dances. Yet it is these very things that allowed him to attain the spontaneity he seeks.

There are other aspects of Zen that resonate with Cunningham's attitudes and his work. Watts speaks of Zen being located in the concrete and of art not being artificial but a work of nature. Cunningham was describing a Zen attitude when he wrote: "A thing is just that thing. It is good that each thing be accorded this recognition and this love. Of course, the world being what it is—or the way we are coming to understand it now—we know that each thing is also every other thing, either actually or potentially. So we don't, it seems to me, have to worry ourselves about providing relationships and continuities and orders and structures—they cannot be avoided. They are the nature of things" ([1955] 1978: 310). Zen does not divide the world into binaries; rather, all things are related. And since everything is related, humans are an integral part of their environment. "Thus, our stark divisions of spirit and nature, subject and object, good and evil, artists and medium are quite foreign to this culture" (Watts 1957: 170). The concreteness that Zen emphasizes means that much of Zen art is nonrepresentational. Since the work of art is "that thing," as Cunningham described it, it is not necessary for it to represent something else.

The concreteness of Zen is closely related to direct action. Watts says that Zen masters speak as little as possible about Zen because words are abstractions, and they prefer to show its principles by the concreteness of action (1957: 127). A story that Cunningham has related on many occasions illustrates the point. During a class Cunningham was teaching, company member Marianne Preger asked how to do a certain movement. Cunningham finally said, "Marianne, the only way to do it is to do it" (1985: 48).

For Cunningham, dancing is instinctive from the standpoint that it is not about ideas but about action. In 1955 he wrote: "If a dancer dances—which is not the same as having theories about dancing or wishing to dance or trying to dance or remembering in his body someone else's dance—but if a dancer dances, everything is there. The meaning is there, if that's what you want" ([1955] 1978: 310). In speaking to Jacqueline Lesschaeve, Cunningham noted that some dancers come to study with him because they are attracted to the ideas of his dances, particularly the use of chance, but because they are involved with intellectual processes, they cannot understand the act of dancing. "In most people, there's such a split between instinct and intellect. A technique class should, in a way, within a certain scale, put them together so that both are working in unison" (1985: 72–73).

In Zen, direct action leads to the possibility of freedom. But action is not mere impetuosity; it is assumed the actor has spent long hours practicing Zen principles. With this discipline one can act without the danger of paralyzing abstractions that come with thought. Watts comments: "The marvel can only be described as the peculiar sensation of freedom in action which arises when the world is no longer felt to be some sort of obstacle standing over and against one" (1957: 132). Cunningham noted: "I find that it is the connection with the immediacy of the action, the single instant, that gives the feeling of man's freedom. The body shooting into space is not an idea of man's freedom, but is the body shooting into space" ([1955] 1978: 311–312). Cunningham's writings suggest that he saw parallels between dance and Zen practices; or perhaps, he considered dance itself a Zen practice, since, as Watts notes, in Japan every profession and craft was at one time considered a lay method of learning the principles embodied in Taoism, Zen, and Confucianism (1957: 171).

There is one further aspect of action in Zen that is important in Cunningham's working methods, which is commitment or follow-through—in other words, an action made unhesitatingly and wholeheartedly (Watts 1957: 148). In his 1955 essay, Cunningham mentioned the necessity of this kind of commitment to the dance. "This is not feeling about something, this is a whipping of the mind and body into an action that is so intense, that for the brief moment involved, the mind and body are one. The dancer knows how solidly he must be aware of this centering when he dances. And it is just this very fusion at a white heat that gives the look of objectivity and serenity that a fine dancer has" ([1955] 1978: 311).

Summerspace, which Cunningham choreographed in 1958, exemplifies many of the points of contact with Zen and dada that have been made here. When Cunningham created the work, he said he wanted it to deal with space: "the principal momentum was a concern for steps that carry one through a space, and not only into it" (1966: 52). He had in mind the way birds alight and then move on as they pass in flight or automobiles move relentlessly along freeways and cloverleaves. As a starting point for the structure of *Summerspace*, Cunningham drew twenty-one lines across the stage that corresponded to six wing spaces for entrances and exits, devising a movement sequence for each line. Each sequence was devoted to a certain kind of movement, such as turns, runs, skips, or leaps. He then used chance procedures to determine the direction each sequence would take, its speed, its height or depth (performed in the air or on the ground), how space was covered (for example in a straight line, diagonal or circle), number of dancers performing an action, whether they did it together or separately, and whether they ended the action on or off the stage. Again, the controlled accident allowed Cunningham room to dictate the choice of steps and the elements devoted to chance. The musical score was composed by Morton Feldman, and the designs were, as mentioned earlier, the pointillist backdrop and leotard costumes by Rauschenberg in bright, fresh colors.

In *Summerspace* the felicitous workings of the controlled accident can be seen in the meeting of Feldman's shimmering score, the dappled set and costumes, and the movement, with its constant shifts of direction and trajectories through the stage space. Whether one wishes to call it a dada method or Zen, the cause-and-effect logic of the dance is broken by the chance procedures, making constantly unexpected meetings and juxtapositions both among the dancers' groups and spacing and within the movement sequences themselves. As for the dancing, a film exists of excerpts from the first performances of *Summerspace* at the 1958 American Dance Festival at Connecticut College.[4] The film is without sound and in black and white, but even this inadequate record cannot diminish the impact of the dancers' performance. Carolyn Brown, Viola Farber, Remy Charlip, Cynthia Stone, Marilyn Wood, and Cunningham move in unhesitating action, apparently unblocked by any second guess-

Viola Farber and Carolyn Brown in Merce Cunningham's *Summerspace* (1958). *Photo: Richard Rutledge. Courtesy of the Cunningham Dance Foundation.*

ing about how they look or what they are doing. Their comportment is upright but relaxed. They dance with unhurried clarity, each immersed in the work in a way that looks free and unburdened; they are alert and completely at home in their environment.[5]

Although Zen Buddhism and modernism may seem strange bed-fellows, they are compatible in two important ways: they both abjure causality, and they both distrust language. Modernists sought to disrupt ideas of causality as part of an antirationalization agenda, while Zen practitioners view causality as the wrong-thinking that separates the world into binaries. Zen holds to a relational view, or as Cunningham put it, each thing as part of everything else. Above all, however, Zen looks upon language as a rational system much as modernism does. In *An Introduction to Zen Buddhism* ([1934] 1964) Daisetz Suzuki wrote: "Zen is decidedly not a system founded upon logic and analysis. If anything, it is the antipode to logic, by which I mean the dualistic mode of thinking" (ibid.: 38). Words are words and nothing more, Suzuki declared: "Zen deals with facts and not with their logical, verbal, prejudiced, and lame representations" (ibid.: 61). "The reason why Zen is so vehement in its attack on logic, and why the present work treats first of the illogical aspect of Zen, is that logic has so pervasively entered into life as to make most of us conclude that logic is life and without it life has no significance" (ibid.: 63). On the contrary, Suzuki said, logic chains the spirit. Logic must be conquered in order to see the whole of reality, "which refuses to be tied up to names" (ibid.: 60). Dualities divide the soul against itself; they cause discord, contradictions, and antagonism. Zen attempts to make the whole of reality apparent.

This splitting of mind from the totality of mind-body causes other problems. According to Watts, Zen teaches that there is no "myself" apart from experience. It is an illusion for the mind to try to stand apart from experience (1957: 121). Language aids this abstraction from reality. Zen is wary of language as a system of abstract signs that inhibits uncontrived action: "spontaneity or naturalness (*tzu-jan*) . . . is the unmistakable tone of sincerity marking the action which is not studied and contrived" (ibid.: 133). In order to practice Zen, it is necessary to switch from the symbolic to the concrete, from words to action. Watts speaks about the "fatal confusion of fact and symbol" in splitting the mind from itself. "To make an end of the illusion, the mind must stop trying to act upon itself, upon its stream of experiences, from the standpoint of the idea of itself which we call the ego" (ibid.). The Zen practitioner understands "the importance of avoiding confusion between words and signs, on the one hand, and the infinitely variable 'unspeakable' world on the other" (1957: 130). Modernists, on their side, viewed language as a system of signs that had been fully rationalized. Dada and surrealist artists tried to disrupt the logic of language through strategies that included chance procedures, collage, and improvisation.

Zen gave Cunningham an alternative to Western philosophies of duality, and chance procedures gave him a method for escaping the causal logic of dance meaning. As such, these practices constituted a form of resistance in his work. However, as noted earlier, critics did not recognize the critical aspect of Cunningham's dances, even when Cunningham and his supporters (particularly Cage) spoke about them. Nor was Zen little known at the time. Zen philosophy, calligraphy, and poetry were all extremely popular in the early postwar years. The Beat poets and artists were using Zen extensively in their work in the late 1940s and '50s, and Watts and Suzuki, among others, had written numerous books and articles about Zen, which had become popular among a wide public. However, commentators focused on what they saw as the lack of emotion in Cunningham's dances, their coldness, and their meaninglessness, which set them in opposition to expressional modern dance.

A *Dance Observer* review by Nik Krevitsky in 1951 illustrates this point. In it he struggled to come to grips with Cunningham's first chance piece, *Sixteen Dances for Soloist and Company of Three*. Krevitsky noted that the work lacked continuity and meaning, but he didn't extrapolate from this observation. Rather, he wondered why Cunningham could not have given more hint of what the dance was about in the title, instead of naming it so objectively and cryptically. Even as a pure dance piece, he said, "we find many of the sequences completely disturbing from the standpoint of development or of mood" (1951a: 41). Krevitsky did not suggest that the meaninglessness of *Sixteen Dances* was due to the choreographer's inexperience or ineptness; the absence of meaning appeared to him to be willful. Krevitsky twice spoke of the work's being aimed at a select few who shared a philosophy of art similar to Cunningham's. In emphasizing the choreographer's lack of desire to communicate and his concern with a small audience of peers, Krevitsky placed *Sixteen Dances* in the realm of vanguard modernism, but his comments did not in any way reflect the view that the piece might have offered an alternative to the rationalized workings of Western society. This was the general attitude of commentators, who focused on those aspects of Cunningham's work that tied it to a new objectivist vanguard while ignoring or simply not seeing resistant qualities in it.

Alwin Nikolais (1910–1993), like Cunningham, saw his work accepted as part of a new modernist vanguard while being denied a critical component. Nikolais developed a dance that rejected narrative subject matter and the communication of emotion. It also gave movement, sound, and light an equal place on the stage. Nikolais formulated a dance theory rather than a technique, and working methods that gave improvisation a central place. In addition he articulated an overarching philosophy, embodied in his dance, that stressed human beings' place in a larger universe. Nikolais wished to show, in his words, "man being a fellow traveler within the total universal mechanism rather than the god from which all things flowed" (1971a: 11). In 1958, he wrote an essay entitled "The New Dimension of Dance" that explained his principles.[6] Speaking of new directions in the arts he wrote: "The arts, we find, are now becoming vitally concerned with the direct and poignant translation of those abstract elements which characterize and underline an art subject" (1958: 43). The new modern dance was no longer concerned with placing the individual at the center of attention, of probing psychological and emotional essences. "Man now realizes his presence within a universe rather than a world." Nikolais went on to say, "the major contemporary significance of this is the greater freedom from the literal and peripheral self of man. This freedom, indeed, is one of the striking and appealing characteristics of the new art" (ibid.). What it left the artist free to do was to explore more fundamental energies than the human psyche.

While acknowledging the importance of the Bennington pioneers in exploring the basis of human emotions, Nikolais asserted that modern dancers had nonetheless appeared as stylized characters through which a psychological drama transpired. "The character still remained literally and dominantly present." Like other objectivists, Nikolais saw in expressional modern dance representation rather than embodiment. Equally important in his argument was the fact that the dance character dwarfed its surroundings. In the new dance,

> the character or dance hero is no longer dominant. The new dance figure is significant more in its instrumental sensitivity and capacity to speak directly in terms of motion, shape, time and space. . . . It is the poetry of these elements speaking directly out of themselves and their interrelationships rather than through a dominant dance character or figure. The dance figure may often be present, but if it is, it is usually in equilibrium with the aggregate of all elements in operation rather than dominant or emotionally intrusive upon it. (1958: 44)

Nikolais said that subject matter in the new dance was often non-objective; consequently movement had less dramatic tension and dissonance now that "peripheral emotion" had been eliminated. The new dance might, for example, include long periods of pause, comparable to silence in music. Peripheral emotions such as sorrow, joy, and rage were exchanged for primary emotions that were abstract feelings of heavy, light, thick, thin, large, small, fast, slow, and so forth. These were more basic than peripheral emotions, in fact were the ingredients of them. The use of these primary emotive factors was to make humans "more congenially aligned and relative to a greater natural orbit rather than an unbalanced human island" (ibid.). In this way individuals could understand that they were part of an integrated totality rather than feeling isolated and alone.

The performer of this new dance did not seek to impose his will on it but left ego behind, making himself "pliantly available to his impulsions" (1958: 45). "He stays totally engrossed in the motional content, without personal emotional point of view towards the action, but, rather, sentiently and kinetically involved in its unfolding. In this way the motion speaks—directly and clearly of itself—to both dancer and beholder. Its emotional content is born out of itself, rather than from any external emotive factors grafted upon it" (1958: 46).

As for spectatorship, Nikolais conceded that the new dance he described might initially be difficult for viewers to understand, because it did not conform to familiar practices. However, such a dance opened the way to new freedom by "allowing the audience esthetic generation of broader scope and personal associative experience" and by "plunging the onlooker into more deep-seated visions and connotations" (1958: 45).

Clearly, many of his ideas put Nikolais in opposition to expressional modern dance, but if there were any doubt, he made it explicit when he said: "New Modern Dance distinguishes itself from the Bennington period in all areas. Subject, method, composition, technique, titles, costume, accompaniment, all differ. We find the dancer, like the painter, discovering directness of vocabulary immediately through the sentient values of his media" (1958: 43–44). In opposing expressional modern dance, Nikolais was not just engaging in modernist position taking, trading one set of values for another in order to differentiate himself from the past. Nor did he simply believe that psychological dance had run its course. Nikolais viewed the basic assumptions of expressional modern dance, and by extension of society at large, as wrong. Humans were not the center of things; they were not meant to dominate their environment and each other but to exist harmoniously as one of many. This was not an idea that fit comfortably with prevailing Western ideologies, based as they were on technological progress and the conquest of nature.

World War II played a large role in the development of Nikolais's ideas. Murray Louis has commented that any belief Nikolais may have had about the omnipotence of man faded after serving on the European front in World War II.[7] Claudia Gitelman, quoting Nikolais, writes further that his "turn away from personal and emotive art was sealed by the 'apocalyptic explosion [of the atom] bringing awareness of invisible realities of nature'" (Gitelman 2000: 204). And Susan Buirge, who danced with Nikolais in the 1960s, also noted that Nikolais spoke frequently of the impossibility of dance ever being the same after the explosion of the atomic bomb.[8] For him, the days were gone when a modern dance could be content with representing what amounted to emotional problems; a radical rethinking of art was in order.

Nikolais did not arrive at his concept of a new modern dance overnight. It was part of a process that percolated over a decade of work, beginning after the war. Nikolais came to dance through music (Louis 1960, 1980; Grauert 1999). Born in Southington, Connecticut, of German and Russian immigrant parents, he studied piano as a child. At sixteen he became a pianist for silent movies, then eventually worked with several acting companies, doing a variety of jobs. He then moved to Hartford where he took over the directorship of the Hartford Marionette Theatre. His dance studies started after seeing a performance by Mary Wigman. It was her percussion orchestra that interested him, but when Nikolais discovered Truda Kaschmann, a Hartford dancer who had studied with Wigman, he agreed to take dance classes as a means of learning more about the percussion instruments he had heard. In 1938, Nikolais started spending the summers at Bennington, working with Humphrey, Weidman, Graham, Horst, and Holm. He then opened a studio of his own in Hartford. His dance activities ended abruptly with the war. When Nikolais returned from the army in the mid-1940s, he settled on Holm as his principal teacher, and she soon asked him to serve as her assistant. In 1949, Nikolais was offered the directorship of the dance department at the Henry Street Playhouse on the Lower East Side, which he accepted.

Nikolais's move to the Playhouse was crucial to the evolution of his

Alwin Nikolais speaking to students at the Henry Street Playhouse in the early 1950s.
Photo: Gene Dauber. Courtesy of the Nikolais/Louis Foundation for Dance.

ideas. There he was able to experiment with light and sound while developing a school and a system of instruction with students who became his company. His advanced class consisted of a handful of pupils, including Phyllis Lamhut and Gladys Bailin. Murray Louis soon joined them after leaving the navy. Nikolais also had an assistant, Ruth Grauert, who had worked with him in Hartford and was key to helping him realize his technical ideas as well as in aiding him with a number of organizational tasks. The dancers of the soon-to-be-created Henry Street Playhouse Dance Company were extremely young; Louis was the oldest at twenty-two, and Lamhut was still in high school. Nikolais was teaching them how to dance as he was developing his approach to movement and choreography. But although inexperienced, the youngsters were energetic and eager to experiment. Nikolais's approach aimed at training creative artists and not just dancers, so he required students to attend technique, theory, composition, percussion, and notation classes. He routinely shared concert programs with his company members, and they also had the opportunity to show their work in their own concerts.

Nikolais stopped dancing soon after arriving at Henry Street. He had come to dance late and said that he never felt comfortable as a dancer, preferring choreography.[9] Consequently, unlike most modern dancers his work did not revolve around himself or the concept of a star performer. This disposal of a central dancer-creator, reflected even in the name of his company, reinforced his philosophical ideas, since it enabled him to deconstruct the notion of the heroic individual, built into the very structure of modern dance companies and works.

Nikolais's working methods grew out of the heritage of Holm, Wigman, and Laban, to which he added his own ideas in order to attain the directness, immediacy, and clarity of movement he wanted. His aim was not to teach steps to be learned as a factory worker might learn the motions of an assigned task. It was rather to teach a theory of motion that would enable his dancers to help produce his vision on stage. He therefore did not develop a dance technique, per se. In what was called the technique class he gave exercises for general strengthening and at the same time attempted to eliminate the personal tensions, rigidities, and affectations in the bodies of his students that he felt impeded them from achieving the kind of direct movement he sought.[10] Classes were usually arranged around a central theme: for example, rotations, directional change, shifts of levels, or impulses in particular parts of the body.

The technique class paved the way for the real work, which took place in the theory class that followed, where experimentation through improvisation was a key element. Nikolais's theory was based on a number of premises, among the most important being "decentralization." Decentralization demanded a fluid center and flexible placement, contrasting with the single, unvarying center of ballet and most modern dance. It also called for the dancer to make the self available to the movement rather than imposing the ego upon it. With a fluid center, the dancer learned to quickly shift his or her center of movement and balance while remaining in a relaxed body posture. According to Murray Louis, "moving the center to any part of the body necessitated an unusually quick and direct thinking. These shifts prevented the energy from becoming rooted. They also brought into prominence parts of the body (chest, hips, back) other than the extremities. The resulting movement seemed unpredictably and rhythmically complex" (1980: 138).

Decentralization is made particularly clear in Nikolais's solo for Louis, entitled "Fixation," from *Allegory* (1959).[11] The dance is set in a highly constricted boxlike space in which the dancer can only move a few feet in any direction. It consists of sequences of repeated, often subtle isolations of the body. The first sequence begins with Louis, turned slightly to the side, articulating breathlike movements that start in the pelvis and move up the body to his torso, chest, and shoulders. Then he executes a large, sweeping kick as his arms come over his head, echoing the circular motion of the leg. Next, he resumes a straight standing position, shakes his arms and hands rapidly in front of him, and executes a big bent-legged jump. He repeats this sequence several times, all at rapid speed. He then moves on to sequences that explore different parts of the body in jumps, turns, and crouches. Now the knees receive attention, now the head, now the chest. In all of this Louis's balance and weight shift constantly. The dance has a precise, at times mechanical, yet highly energized look about it, reinforced by a percussive score. The movement is lightning fast, the spine whipping, arms darting, yet the individual isolations of movement are always lucid, and the body posture never looks tense, giving the impression that Louis is free to move in any direction. The qualities elicited by decentralization become apparent in the flexibility and clarity of movement Louis achieves within the extreme spatial limitations of the dance.

Nikolais's theory sessions explored the theme of that day's technique class. For example, if the theme had been rotations of the body, the dancers would then improvise accordingly. This was often done in small groups that would build responsiveness and cooperation within the group. Louis noted that the improvisation in theory sessions was controlled, from the standpoint that if the dancers did not improvise according to specific theoretical concepts, it implied they did not understand the concept, and they were then corrected.[12]

Nikolais taught improvisation to his dancers as a tool for choreography, since he expected them to create dances. He also asked his company to use improvisational methods when he was producing his own choreography. Phyllis Lamhut recalled that Nikolais often brought a prop or image—sometimes a painting or sketch—to a rehearsal, and they would begin to experiment from there.[13] She used as an example the dance "Discs," from *Kaleidoscope*. Nikolais, she said, brought metal discs about sixteen inches in diameter to the studio, asked the dancers to strap them on their feet and explore what they could do. After they experimented with a great deal of movement, Nikolais chose what he thought might work best, added his own ideas, sent the dancers back for more exploration, and eventually set the resulting dance. This was his usual working process. His dances were created collaboratively within the parameters of his dance theory. However, he always had the final word on all elements.[14]

Although Nikolais's theory constituted a rational system, its overall aim was to unfix habits and rigidities rather than impose them. In particular, his use of improvisation was meant to give direct access to the motional content that lay beneath emotional representation. Once again it was the hidden truth of movement (or motion, as Nikolais preferred to call it) that was sought, and it was located through a method that circumvented conscious processes. In Nikolais's words, "the subject is guided by felt judgment rather than by objective or cerebrally dominated choice" (1958: 44). Murray Louis has noted that improvisation demanded instant choreography and performance. Action occurred too quickly for conscious thought to be brought into play, which in turn created flexibility and enhanced bodily intelligence or "felt-judgment." Nikolais's use of improvisation can be traced through his German dance heritage, that is, through Holm to Wigman and Laban. And here there are links to the Zurich dada group, which included several of Laban's students, among them Sophie Taeuber, Suzanne Perrottet, and Claire Walther (Richter 1965: 31, 45, 69–70, 77, 79; Prevots 1985; Manning 1993: 68–69). Like chance procedures and free association, improvisation played a role in what Hans Richter called the dadaists' "conscious break with rationality" (Richter 1965: 57). Nikolais also used a break with rationality to gain access to what he believed was direct movement, free from the taint of representation.

Nikolais employed sound and light to aid in the task of making his philosophy visible on the stage. He had been attracted to dance through percussion, and he used it in combination with the piano in his teaching. However, he did not begin his choreographic career using his own scores. According to Louis, Nikolais gradually became frustrated with trying to obtain appropriate musical compositions by others and consequently began to create his own. He started with scores for percussion and piano then, with the advent of the tape recorder, he was able to produce *musique concrète* and finally electronic compositions (he is credited as the first owner of a Moog synthesizer).[15] These scores, Nikolais said, emphasized a nonliteral response in the audience and encouraged "more direct sense appeal" (1958: 45). Normally Nikolais created his choreography, the dancers moving in silence or to percussion, then he composed a score for it. In this sense, the sound and dance had closer links than they did in Cunningham's work. Early on, his scores also tended to have a strong pulse, but gradually he deemphasized this element, making the sound less conspicuously supportive, then independent.

Nikolais not only discouraged ties to literal meaning through his movement processes and sound scores, he further dissolved these connections through his use of light and color. In his early work Nikolais disrupted the traditional hierarchy of the stage space, which focuses attention on the center and which is normally supported by lighting. His stage was an open area of abstract color and light that humans and props might inhabit but, true to his philosophy, did not dominate. He achieved his effects by placing lights at many unusual angles, including low in the wings, which streaked the stage with light. He also used gels in a variety of colors. Later, Nikolais would create fantastic lighting designs with projections of great sophistication—in the early days the effects he created were far more rudimentary, although no less experimental for their time. Ruth Grauert recalled that he would suggest a new design he wanted to achieve, and Richie Brown, the technical director at the Playhouse, would go to the cellar and improvise lights from whatever he could find. Murray Louis noted that sometimes the dancers operated lights when they went offstage to help create a desired effect.[16]

A glance at Nikolais's early programs at Henry Street demonstrates how he was developing his dancers and his dance in the direction his mature work would take. A program in May 1950 included three *Technical Etudes* ("Walking," "Curve Study," and "Fall Study") as well as *Etudes Composed by the Dancers*. The studies may have been extensions of his technique and theory classes, indicating the point his young dancers had reached in their training. But they also suggest the experimental nature of his work at that time as Nikolais sought to realize his ideas in motion. The fact that he produced a program that featured both his dances and that of his students was also typical. As noted, he encouraged his dancers to experiment along with him.

Noumenon is usually considered the first of Nikolais's new dance works. It was premiered on 9 November 1951 and performed by Beverly Schmidt and Dorothy Vislocky. The dancers were completely covered in stretch fabric. They used stools as props to sit and stand on, which enabled them to enlarge their range of movement and allowed them to take ever-changing shapes. In this case, Nikolais chose to reconfigure the human body through costumes, but although he always considered such changes in body shape an option, he as frequently revealed the body as concealed it. One of the costumes he favored most was based on a unitard or leotard and tights, which took advantage of new technologies in stretchable synthetic fabrics.[17] The use of such costuming in performance was unusual, but not singular. In the early 1950s, Balanchine began to dress his dancers in practice clothes for some of his works, and Cunningham, too, used leotards in most of his dances. However, these skinlike costumes were a mark of difference in objectivist dance. The usual costumes for modern dancers were skirts for women and trousers and shirts for men. Leotards and tights put the emphasis on movement and, since they were practice clothes, on the work of dance, rather than on representational elements or thematic or narrative subject matter. They also made it possible to see movement more clearly, particularly small steps and gestures that previously would have been hidden in less closely fitting garments.

On 26 January 1953 Nikolais introduced *Etudes II: Masks, Props, and Mobiles,* in which he continued to develop his ideas. The title did not indicate a specific work; it was simply a general description of independent dances by Nikolais and company members. In this case it included *Aqueouscape* and *Noumenon,* now called *Noumenom Mobilis,* by Nikolais. There were also dances by the company, among them *Enclave* and *Harlequinade* by Gladys Bailin, *Annoyous Insectator* by Phyllis Lamhut, and *Antechamber* by Murray Louis. On 10 December 1955 *Masks—Props—Mobiles* made another appearance, this time without "Etudes II" attached to the title and with slightly different punctuation. It also carried a declaration of intent: "An experimental program in which the dancers are depersonalized or in which their motions are extended into external materials."[18] The dances included *Noumenom Mobilis, Web, Aqueouscape,* and *Tournament* by Nikolais, along with *White Figure* and *Red Hoop* by Beverly Schmidt, *Belonging to the Night* and *Polychrome* by Murray Louis, and *Paraphrenalia* by Dorothy Vislocky. Nikolais often changed or developed dances and ideas from concert to concert, which is evident here. However, *Masks—Props—Mobiles* shows a gradual development of his philosophy and his dance. The 1953 incarnation was simply a group of dances with little visible connection, whereas the 1955 version had a clear objective and was more integrated in conception while still comprising dances by both Nikolais and the company. Nikolais's notion of depersonalization and of extending motion into external materials would receive significant amplification the following year in

From left, Murray Louis, Gladys Bailin, and Coral Martindale in "Straps" from Alwin Nikolais's *Kaleidoscope* (1956). *Photo: David Berlin. Courtesy of the Nikolais/Louis Foundation for Dance.*

Kaleidoscope, his first major experimental work. *Masks—Props—Mobiles* also included *Tournament*, which would become "Capes" in *Kaleidoscope*.

Kaleidoscope was a breakthrough for Nikolais, as the company was invited to perform it in August 1956 at the ninth American Dance Festival in New London, Connecticut. The American Dance Festival had been started in 1948 as a showcase for modern dance. The José Limón Dance Company was in residence each year along with guest artists. The latter were usually drawn from the modern dance mainstream, although Cunningham had appeared in 1950. Nikolais was the first objectivist since that time to be invited.

Kaleidoscope consisted of eight dances, all by Nikolais, that were related to each other primarily in their use of props. Otherwise each dance was conceived as an independent entity. Nikolais considered this kind of arrangement to be a collage of unrelated material whose juxtaposition nonetheless produced a totality (1961b: 31). The dances in

Kaleidoscope consisted of "Discs," "Pole," "Box" (soon to be replaced by "Paddles"), "Skirts," "Bird," "Hoop," "Straps," and "Capes." *Kaleidoscope* featured Nikolais's lighting, but he had not yet reached the point of composing the entire sound score himself. Compositions by John Cage, Edgard Varèse, and Carlos Chavez were included, in addition to Nikolais's own work. The dancers wore unitards that were painted in variegated colors extending over the face, hands, and feet. They also wore headpieces that curved upward in a tail behind the head. The effect of the costumes and makeup was to integrate the group and depersonalize it. However, although the costumes depersonalized the dancers in the sense of muting their individuality, they did not disguise sexual differences. These were made amply visible by the body-hugging unitards. I would suggest that, in keeping with his philosophical aims, Nikolais was not so much interested in suppressing sexuality as in emphasizing the dancers' relationship to a larger whole. Nikolais made his position clear when he told an interviewer that his intention was not to erase sex from his work. He said he wished to put sex in a neutral position instead of making it a center of focus, as expressional dancers had done (Nikolais 1973–1974: 41).

In *Kaleidoscope* the dancers used props to extend or add elements to their movement.[19] For example in "Discs," referred to earlier, the seven dancers wore a metal disc attached to one foot. The dancers employed the discs in a variety of ways, sometimes even balancing on the edges. But they also used the discs as percussive instruments to punctuate their movement and to act in concert with the percussion score composed by Nikolais. In "Pole," a duet for Murray Louis and Gladys Bailin set to Japanese koto music, the two dancers balanced a pole between them, moving it from shoulders, to arms, to feet in numerous ingenious ways while rarely ceasing their slow, dreamlike dance. Although one of them would occasionally take over the pole while the other moved out independently, for the most part the pole acted as an object that bound them together and which they manipulated with graceful cooperation. "Straps" had three dancers with loops of elastic around their waists that extended into the wings where they were attached to supports. The dancers were able to produce movements, such as slow falls and cantilevered stretches, that would have been impossible had they been unaided by the straps. In these various ways, Nikolais enlarged the movement of the dance beyond the individual body to create what he called an "abstract protagonist" (1961b: 31).

From left, Murray Louis, Phyllis Lamhut, Gladys Bailin, Dorothy Vislocky, Beverly Schmidt, Bill Frank, and Coral Martindale in "Discs" from Alwin Nikolais's *Kaleidoscope* (1956). *Photo: David Berlin. Courtesy of the Nikolais/Louis Foundation for Dance.*

However, this protagonist was not reduced to an abstract shape; the human body was everywhere in evidence. In "Pole," for example, Bailin and Louis were perfectly recognizable as a man and woman, but their movement vocabulary gave none of the usual cues that in expressional modern dance would have conveyed ideas of a gendered relationship between them. This absence allowed attention to be focused on their general "humanness." What was emphasized was the balance the dancers attained between themselves and the object they held, and the relationship of the shapes they made in collaboration with that object to the surrounding space. Throughout the work Nikolais stressed the notion of human integration with the surrounding environment and how that integration could enlarge human capabilities. *Kaleidoscope* reinforced Nikolais's contention that new concepts of motion, shape, time, light, space, color, and sound would not dehumanize "man," but rather, according to Nikolais, "en-humanize" him. "His power to 'identify-with' is his most vital human facility and to deny it would deny him his greatest scope of love, the essence of art and life itself" (Nikolais 1957: 31).

Kaleidoscope was an early work and was still crude in certain technical

aspects and in the simplicity of much of its dance vocabulary and structure. Nikolais also did not altogether give up narrative. For example,
Kaleidoscope contained two dances that were thematic. "Skirts" was a
quixotic comment on fashion, while "Bird" depicted two little girls who,
while playing, find a bird. They try to capture it and in the process kill
it. With the unconscious cruelty of children, they then resume their
play. Despite these lapses from his stated aims, there is no doubt that
Kaleidoscope moved Nikolais closer to realizing his philosophy through
a unified theater. This was apparent not only in his more accomplished
melding of sound, light, and movement, but in the work's greater unity
of concept and in Nikolais's increasing control of all the major elements
of the production.

Although critics recognized Nikolais's work of the 1950s as experimental and opposed to expressional modern dance, they did not acknowledge his philosophical ideas. Instead, they spoke of dehumanization and lack of emotion. Some reviews were positive, others negative.
In negative reviews critics found fault both with Nikolais's objectivist
aesthetic and with the fact that he gave equal weight to light, sound, and
movement. It should be noted though, that as much as critics commented on the experimental nature of his work and complained about
the equality of elements in it, they accepted it as modern dance. Nikolais's years with Holm and the many aspects of his dance that were based
in her teaching assured him of a place in the modern dance fold. No one
accused Nikolais of breaking with expressional models so completely
that he had created a new genre, as early modern dancers had done in
their rejection of ballet.

Even when reviews of Nikolais's work were positive, they were much
the same as negative ones in their focus on aesthetic elements. Doris
Rudko of *Dance Observer* described *Masks—Props—Mobiles* as "a re-
freshing, highly theatrical evening of dehumanized dance" (1956: 28),
while Walter Sorell wrote of Nikolais in *Dance Magazine:*

> It seems that, in his opinion, the expressiveness of the modern dance has
> gone too much in the direction of soul-searching and caught itself in the
> complex snares of psychological problems. He offers no problem themes.
> He dehumanizes his dancers and makes them part of the external mate-
> rial he chooses for the development of an idea. His ideas are those of a
> sculptor or painter, not primarily of a dancer. And he achieves stunning
> images and unconventional designs with the help of props, masks, cos-

tumes and lighting. He seems to visualize an image, conceive and circumscribe a basic design for it. Then he proceeds painstakingly to exhaust its movement possibilities. Though sometimes the impression is that he uses movement sparingly, there is not one static moment. (1956: 70)

In stressing experimentation, dehumanization, and lack of emotion in Nikolais's work, critics placed it in opposition to the old expressional modern dance and in this way positioned it to assume the mantle of a new vanguard. However, in failing to recognize its philosophical base, they robbed the dance of its critical power. In this way, Nikolais's and Cunningham's work met a similar fate.

In probing issues in these artists' work, it is necessary to mention one other point. It has been suggested that their attraction to "pure" dance emanated from a desire to hide or encode or otherwise deal with their homosexuality at a time of intense homophobia. Pure dance, so the argument goes, allowed them to suppress romantic relationships in male-female partnering while at the same time closeting their own sexual orientation by continuing to make dances in which couples were inevitably paired as male and female (Burt 1995: 144; Kowal 1999: 179–180; Foster 2001: 175–178; Manning 2004: 209–210). Although I don't disagree that homosexuality may well have played a role in Nikolais's and Cunningham's muting of relationships, I have tried to show that there were more compelling reasons for their turning away from expressional models. On the one hand, objectivism provided a means of fostering a new vanguard, which was the path to success in the field; and on the other, it opened ways of challenging means-ends logic and of finding alternatives to it, which were modernist imperatives. It should also be pointed out that all objectivists, no matter what their gender or sexual orientation, eschewed overt meaning in their work, usually with the aid of depersonalization, while a number of homosexual choreographers continued to embrace expressional modern dance, even in the homophobic postwar years.

If commentators focused attention on those aspects of Cunningham's and Nikolais's work that linked it formally to a new vanguard while ignoring its critical aspects, the fact remains that the two choreographers offered particularly compelling reasons for calling attention to aesthetic elements in their work. The most obvious of these was provided by the dances themselves, in which the choreographers did not just abandon themes and plot lines, but turned their backs on the need to communicate emotion. In addition, both Cunningham and Nikolais spoke out verbally and in writing against the old modern dance, placing themselves in opposition to it. Sometimes this was done obliquely, sometimes with a direct attack. In stating their views the two men not only questioned an expressional aesthetic, they went further, couching their opposition in gendered terms that also challenged women's leadership of the field, a leadership which at that time was imbedded in expressional dance. They did this by associating expressional modernism with emotion (the realm of women) and objectivism with action (the realm of men). Feminist scholars have frequently pointed out, as Simon Williams and Gillian Bendelow note, that "emotions have tended to be dismissed as private, 'irrational,' inner sensations that have been tied, historically to women's 'dangerous desires' and 'hysterial bodies'" (Williams and Bendelow 1998: 131; see also Sydie 1987: 3; Laqueur 1987: 1–41), while the sphere of action, according to Sherry Ortner (1974), is seen as a male preserve that goes on outside the domestic sphere. Nikolais alluded to this idea when he wrote that, "the previous period of dance dealt with strong emotionalism and was dominantly in the hands of the female. This new dance level of abstraction seems to find the male choreographer in control" (1961a: 324; see also 1965: 65).

Nikolais sometimes compared the directions of the new dance as a response to scientific discoveries, thus tying it, however vaguely, to science itself. Cunningham described his working methods in the language of the skilled artisan. No longer did the choreographer have to agonize through a painful process of creation. He could act decisively, without indulging in overwrought feeling. Although both Cunningham and Graham claimed their choreography was based in movement, Cunningham explained dance movement in a practical fashion: "In my choreographic work, the basis for the dances is movement, that is, the human body moving in time-space" (1980: 52), while Graham explained dance movement in emotional terms: "Each art has an instrument and a medium. The instrument of the dance is the human body; the medium is movement. The body has always been to me a thrilling wonder, a dynamo of energy, exciting, courageous, powerful; a delicately balanced logic and proportion" (Graham [1941] 1980: 44–45). Similarly, Cunningham took a workmanlike approach in describing his choreographic method: "So in starting to choreograph, I begin with movements, steps, if you like, in working by myself or with the members of my company, and from that, the dance continues" (Cunningham 1980: 52). Graham, on the other hand, remarked: "If I was working on a new piece I would fix a red ribbon to the door, which signified that no one was to enter the studio. You did not want to be invaded when you were in the holy of holies, which it was when you were trying to create a new dance" (Graham 1991: 136).

It would not do to push the argument of gendered opposition too far, as both Nikolais and Cunningham viewed their dance as intuitive and not intellectual. Also, expressional dancers, themselves, had tried to masculinize modern dance. As Mark Franko has pointed out, Martha Graham identified modern dance as a virile form in some of her statements in the 1930s (Franko 1995: 38–57), while after the war José Limón called for a distinctly male "virile dance" to help save the human race from atomic extinction (Limón 1951). However, Cunningham and Nikolais in their use of a language of action as opposed to emotion employed masculine cues specifically against expressional dance and as a means of differentiating objectivism from it. At the same time, their attack, however indirectly, also challenged women's domination of the modern dance genre. The generation of modern dancers that came of age in the 1950s was the first to include a large contingent of men, and a number of them were attracted to a nonnarrative dance, including James Waring, Paul Sanasardo, David Gordon, Murray Louis, and Paul Taylor. Also notable was Erick Hawkins, whose early work was indebted to Graham, but who adopted an objectivist approach in the 1950s.

If Cunningham and Nikolais differentiated themselves from expressional dance, they had supporters acting on their behalf who also stressed differences between the new and old modern dance. Nikolais had, in particular, Murray Louis, a highly articulate spokesman, as well as a brilliant dancer. In 1956, Louis went to John Martin and convinced him to pay Henry Street a visit. Martin came and wrote two Sunday articles on Nikolais and his work, a powerful endorsement (Martin 1956a, 1956b). These lengthy pieces were unusual in Martin's newspaper work. They came at a crucial time in Nikolais's career and without doubt had an impact on it. In particular Martin extolled Nikolais's use of improvisation and the fact that he did not teach a technique. These were in line with the theoretical basis of German modern dance that Martin had long admired. Although he commented that Nikolais and his dancers were in love with movement for its own sake, he assumed that this would nonetheless lead to an authentic dance. Martin's assessment of Nikolais's work indicates how far he had traveled from his radically antiobjectivist views of the 1930s. At the same time, Martin focused on the aesthetic rather than the philosophical aspects of Nikolais's dance.

The next year, Nikolais himself was able to contribute a Sunday piece to the *New York Times*, an unusual opportunity that may well have been influenced by Martin's support. In the article he attacked the old modern dance as mired in sexual psychosis, a dance in which "relations and styles were dominantly promiscuous and the world was only a gigantic brothel. To interpret it otherwise was to deny both humanism and dance" (Nikolais 1957: 31).[20] This characterization had some of the outrageous aggressiveness of dada and surrealist manifestos. Nikolais then went on to describe a new dance, essentially his own, that would "create esthetic entities out of fresh concepts of motion, shape, time, light, space, color and sound." This was the kind of statement, appearing as it did in the pages of the *Times*, that was likely to capture the attention of the dance community, and it undoubtedly did, as Nikolais was one of the vanguardists anointed by *Dance Magazine* at the end of the year. Louis was less radical in his writing, but he explained Nikolais's work in a number of articles over the ensuing years.

Cunningham also had others who helped promote the oppositional aspects of his work. Denby was one of the few critics to write positively of Merce Cunningham's dance in the 1940s, recognizing in it a rejection of literary elements that Denby appreciated. He asked only that Cunningham be bolder, a request that Cunningham soon obliged (Denby [1944b] 1986: 207–208; [1945] 1986: 279–280). David Vaughan, a young transplanted English choreographer, was an eloquent defender of objectivism who in time became Cunningham's archivist. He organized the symposium that was recorded in the *Dance Magazine* series in 1957 and that included Cunningham. He also wrote an introduction to the symposium that plainly set out the goals of objectivism. These were stated in positive terms, but they nonetheless placed objectivism in opposition to expressional modern dance and as such positioned it as a rival to the old vanguard. Vaughan was more direct in a letter to the editor of *Dance Magazine* in July 1958 in which he complained of Doris Hering's enthusiastic response to Martha Graham's season at the Adelphi Theatre. The details of Vaughan's argument were a summary of objectivist criticism of the old modern dance, now voiced in specifically oppositional terms: he found the dance less important in Graham's work than the narrative; the need to communicate led only to incomprehensible symbolism that dance was not equipped to convey; the atmosphere of the dances was reminiscent of what "prevails in an analyst's consulting-room"; Graham's dance was not classic, which presents the individual in relation to others and to the universe, but romantic, which is "concerned exclusively with the individual in relation to himself" (1958: 26–27). In short, Graham's work was not concerned with dance, but with storytelling and self-absorbed psychology.

While both Cunningham and Nikolais could muster support in the dance field that helped put them in leading vanguard positions, Cunningham had certain advantages because he was part of a circle of artists that extended far beyond the dance world and whose connections put him in touch with the newest trends in music and art. Cage seemed to know everyone of importance in the musical world who passed through New York, and Robert Rauschenberg, although not yet famous, introduced Cunningham to important people in the art world. Cunningham's audience was made up to a large degree of these artists and musicians so that his work was known and spoken of outside the confines of the dance world (Cunningham 1985: 45). This gave him wider exposure and also kept him abreast of the latest developments in the world of vanguard art. Nikolais, on the other hand, had isolated himself at Henry Street, far down on the Lower East Side. However, although cut off from the center of vanguard activity, he had the advantage of Henry Street itself, a theater, funding, and a stable environment. This was nearly unheard of in the modern dance world where choreographers (including Cunningham) struggled to give one concert a year with a few hours of rehearsal in the theater in which they were to perform. Nor did this advantage go unnoticed. *Dance Observer*, whose writers were increasingly critical of Nikolais's work, referred in one review to the "clique" at Henry Street (Telberg 1959: 73). Despite such carping, there is little doubt that the stability of Henry Street contributed significantly to the development of Nikolais's work.

In all then, Nikolais and Cunningham were instrumental in establishing a new vanguard and were supported in their quest by others in the field. This support sometimes came from surprising sources, such as John Martin in the case of Nikolais and to a lesser extent Denby in the case of Cunningham. But whatever the source, the overriding element in both the defense of objectivism and its critique was the aesthetic aspect of its rejection of expressional models. As much as Nikolais and

Cunningham might have attempted to embody alternative visions of society in their dances, it was not acknowledged.

The success of objectivism offers a telling example of how a field refracts general social conditions through its own history and needs. Objectivism solved a number of modern dance's problems: First, it renewed the genre without destroying it. Lincoln Kirstein had long argued that because modern dance was a complete break from the past and was dependent on personalities rather than an impersonal vocabulary, it was not viable. Objectivism proved him wrong.[21] It did so by retaining enough of the forms and structures of expressional dance to still be recognizable as modern dance. These elements included framing devices that ranged from the ways in which concerts were structured to where they took place. Objectivists still appeared in the theaters that modern dancers had long inhabited and many also shared programs with expressional dancers, as Cunningham did with Erdman in the 1940s, Nikolais with Nina Fonaroff and others in the early 1950s, and Merle Marsicano with Mary Anthony in the mid-1950s. As pointed out, objectivists also preserved parts of expressional vocabulary and technique. Cunningham maintained the sense of weight and torso flexibility that marked modern dance, while Nikolais carried forward many aspects of Holm's approach to movement, including an emphasis on improvisation. Both Cunningham and Nikolais also retained the use of bare feet, one of the most visible and characteristic elements of expressional modern dance.

Yet while some aspects of expressional dance were preserved, others were prominently rejected, the most crucial being the communication of essentialized emotion, which was at the heart of expressional dance. Objectivists succeeded in attacking this central tenet without destroying modern dance as a whole by laying down their challenge in modernist terms. That is to say, they focused attention on movement as dance's acknowledged, essential element. This pushed the genre away from narrative and illustration toward which it had been drifting and which threatened its modernist credentials. Objectivists made it clear that the desire to communicate meaning, abstracted though it may have been, was a liability for modern dance, and they submitted that what they offered was closer to modernist goals.

The second problem to be solved by objectivism was modern dance's need to disarm rivals in order to maintain its vanguard position in the field. Objectivism thwarted competition from both commercial media and ballet by adopting extreme forms that neither was eager to co-opt. Although ballet and Broadway choreographers might borrow movement and even thematic material from modern dance, they had no desire to adopt radical methods like improvisation and chance procedures or to produce the kinds of works that resulted from such methods. Nor did they wish to create a level of depersonalization that meant abandoning all romantic relationships on the stage, or to make music and dance completely independent of one another.

Finally, objectivism could be viewed as a new vanguard without raising the specter of critique, which helped keep modern dance from scrutiny by more powerful social forces and at the same time served to acquiesce to those forces. Here one might ponder how successful objectivism would have been if modern dance's need for a new vanguard had not intersected with Cold War constraints: in part, it may have been the idea of secrecy engendered by the Cold War that channeled practice and reception in an objectivist direction. For although abstraction gave every spectator the right to create his or her own meaning, it also hid meaning. This seemed to make resistance possible, but secrecy contained a contradiction because whatever resistance existed was likely to be unrecognizable or ignored. Another contradiction existed in modernists' drive for autonomy. Objectivists sought a "pure" dance in order to remain free of outside influence, but their art's lack of overt signs of protest, indeed its apparent lack of all meaning, dovetailed agreeably with state institutional policies and desires.

Not that the muting of opposition had to be imposed from outside, it was common enough within dance itself, whether it stemmed from a desire to protect a vulnerable art or simply to maintain the status quo. Frequently suppression came through an appeal to the very rules that were supposed to keep dance free. As we have seen, choreographers who attempted overt protest were labeled "literal" and eliminated from the ranks of modernists, while those who opted for coded protest were disregarded. Artists who dealt with difference also encountered formidable difficulties. At various times, modernist rules that demanded the embodiment of universal experience were invoked either to emphasize or silence difference. Particularly poignant was the inability of commentators to acknowledge the protest in African-American dance—not that of long-accepted narratives of past iniquities but the protest against continuing discrimination that was implicit in Dunham's insistence on sexuality as a legitimate element of dance and in Primus's and Beatty's equal insistence on virtuosity as an expressive means open to black artists.

In addition to silence, commentators also used the language of aesthetics throughout the postwar period as a way of deflecting critical debate, whether by directly censuring dances in which protest was clearly present, or by reducing dances to formal concerns alone. The use of aesthetics as a weapon against critique was facilitated by the very rules of modernism, which tended to favor form both as a means of placing control in the artist's hands and as a means of defeating narrative and illustration. Objectivism, which had no overt subject matter except dance itself, encouraged the use of a reductivist aesthetic language to describe it and its intentions.

Was there, then, no way within the confines of modernism to resist or protest the forces that modernism ostensibly opposed? Was modernism, in fact, nothing more than an enforcer of the status quo disguised as an oppositional "avant-garde"? I want to return for a moment to Clement Greenberg's modernist theory as a somewhat circuitous way of addressing that question. As will be recalled, Greenberg defined modernism as "the use of characteristic methods of a discipline to criticize the discipline itself, not in order to subvert it but in order to entrench it more firmly in its area of competence" ([1960] 1993b: 85). The point of this self-criticism was to avoid a "leveling down" by "demonstrating that the kind of experience they [each art] offered was valuable in its own right and not to be obtained from any other activity" (ibid.: 86). For Greenberg, any resistance that adhered to modernist art existed in its refusal to yield to leveling processes through a constant reexamination of formal methods and materials and the elimination of any aspect that did not reinforce a particular art's essential elements. The rejection of politics was a given in this dedication to art's purification.

Certainly modern dancers feared the culture industry. However, it is debatable whether the fear was as much one of contamination from below as one of seduction and co-option from more powerful forces. There is in Greenberg a contempt for the lower orders that is seldom felt in the theory or practice of modern dance. Dancers feared the culture industry because, in its power, it offered economic stability and fame. But they also feared the legitimized high-art of ballet that threatened to overwhelm and consume a weaker modern dance. Both ballet and entertainment were viewed as aspects of entrenched power.

Dancers would have found other points of disagreement with Greenberg, the most important having to do with the role of representation in art. Greenberg attempted to circumvent representation in painting by allowing it to include only those elements that could be found nowhere else. This would give painting autonomy, but the price it would have to pay was separation from life. Dancers, however, felt that dance's essential element, the element that set it apart from literature and painting, could not be separated from life. The embodied nature of dance movement always intimated meaning, no matter how free it was of representation. Although it might be presumed that this attachment to life would prevent dance from achieving independence, there was an answer: because all humans shared embodiment, no education or conditioning was needed to respond to it. This was quite different from Greenberg's idea, expressed in *Avant-Garde and Kitsch*, that genuine art required reflection to make its effects ([1939] 1986a: 1:16). As far as modern dance theory was concerned, any kind of intellectual mediation made for an adulterated response. Dance could only be "understood" body to body through kinesthetic sympathy. In addition, any possibility of resistance or protest in dance could only be attained through movement freed of rationalized processes, most evident in language and illustration. Therefore, the fact that resistance, per se, did not enter written discourse was of little consequence. Resistance lay in practice, the activity of dancing, not in the representation of protest in dance nor in written or spoken responses to it. Resistance lay in Dunham's grinding hips, Primus's leap, Beatty's balletic extensions, Sokolow's gestures of madness, in the unpredictability of Nikolais's decentralized movement and Cunningham's controlled accidents. This was movement to confront the accepted, to destabilize the familiar and comfortable. And it would make itself felt through corporeal means.

This solution to the dual problem of freedom and resistance may seem at best idealistic and at worst conveniently constructed to work both ways. One may question how effective a concept of resistance through bodily practice might be and think how easily it fits the role of malleable tool for dominant ideologies. On the other hand, the social sciences have shown how much of human behavior is dependent on unconscious corporeal learning and teaching, and if such bodily practices are used to reinforce the status quo, they are also employed as instruments of change. In the final analysis, too, modernists were idealistic; they believed art could change society.

Modernist intentions are doomed to remain ambiguous and contradictory; these are accounted for in the structure and practice of modernism itself. But if the desire for acceptance is part of modernism, so
is the desire to oppose. Opposition, though, must occur however it
can, and the postwar period was not one in which opposition was easy.
Possibilities were limited not only by modernist rules but by the pressures of the larger social world, not least of which was the increasing co-
option of modernist form by institutions of power. The difficulties that
beset postwar modern dancers were many and serious, yet there can be
no doubt that dancers struggled to solve those problems within the
choices they thought possible. If their solutions were not free of contradiction, their faith in embodied movement nevertheless demonstrates
the power they felt existed in their medium and how that power could
be exercised even in the face of oppression.

Notes

Introduction

1. Examples include Ramsay Burt's *The Male Dancer: Bodies, Spectacle, Sexualities* (1995) and Sally Banes's *Dancing Women: Female Bodies on Stage* (1998), which address gender issues within a broad range of modern dance; Naomi Jackson's *Converging Movements: Modern Dance and Jewish Culture at the 92nd Street Y* (2000), which focuses on the lively interaction between modern dance and Jewish concerns at the Y from the 1930s onward; and Susan Manning's *Modern Dance, Negro Dance: Race in Motion* (2004), which traces the convergence of modern dance and African-American concert dance from the 1930s into the 1960s.

2. These are, most importantly, Naima Prevots's *Dance for Export: Cultural Diplomacy and the Cold War* (1998), which examines the American government's sponsorship of dance tours abroad during the Cold War, and Rebekah Kowal's dissertation, *Modern Dance and American Culture in the Early Cold War Years* (1999), which offers interpretations of the work of Martha Graham, Merce Cunningham, Alwin Nikolais, Paul Taylor, and Ann(a) Halprin in light of Cold War politics.

3. Mark Franko's reevaluation of a modernist narrative of modern dance history in *Dancing Modernism/Performing Politics* is among the few works to consider modernism itself in detail, although his project centers on the politics of modernist interpretation. Also, as in most dance research, his work reaches across a spectrum of modern dance rather than focusing on postwar modernism per se.

4. Since, as has often been said, there are many modernisms, I am not going to attempt to deal with a comprehensive treatment of the subject. Rather, I have chosen specific, accepted elements of modernism on which to focus in this study, including issues of representation and autonomy.

5. A number of anthologies document the modernist debates within art history, including Frascina 1985, Guilbaut 1990, Frascina and Harrison 1987, and Harrison and Wood 1993. Nor do the issues surrounding modernism appear

to be settled; see, for example, Clark 1998 (371–404) for a recent analysis of abstract expressionism.

6. Antonin Artaud reflected this uncertainty when he wrote in *The Theater and Its Double:* "If confusion is the sign of the times, I see at the root of this confusion a rupture between things and words, between things and the ideas and signs that are their representation" ([1938] 1958: 7).

7. I use the term "objectivist" after Susan Foster, who employs it to describe the dance of Merce Cunningham and other choreographers who favored what she refers to as the "activity of moving" in opposition to "expressionist dance" (1986: 167). Although "formalist" is also often used to describe the work of such choreographers, "objectivist" to my mind is less loaded. At the same time, I will use Martin's term "expressional" modern dance when differentiating older modern dance from the new objectivism.

8. This can readily be seen simply by comparing the increasing number of articles on dance listed in the *Readers' Guide to Periodicals* from the 1930s through the 1950s.

9. In particular, Balanchine's article entitled "Ballet Goes Native," published in *Dance* in 1937 has Denby's cadence and phrasing. It appeared in the December issue of the magazine, eight months after Denby had written a perceptive and complimentary review of Balanchine's choreography (Denby [1937] 1986: 44–46).

10. Hering had done freelance work for *Dance Magazine* beginning in 1945 (Doris Hering, personal interview with author, 17 September 2004).

Chapter 1. The Trouble with Modern Dance

1. Foote included in this category not just artists such as Martha Graham and Doris Humphrey but "modern" ballet choreographers Agnes de Mille, Antony Tudor, and Jerome Robbins.

2. Just how porous, Foote himself could attest. In addition to being a *Dance Observer* editor, Foote was an aspiring Broadway actor. Although he had little success on the stage, he eventually won fame as a television and Hollywood screenwriter (*To Kill a Mockingbird, Tender Mercies*) and Pulitzer Prize–winning playwright (*The Trip to Bountiful, The Young Man from Atlanta*).

3. See Jane Feuer's *The Hollywood Musical* (1993) for an interesting discussion of how American ballet, in incorporating folk and modern dance elements, made itself more accessible to a mass audience, thereby winning a prominent place in Broadway and Hollywood musicals after the war.

4. See Rosenbaum 1943 and Terry 1947b for the economic plight of dancers and the relationship of high-art dance to commercial work.

5. Regionalists included, most prominently, Grant Wood, Thomas Hart Benton, and John Steuart Curry (Dennis 1998; Corn 1985; Doss 1991).

6. The synthesis of idioms was institutionalized in the dance curriculum developed by Martha Hill for the Juilliard dance program initiated in 1951.

7. Undated program for Choreographers' Workshop, Dance Collection, New York Public Library. In this case, the workshop presented Bettis's *As I Lay Dying* with Horton Foote's *Goodbye to Richmond*, which had been commissioned by the Neighborhood Playhouse. These were billed as "two dance plays." Choreographers' Workshop was founded in 1946 by Trudy Goth, Patricia Newman, and Atty van den Berg to showcase the work of young choreographers (Hering 1947).

8. Analysis of *The Moor's Pavane* is based on a performance by the José Limón Dance Company (1955–1957 video) in *José Limón: Three Modern Dance Classics*, Canada: CBC Production.

9. Limon called his characters The Moor, His Friend, His Friend's Wife, and The Moor's Wife, which correspond to Shakespeare's Othello, Iago, Emilia, and Desdemona. I have used Shakespeare's designations for the sake of clarity and brevity.

Chapter 2. Ballet's Challenge

1. Although the pamphlet does not identify the writer, its style is unmistakably that of Kirstein, and his authorship is generally accepted. The pamphlet, from a private collection, was produced for Ballet Society in 1946 and was included in the exhibition *Dance for a City: Fifty Years of the New York City Ballet*, organized by Lynn Garafola and Eric Foner at the New York Historical Society, 20 April to 15 August 1999.

2. The Ballet Russe de Monte Carlo had begun its existence in Europe in the 1930s but made the United States its home after the advent of World War II (Anderson 1981).

3. Despite his written attacks, Kirstein's actual relationship with the genre was more ambivalent. He invited Iris Mabry and Merce Cunningham to show or contribute work to Ballet Society, and he asked Talley Beatty to dance in Lew Christensen's *Blackface* in 1947. He also knew Graham well, spending time at her studio and writing favorably about her in an essay for Merle Armitage's book, *Martha Graham: The Early Years* (1937). In addition, Kirstein invited Graham to choreograph half of *Episodes* in 1959, the other half choreographed by Balanchine.

4. Although Kirstein here sounds much like Greenberg, the two had little time for each other. Kirstein, an advocate of surrealism and neoromanticism, wrote an article in 1948 condemning abstract expressionism and arguing against Greenberg (Kirstein 1948). Greenberg, for his part, had contempt for Kirstein. On the one occasion in which he mentioned Kirstein in writing, it was to disparage him and his taste for neoromanticism (Greenberg ([1950] 1993a: 59–62).

It is an interesting footnote to a footnote that the only time Greenberg ventured into the field of dance was to write a review defending Tudor's *Dim Luster* ([1945] 1986c: 36–39). Apparently, his high-modernist purity did not extend to ballet.

5. For an analysis of the relationship of New York City Ballet and the Rockefeller Foundation, see Garafola 2002.

6. Kirstein founded Ballet Caravan in 1936 to provide work for the American Ballet dancers during the time they were not needed by the Metropolitan Opera. American Ballet had won the contract to become the resident company at the Met, but it soon became apparent that it would not be allowed to develop there. After the demise of American Ballet in 1938, Kirstein made Ballet Caravan a full-time touring group. Ballet Caravan's name was changed to American Ballet Caravan in 1941 and joined with the remnants of American Ballet for a Latin American tour that year. The entire enterprise was disbanded after the company returned to the United States (Kirstein 1973: 43–81; Garafola 1999: 4–5).

7. Balanchine tried to commission a score from Hindemith in 1937, but the composer refused. He agreed in 1940 when his financial situation changed (Buckle 1988: 162).

8. The analysis of *The Four Temperaments* is based on a silent Ballet Society rehearsal film of parts of the ballet (1946 film) with most of the original cast. This film includes the original finale. Also used were two performances by New York City Ballet made under Balanchine's direction: a Radio Canada production (1961 film) and a *Dance in America* production (1977 video); also two videos made of New York City Ballet at the New York State Theatre, Lincoln Center (1993 video), one a close-up and the other a full-stage view of the same performance. All are at the Dance Collection, New York Public Library for the Performing Arts. Unless otherwise noted, I will refer to the 1977 video, since it is commercially available and therefore the most easily accessible.

9. For a nuanced analysis of Balanchine's use of music in his work, see Jordan 2000.

10. Dance theorist Evan Alderson calls such movement associations "dance metaphors" (Alderson 1983).

11. See Banes (1999) for an analysis of modern dance influences on Balanchine's choreography.

12. See also Duell 1987; Ashley 1987; and Wilde 1987, all of whom participated in a panel discussion that was expanded for the first in a series of articles entitled "Celebrating *The Four Temperaments*," published in *Ballet Review* (Winter 1987, Spring 1987, and Spring 1988).

13. On surrealist aims and methods, see Breton 1972 and 1978; and Nadeau 1989. On surrealists in the United States, see Sawin 1997.

14. It should be added that by the time the surrealists reached America's

shores, their own use of the methods described here had lost most of their subversive edge. By the end of the 1930s, the majority of the surrealist artists were showing in important galleries and publishing with major houses, that is they had already achieved consecration (see Richard Martin 1987; Sawin 1997; and Brandon 1999).

15. In an article written in 1987, feminist dance historian Ann Daly argued that Balanchine portrayed women as passive instruments in the hands of men, using as her primary examples the thematic duets from *The Four Temperaments*. Although other commentators disagreed, arguing from a wider range of Balanchine ballets, the violent manipulation of women in *The Four Temperaments* had long been noted as one of the work's most striking features (Daly 1987; Jordan and Thomas 1994; and Siegel 1997).

Chapter 3. Modernist Theory: John Martin, Edwin Denby, John Cage

1. Cage is considered here only in his interaction with dance and dancers in the 1940s and '50s. Sally Banes and Noël Carroll have argued that Cage's vanguardism in his own compositions outstripped Cunningham's. Marjorie Perloff has also defended the radicalism of Cage's work (Banes and Carroll 2005; Perloff 1989).

2. For biographical information on John Martin, see Sabin 1946; Hering 1952; Anderson 1989; and the unsigned *New York Times* obituary, "John Martin Is Dead," 21 May 1985.

3. Richard Boleslavsky was an alumnus of the Moscow Arts Theatre and is credited with introducing the ideas of Constantin Stanislavski to the United States.

4. See Damasio (2003) for a leading neurologist's theory of how emotion is manifested. Damasio's theory is similar to Martin's to the degree that Damasio posits that a physical action (for example, blinking or clenching) occurs first and then a feeling about it is produced.

5. Martin's criticism did not always reflect his theory. For example, he praised narrative works by Graham, Maslow, and Limón.

6. The chronology of the Franco-Russian companies that emerged in the wake of Diaghilev's death in 1929 is confusing because the company names (including spellings) and personnel changed frequently. Often choreographers and dancers worked for a season or two in one troupe and then another. The first company, Les Ballets Russes de Monte Carlo, was founded in 1932 and was headed by Colonel W. de Basil and, until 1934, by René Blum. Another company, the Ballet Russe de Monte Carlo, was founded in 1938 with Sergei Denham as director. This company based itself in the United States during the war, while the de Basil troupe toured Australia and Latin America. The de Basil troupe returned to Europe after the war and disbanded in 1948. Denham's

Ballet Russe remained an American company until its demise in 1962 (Anderson 1981; García-Márquez 1990; Hurok 1947, 1953).

7. Although Tudor was English, he moved to the United States in 1939 and lived and worked there for most of his career until his death in 1987 (Perlmutter 1991; Chazin-Bennahum 1994). Denby initially responded favorably to Tudor's ballets, but he soon began to have reservations about them (see Denby [1942] 1986: 93–95; [1943b] 1986: 129–131; and Jordan 2000).

8. A time art is defined as follows: "The physical conditions in which all the arts have their existence, so far as they become communicable to the human senses, are either space (painting, sculpture, etc.) or time, or both (drama and in a sense all literature)" (Blom 1971: 701). Dance also would be categorized as an art of both time and space, although Cage, as a musician, is here considering it in terms of time.

Chapter 4. Embodying Community

1. The analysis here is based on *The Village I Knew* (1977 video), performed by the Sophie Maslow Dance Company at the Theatre of Riverside Church, Dance Collection, New York Public Library for the Performing Arts. Maslow originally choreographed some of the dances for *The Village I Knew* as *Festival* in 1949. She enlarged the work in 1950.

2. The New Dance Group had long made racial integration a policy and Maslow embraced it too. In fact the inclusion of McKayle and Aul in Maslow's work was itself a political act and commitment. Maslow has said that having a mixed company eliminated an entire area of touring for her in the South and made it difficult in the North where blacks were not allowed to stay in most white hotels or eat in white restaurants, among a number of forms of discrimination (Maslow 1984).

3. Although it is not clear from McKayle's account under what circumstances Martin made this comment, he made a similar remark in less inflammatory language in *John Martin's Book of the Dance* (1963: 189).

4. Sokolow continued to explore Jewish themes in the 1950s and beyond, both on the stage and for television. Her best known of these later works was *Dreams*, which she created in 1961 and which dealt with the horrors of the holocaust.

5. The analysis of *Kaddish* is drawn from *Kaddish* (1990 video), Deborah Zall soloist, Dance Collection, New York Public Library for the Performing Arts. The analysis of *Lamentation* is drawn from a film of excerpts from the dance with Graham as soloist and from a complete version of the dance with Peggy Lyman as soloist: *Lamentation* (1943 film), Martha Graham soloist and with an introduction by John Martin, Harmon Foundation production, Dance Collection, New York Public Library for the Performing Arts; *Lamentation* (1976

video), Peggy Lyman soloist, Martha Graham Dance Company, Dance in America production, Dance Collection, New York Public Library for the Performing Arts.

6. This analysis of *Rooms* is based on two video recordings, one of excerpts, one complete: *Rooms* (1966 video) excerpts, Anna Sokolow Dance Company, telecast on WNET-TV, New York, Jac Venza, producer (the dances "Dream," "Daydream," and "The End?" are omitted); *Rooms* (1975 video) complete, Contemporary Dance System, performed at American Place Theatre. Both at the Dance Collection, New York Public Library for the Performing Arts.

7. Program, Dance Recital by Anna Sokolow and Dance Unit of the New Dance League, 92nd Street Y, 28 February 1937, 92nd Street YW-WMHA Archives.

8. This analysis is based on *Session for Six* (1964 video), Juilliard Dance Ensemble, Dance Collection, New York Public Library.

9. The twist became popular in 1960 when Chubby Checker released his hit record "The Twist," but the dance grew out of the jitterbug of the 1940s and the variations that teenagers gave it in the 1950s. Sokolow's *Opus* works parallel the development of late '50s dances into the twist.

10. The analysis of *Opus '63* is based on a performance by the Juilliard Dance Ensemble (1963 video) and of *Opus '65* on a performance by the City Center Joffrey Ballet (1967 video), both at the Dance Collection, New York Public Library for the Performing Arts.

Chapter 5. African-American Vanguardism: 1940s

1. See, for example, Aschenbrenner 1981, 2002; Perpener 2001; DeFrantz 2002, 2004; Gottschild 1988, 1996; and Manning 2004.

2. See Aschenbrenner 2002 for a detailed analysis of the relationship of anthropology to Dunham's life and work. For biographical material and information on Dunham's early career, see Beckford 1979; Perpener 2001; Aschenbrenner 2002; Barzel 1983; and Manning 2004.

3. Adjustments were soon made in the program, perhaps because critics found *Bre'r Rabbit* weak. Dunham dropped the story line of the work and excerpted dances from it to make what she entitled *Plantation and Minstrel Dances from the Ballet Bre'r Rabbit*. She also changed the order of the last two suites, making the exciting *Le Jazz "Hot"* the finale.

4. The duet from *L'Ag'Ya* is shown in *Katherine Dunham Company* (1941–1944 video) [presented by] the Katherine Dunham Centers for Arts and Humanities, choreography and direction by Katherine Dunham. Dance Collection, New York Public Library for the Performing Arts.

5. *Choros #1* and *Rhumba Jive* (usually listed on printed programs as *Rumba with a Little Jive Mixed In*) can be seen in *Katherine Dunham Company*

(1941–1944 video) [presented by] the Katherine Dunham Centers for Arts and Humanities, choreography and direction by Katherine Dunham, as well as in *Katherine Dunham Company Tropical Revue* (1947 video): [presented by] the Katherine Dunham Centers for Arts and Humanities, choreography and direction by Katherine Dunham. The latter film was made by Ann Barzel of a performance at the Studebaker Theater, Chicago. Both films are in the Dance Collection, New York Public Library for the Performing Arts.

6. The authorship of this review is not altogether clear, considering the pseudonyms routinely used by critics writing in leftist publications. The *Daily Worker* review is almost identical to parts of one written on 1 March 1940 in *TAC*, a leftist magazine that ceased publication in 1942. Susan Manning states that circumstantial evidence points to Edna Ocko as the writer of *TAC*'s unsigned review (Manning 2004: 258–259n153). If so, it is likely Ocko wrote the *Daily Worker* review, as well. Ocko wrote often for the *Daily Worker* as well as *TAC* and other of the leftist publications. If Ocko (or the same author) wrote both reviews, it would mean that essentially there was one opinion representing leftist views of *Tropics and Le Jazz "Hot,"* since Owen Burke only mentioned the Dunham season in passing in *New Masses* (Burke 1940: 30).

7. Printed program, Katherine Dunham and her company in a tropical revue, 19 September 1943, Martin Beck Theatre, New York. Dance Collection, New York Public Library for the Performing Arts.

8. This interest in psychology and sociology may have been prompted by her friendship with Erich Fromm, whom Dunham met at the University of Chicago and who remained a friend and mentor for many years.

9. Among those who spoke of the intrusion of extraneous elements in the program were George Freedley of the *New York Morning Telegraph*, Fredi Washington of the *People's Voice*, Edwin Denby in the *New York Herald Tribune*, and John Martin in the *New York Times*. Although Martin mentioned intrusive elements in Primus's concert, he wrote a generally laudatory review under the headline, "Brilliant Dancing by Pearl Primus" (Martin 1944b). Martin was an admirer of Primus's work and continued to support her through news articles and reviews when others were less positive.

10. This work, called *Block Party*, was to have had music by Virgil Thomson. However, it was never completed (Beatty 1990; Nash 1992: 13).

11. The analysis of *Southern Landscape* is based on a performance by the Philadelphia Dance Company (Philadanco), Joan Brown, director, in *A Memorial, Tribute, Celebration of the Life and Art of Choreographer/Dancer Mr. Talley Beatty* (1995 video), Dr. Glory Van Scott, producer; and "Mourner's Bench" (1948 film), choreographed and performed by Talley Beatty. Both are in the Dance Collection, New York Public Library for the Performing Arts. According to Joan Brown, the Elie Siegmeister score was lost, and Beatty set *Southern*

Landscape to spirituals, folk, and contemporary songs when he revived it for her company. Personal interview, 15 September 2004.

12. Beatty in *The New Dance Group Gala Concert* (1994 video). American Dance Guild Production, New York.

13. Printed program, Talley Beatty and Company, 24 October 1948. The Dance Center of the YW-WMHA, 92nd Street and Lexington Avenue, New York. 92nd Street YW-YMHA Archives.

14. Personal interview, Joe Nash, New York City, 16 July 2002. In the last section of the Philadelphia Dance Company production, Beatty changed not just the choreography and music but the concept as well. He now titled the segment "Runagate Variations." A runagate was an escaped slave. Therefore, the new finale, with its implication of flight to the North and freedom, appears more optimistic than the original "Settin' Up," which continued the work's overall mood of resignation and sorrow.

15. It should be noted that Smith had been a critic for the *Chicago Tribune* and knew of Beatty as a young dancer. According to Beatty, Smith had seen him perform with Dunham while he was still in middle school and provided him with a scholarship to attend ballet classes with Edna McCrae while Dunham was in Haiti (Beatty 1990).

16. The analysis of *Ophelia* is based on a performance in *Dance and Myth: The World of Jean Erdman*, part 1, "Early Solos" (1993 video), National Video Industries.

17. This pose was found among Louis Horst's "medievalist" forms in his composition classes and was frequently used by dancers who had studied with him. See Horst and Russell [1961] 1987: 76–86, and illustration on 80.

18. Erdman's quote is from *Dance and Myth: The World of Jean Erdman*, part 1, "Early Solos" (1993 video), National Video Industries. The analysis of *Hamadryad* is based on a performance in the same video.

Chapter 6. African-American Vanguardism: 1950s

1. The black press seldom covered modern dance concerts in the 1950s, so written discourse centered almost exclusively on white reception. It is worth noting, however, that the *Amsterdam News* and *New York Age* frequently ran announcements of concerts by both black and white choreographers at the 92nd Street Y. Although this may have been due to some extent to the Y's uptown location, it also supports Naomi Jackson's contention that the Y reached out to black artists and audiences. It equally suggests that the city's African-American newspapers thought news of these concerts would be of interest to their readers.

2. The title of the dance work came from a chain gang song and referred

to the arched head of a pick, one of the tools prisoners used along with sledge-hammers to break rock.

3. The analysis of *Rainbow Round My Shoulder* is based on a 1959 perform-ance recorded in *Donald McKayle: Early Work* (1999 video), John Desmond, di-rector, produced by John McGiffert, Creative Arts Television Archive; also performances recorded in *Revelations [and] Rainbow Round My Shoulder* (1973 video), Alvin Ailey American Dance Theater; and *Alvin Ailey American Dance Theatre: Three by Three* (1985). All videos are in the Dance Collection, New York Public Library for the Performing Arts.

4. Donald McKayle, personal conversation, 26 November 2004, New York.

5. Only the dance press covered the early performances of *Rainbow Round My Shoulder*. Of the black press, *New York Age* ran an announcement of the opening (9 May 1959: 12) and the *Amsterdam News* ran an announcement after the fact (16 May 1959: 16), but neither newspaper covered the event.

6. The analysis of *The Road of the Phoebe Snow* is based on a rehearsal per-formance by the Alvin Ailey Dance Theatre (1969 video) and a performance by the Alvin Ailey Repertory Ensemble (1983 video) presented by the Riverside Dance Festival. Both videos are in the Dance Collection, New York Public Library for the Performing Arts.

7. In the late 1970s, a young Bill T. Jones took note of this development and delivered blistering attacks against the audiences who encouraged it. In a series of solos he seduced (mostly white) spectators with beautiful movement then ag-gressively confronted them in words and movement (Jones 1995; Morris 2001).

Chapter 7. Objectivism's Consonance

1. It should be emphasized that in this chapter I am speaking of the work of Nikolais and Cunningham in the 1940s and '50s. It is reasonable to assume that their ideas, interests, and priorities might change over the course of their careers.

2. *Septet* (1964 film), Cunningham Dance Foundation Archives, New York City.

3. Years later, Cunningham was still speaking of his dance in concrete terms. In 2005, the Cunningham company Web-site prominently featured a quote by Cunningham stating, "there's no thinking involved in my choreography. . . . I don't work through images or ideas—I work through the body."

4. *Summerspace* (1958 video), filmed at the American Dance Festival, Con-necticut College. Cunningham Dance Foundation Archives, New York City.

5. Unfortunately, this quality has been lost, as a comparison to a video performance of *Summerspace* made at Berkeley, California, in 2000 attests (Cunningham Dance Foundation Archives, New York City). The Cunningham dancers now perform the work as an exercise in mannered virtuosity.

6. A year earlier Nikolais had written a similar but less complete explanation of his ideas in a piece for the *New York Times* (Nikolais 1957).

7. Murray Louis, personal interview, 16 August 2003, New York.

8. Susan Buirge, personal interview, 5 November 2003, Paris.

9. Nikolais commented, "I was always a little ashamed of dancing. Choreography removed that." *Nik and Murray* (1986 video), Dance Collection, New York Public Library for the Performing Arts.

10. Phyllis Lamhut and Susan Buirge commented on how similar these exercises were to Pilates mat exercises. Phyllis Lamhut, personal interview, 28 July 2003, New York; Susan Buirge, personal interview, 5 November 2003, Paris.

11. "Fixation" survives in *A Time to Dance: Alwin Nikolais* (1959 video), Dance Collection, New York Public Library for the Performing Arts. Louis has said the dance's title reflected the repetitiveness of the movement (personal interview, 16 August 2003, New York).

12. Murray Louis, personal interview, 13 August 2003.

13. Phyllis Lamhut, personal interview, 28 July 2003.

14. On stage Nikolais used improvised movement only in limited ways. The dancers might, for example, be asked to do darting movements for a short period of time at a specific location on the stage; otherwise, the dances were generally set. According to Murray Louis, the one major exception to this rule was *Mirrors* (1959), a piece completely improvised on stage by the company. Since improvisation demanded constant, instant spontaneous decisions, Louis said that the work was so exhausting it was only repeated four times and then dropped from the repertory. Murray Louis, personal interview, 16 August 2003.

15. Murray Louis, personal communication, 16 August 2003.

16. Ruth Grauert, transcription of interview with Claudia Gitelman, April 1999, Collection of Claudia Gitelman, New York. Murray Louis, personal interview, 16 August 2003.

17. According to several of his early dancers, Nikolais often said that the invention of synthetic fabric tights that were stretchable but did not sag changed dance technique.

18. Program: The [Henry Street] Playhouse Dance Company, *Etudes II: Masks, Props, and Mobiles*, 26 January 1953. Program: The [Henry Street] Playhouse Dance Company, *Masks—Props—Mobiles*, 10 December 1955. Both are in the Dance Collection, New York Public Library for the Performing Arts.

19. Analysis of *Kaleidoscope* is based on a performance by the Henry Street Playhouse Dance Company (1956 film), which includes five of eight sections, Dance Collection, New York Public Library for the Performing Arts; and on a performance of the entire work from 1956 in the collection of Murray Louis.

20. This was not the only time Nikolais attacked expressional modern dance for being excessively focused on sexuality (1958: 43; 1968; 1971a: 9; 1971b; 1973; 1973–1974: 41–42). His most extensive attack came in a 1961 essay he

contributed to *The Encyclopedia of Sexuality* (1961a) in which he accused the old modern dance of sexual disfunction and illness in the harshest terms.

21. Although objectivist modern dance was soon overtaken by early post-modernism, it is debatable how much of a break with the past postmodernism was. With the passing years, early postmodernism looks more like reformation than revolution, despite manifestos to the contrary.

REFERENCES

Adler, Les K., and Thomas G. Paterson (1970). "Red Fascism: The Merger of Nazi Germany and Soviet Russia in the American Image of Totalitarianism, 1930s–1950s." *American Historical Review* 75 (April): 1,046–1,064.

Adorno, Theodor, and Max Horkheimer ([1944] 1979). *Dialectic of Enlightenment.* Translated by John Cumming. Reprint, London: Verso.

Alderson, Evan (1983). "Metaphor in Dance: The Example of Graham." *Proceedings, Sixth Annual Conference of Dance History Scholars:* 111–118.

Anderson, Edith (1943). "Daring New Dancer Is First Negro to Make YMHA Debut." *Daily Worker* (19 February): 7.

Anderson, Jack (1981). *The One and Only: The Ballet Russe de Monte Carlo.* London: Dance Books.

——— (1989). Introduction to *John Martin: The Dance in Theory.* Princeton, N.J.: Dance Horizons.

Arato, Andrew, and Eike Gebhardt, eds. (1995). *The Essential Frankfurt School Reader.* New York: Continuum.

Armitage, Merle ([1937] 1985). *Martha Graham: The Early Years.* Reprint, New York: Da Capo Press.

Artaud, Antonin ([1938] 1958). *The Theater and Its Double.* Reprint, New York: Grove Press.

Aschenbrenner, Joyce (1981). *Katherine Dunham: Reflections on the Social and Political Contexts of Afro-American Dance. Dance Research Annual XII,* edited by Patricia A. Rowe. New York: Congress on Research in Dance.

——— (2002). *Katherine Dunham: Dancing a Life.* Urbana: University of Illinois Press.

Ashley, Merrill (1982). "Merrill Ashley." In *Striking a Balance: Dancers Talk about Dancing,* edited by Barbara Newman. Boston: Houghton Mifflin.

——— (1984). *Dancing for Balanchine.* New York: Dutton.

Ashley, Merrill, et al. (1987). "Celebrating *The Four Temperaments*—1." *Ballet Review* (Winter): 12–35.

Balanchine, George (1937). "Ballet Goes Native." *Dance* (December): 13. Reprinted (1944) as "The American Dancer." *Dance News* (April): 3, 6.

———— (1945). "Notes on Choreography." *Dance Index* 4, 2–3 (February–March): 20–31.

———— (1951). "Marginal Notes on the Dance." In *The Dance Has Many Faces*, edited by Walter Sorell. Cleveland: World Publishing.

———— (1954). *Balanchine's Complete Stories of the Great Ballets*. Edited by Francis Mason. Garden City, N.Y.: Doubleday.

———— (1961). "Balanchine: An Interview by Ivan Nabokov and Elizabeth Carmichael." *Horizon* (January): 44–56.

———— (1965). "Now Everybody Wants to Get into the Act." *Life* (11 June): 97–102.

———— (1968). *Balanchine's New Complete Stories of the Great Ballets*. Edited by Francis Mason. Garden City, N.Y.: Doubleday.

———— (1984). *By George Balanchine*. New York: San Marco Press.

Balanchine, George, and Francis Mason (1984). *Balanchine's Festival of Ballet*. 2 vols. London: W. H. Allen.

Balcom, Lois (1944a). "What Chance Has the Negro Dancer?" *Dance Observer* (November): 110–111.

———— (1944b). "The Negro Dances Himself." *Dance Observer* (December): 122–124.

Ball, William (1984). *A Sense of Direction*. New York: Drama Book Publishers.

Banes, Sally (1980). *Terpsichore in Sneakers: Post-Modern Dance*. Boston: Houghton Mifflin.

———— (1994). *Writing Dancing in the Age of Postmodernism*. Middletown, Conn.: Wesleyan University Press.

———— (1995). "Images." In *Dance Words*, compiled by Valerie Preston-Dunlop. Chur, Switzerland: Harwood Academic Publishers.

———— (1998). *Dancing Women: Female Bodies on Stage*. London: Routledge.

———— (1999). "Sibling Rivalry: The New York City Ballet and Modern Dance." In *Dance for a City: Fifty Years of the New York City Ballet*, edited by Lynn Garafola, with Eric Foner. New York: Columbia University Press.

Banes, Sally, and Noël Carroll (2005). "Cunningham, Balanchine, and Postmodern Dance." Paper presented at *Dancing from the Center*, Society of Dance History Scholars Conference, 9–12 June. Northwestern University, Evanston, Ill.

Bannerman, Henrietta (1999). "An Overview of the Development of Martha Graham's Movement System (1926–1991)." *Dance Research* 17, 2 (Winter): 9–46.

Barber, Beverly Hillsman (1992). "Pearl Primus: Rebuilding America's Cultural Infrastructure." In *African-American Genius in Modern Dance*, Gerald E. Myers and Stephanie Reinhart, project directors. Durham, N.C.: American Dance Festival.

Barron, Stephanie (1991). *"Degenerate Art": The Fate of the Avant-Garde in Nazi Germany*. Los Angeles: Los Angeles County Museum of Art.

Barzel, Ann (1983). "The Untold Story of the Dunham/Turbyfill Alliance." *Dance Magazine* (December): 91–98.

Beatty, Talley (1990). Unpublished interview conducted by Dawn Lille. Typescript from audio recording. Collection of Dawn Lille, New York.

———— (1993). *Speaking of Dance: Talley Beatty* (video). Interview with Talley Beatty. American Dance Festival production, directed and produced by Douglas Rosenberg. Dance Collection, New York Public Library.

Beckford, Ruth (1979). *Katherine Dunham: A Biography*. New York: Marcel Dekker.

Beiswanger, George W. (1942). "Lobby Thoughts and Jottings." *Dance Observer* (November): 116–117.

———— (1943a). "Dance over the U.S.A." Part 1. *Dance Observer* (January): 4–6.

———— (1943b). "Dance over the U.S.A." Part 2. *Dance Observer* (February): 16–17.

———— (1957). "New London: Residues and Reflections." *Dance Observer* (February): 21–23.

Bell, Daniel ([1960] 1988). *The End of Ideology: On the Exhaustion of Political Ideas in the 1950s*. Reprint, with a new afterword by the author. Cambridge Mass.: Harvard University Press.

Bentley, Eric (1971). *Thirty Years of Treason: Excerpts from Hearings before the House Committee on Un-American Activities, 1938–1968*. New York: Viking Press.

Bernstein, Harry (1958). "Alvin Ailey, Ernest Parham and Companies." *Dance Observer* (June–July): 88.

———— (1959). "Kevin Carlisle, Donald McKayle and Companies." *Dance Observer* (June–July): 92–93.

Bérubé, Allan (1990). *Coming Out under Fire: The History of Gay Men and Women in World War II*. New York: Free Press.

Bettis, Valerie (1945). "Young Dancers State Their Views: As Told to David Zellmer." *Dance Observer* (August–September): 82.

Blom, Eric (1971). *Everyman's Dictionary of Music*, revised by Sir Jack Westrup. New York: New American Library.

Bourdieu, Pierre (1977). *Outline of a Theory of Practice*. Cambridge: Cambridge University Press.

———— (1986). "The Forms of Capital." In *Handbook of Theory and Research for the Sociology of Education*, edited by John G. Richardson. New York: Greenwood Press.

———— (1990a). *In Other Words: Essays towards a Reflexive Sociology*. Palo Alto, Calif.: Stanford University Press.

———— (1990b). *The Logic of Practice*. Palo Alto, Calif.: Stanford University Press.

——— (1993a). *The Field of Cultural Production*. New York: Columbia University Press.

——— (1993b). *Sociology in Question*. London: Sage Publications.

——— (1996). *The Rules of Art*. Cambridge: Polity Press.

Bourdieu, Pierre, and Loïc Wacquant (1992). *An Invitation to Reflexive Sociology*. Chicago: University of Chicago Press.

Brandon, Ruth (1999). *Surreal Lives: The Surrealists, 1917–1945*. London: Macmillan.

Breton, André ([1969] 1993). *Conversations: The Autobiography of Surrealism*. New York: Paragon House.

——— (1972). *Manifestoes of Surrealism*. Ann Arbor: University of Michigan Press.

——— (1978). *André Breton: What Is Surrealism? Selected Writings*. Edited by Franklin Rosemont. New York: Monad Press.

Brinkley, Alan (1996). *End of Reform: New Deal Liberalism in Recession and War*. New York: Vintage Books.

——— (2001). "The Illusion of Unity in Cold War Culture." In *Rethinking Cold War Culture*, edited by Peter J. Kuznick and James Gilbert. Washington, D.C.: Smithsonian Institution Press.

Brodie, Joan (1948). "Choreographers' Workshop." *Dance Observer* (April): 44.

——— (1950). "Talley Beatty and Company." *Dance Observer* (November): 138–139.

Broughton, Shirley (1957). "Close-Up of Modern Dance Today: The Non-Objective Choreographers." *Dance Magazine* (November): 20–23.

Brown, Jean Morrison, ed. (1979). *The Vision of Modern Dance*. Princeton, N.J.: Princeton Book.

Buckle, Richard, in collaboration with John Taras (1988). *George Balanchine, Ballet Master*. New York: Random House.

Bürger, Peter (1984). *Theory of the Avant-Garde*. Minneapolis: University of Minnesota Press.

Burke, Owen (1940). "A Review of Recent Outstanding Performances." *New Masses* (26 March): 30.

Burley, Dan (1940). "Miss Dunham Wins B'way with Dances." *New York Amsterdam News* (24 February): 21.

Burt, Ramsay (1995). *The Male Dancer: Bodies, Spectacle, Sexualities*. London: Routledge.

——— (1998). *Alien Bodies: Representations of Modernity, "Race" and Nation in Early Modern Dance*. London: Routledge.

Butler, Gervase (1937). "American Ballet." *Dance Observer* (June–July): 67.

——— (1943). "Five Dancers." *Dance Observer* (March): 27.

Cage, John (1944). "Grace and Clarity." *Dance Observer* (November): 108–109.

——— (1957). "On This Day." *Dance Observer* (January): 10.

———— (1973). *Silence*. Middletown, Conn.: Wesleyan University Press.

———— (1991). *John Cage: An Anthology*. Edited by Richard Kostelanetz. New York: Da Capo Press.

Campbell, Joseph (1944a). "Betwixt the Cup and the Lip." *Dance Observer* (March): 30–31.

———— (1944b). "Text, or Idea?" *Dance Observer* (June–July): 66, 75.

———— (1945). "The Jubilee of Content and Form." *Dance Observer* (May): 52–53.

Caute, David (1978). *The Great Fear: The Anti-Communist Purge under Truman and Eisenhower*. New York: Simon and Schuster.

Chafe, William (1982). "The Civil Rights Revolution." In *Reshaping America: Society and Institutions, 1945–1960*, edited by Robert Bremner and Gary Reichard. Columbus: Ohio State University Press.

———— (1999). *The Unfinished Journey: America since World War II*. 4th ed. Oxford: Oxford University Press.

Chambers, John Whiteclay (1992). *The Tyranny of Change: America in the Progressive Era, 1900–1917*. New York: Palgrave Macmillan.

Charlip, Remy (1954). "Concerning Merce Cunningham and His Choreography: Composing by Chance." *Dance Magazine* (January): 17–19.

Chazin-Bennahum, Judith (1994). *The Ballets of Antony Tudor: Studies in Psyche and Satire*. Oxford: Oxford University Press.

Chujoy, Anatole (1943). "Dance in Review." *Dance News* (October): 3.

———— (1949). *The Dance Encyclopedia*. New York: A. S. Barnes.

———— (1953). *The New York City Ballet*. New York: Alfred A. Knopf.

Churchill, Allen (1949). "Dancer with a Dream . . ." *Theatre Arts* (March): 34–37.

Clark, T. J. (1984). *The Painting of Modern Life: Paris in the Art of Manet and His Followers*. Princeton, N.J.: Princeton University Press.

———— (1998). *Farewell to an Idea: Episodes from a History of Modernism*. New Haven, Conn.: Yale University Press.

Clark, Vèvè A., and Margaret B. Wilkerson, eds. (1978). *KAISO! Katherine Dunham, an Anthology of Writings*. Berkeley: University of California, Institute for the Study of Social Change.

Cockcroft, Eva (1974). "Abstract Expressionism: Weapon of the Cold War." *Artforum* (June): 39–41.

Cohen, Selma Jeanne (1959). "Donald McKayle, Kevin Carlisle and Cos." *Dance Magazine* (July): 17, 80.

————, ed. (1965). *The Modern Dance: Seven Statements of Belief*. Middletown, Conn.: Wesleyan University Press.

Coleman, Martha (1948). "Talley Beatty, Nina Fonaroff, Yuriko." *Dance Observer* (January): 7.

Collins, Patricia Hill (2004). *Black Sexual Politics: African-Americans, Gender, and the New Racism*. New York: Routledge.

Cooper, John Milton (1992). *Pivotal Decades: The United States, 1900–1920.* New York: W. W. Norton.

Copeland, Roger (1973–1974). "A Conversation with Alwin Nikolais." *Dance Scope* 8, 1 (Fall/Winter): 41–46.

——— (2004). *Merce Cunningham: The Modernizing of Modern Dance.* New York: Routledge.

Corn, Wanda (1985). *Grant Wood: The Regionalist Vision.* New Haven, Conn.: Yale University Press.

Cornfield, Robert, and William MacKay, eds. (1986). *Edwin Denby: Dance Writings.* New York: Alfred A. Knopf.

Craig, Jenifer (2001). "A Redacted Past: Bella Lewitzky Encounters the U.S. Government." Paper presented at the twenty-fourth annual conference of the Society of Dance History Scholars, 21–24 June. Goucher College, Baltimore.

Croce, Arlene (1977). *Afterimages.* New York: Alfred A. Knopf.

——— (1982). *Going to the Dance.* New York: Alfred A. Knopf.

Cunningham, Merce (1951). "The Function of a Technique for Dance." In *The Dance Has Many Faces,* edited by Walter Sorell. New York: World Publishing.

——— ([1955] (1978). "The Impermanent Art." In *Esthetics Contemporary,* edited by Richard Kostelanetz. Buffalo N.Y.: Prometheus Books. Originally published in *7 Arts,* 3, edited by Fernando Puma. Indian Hills, Conn.: Falcon Wing's Press.

——— (1966). "Summerspace Story: How a Dance Came to Be." *Dance Magazine* (June): 52–54.

——— (1968). *Changes: Notes on Choreography.* Edited by Frances Starr. New York: Something Else Press.

——— (1980). "Choreography and the Dance." In *The Dance Anthology,* edited by Cobbett Steinberg. New York: New American Library.

Cunningham, Merce, with Jacqueline Lesschaeve (1985). *The Dancer and the Dance.* New York: Marion Boyars.

Dalfiume, Richard M. (1968). "The 'Forgotten Years' of the Negro Revolution." *Journal of American History* 15 (June): 90–106.

Daly, Ann (1987). "The Balanchine Woman: Of Hummingbirds and Channel Swimmers." *The Drama Review* 31, 1 (Spring): 8–21.

Damasio, Antonio (2003). *Looking for Spinoza: Joy, Sorrow, and the Feeling Brain.* New York: Harcourt.

Dana, Margery (1940). "The Dance." *Daily Worker* (21 February): 7.

Davis, Luther, and John Cleveland (1940). "Russian Genius." *Collier's* (28 December): 22, 36.

DeFrantz, Thomas F., ed. (2002). *Dancing Many Drums: Excavations in African American Dance.* Madison: University of Wisconsin Press.

———— (2004). *Dancing Revelations: Alvin Ailey's Embodiment of African American Culture*. Oxford: Oxford University Press.

D'Emilio, John (1998). *Sexual Politics, Sexual Communities: The Making of a Homosexual Minority in the United States, 1940–1970*. 2nd ed. Chicago: University of Chicago Press.

D'Emilio, John, and Estelle Freedman (1997). *Intimate Matters: A History of Sexuality in America*. 2nd ed. Chicago: University of Chicago Press.

Denby, Edwin ([1937] 1986). "Balanchine's American Ballet." In *Dance Writings*, edited by Robert Cornfield and William MacKay. New York: Alfred A. Knopf: 44–46. Originally published in *Modern Music* (March–April).

———— ([1942] 1986). "Fokine's 'Russian Soldier'; Tudor's 'Pillar of Fire'; Balanchine's Elephant Ballet." In *Dance Writings*, edited by Robert Cornfield and William MacKay. New York: Alfred A. Knopf, 92–95. Originally published in *Modern Music* (May–June 1942).

———— ([1943a] 1986). "Katherine Dunham." In *Dance Writings*, edited by Robert Cornfield and William MacKay. New York: Alfred A. Knopf, 142–143. Originally published in the *New York Herald Tribune* (26 September).

———— ([1943b] 1986). "Tudor and Pantomine." In *Dance Writings*, edited by Robert Cornfield and William MacKay. New York: Alfred A. Knopf, 129–131. Originally published in the *New York Herald Tribune* (11 July).

———— ([1944a] 1986). "A Note on Dance Intelligence." In *Dance Writings*, edited by Robert Cornfield and William MacKay. New York: Alfred A. Knopf, 204–205. Originally published in the *New York Herald Tribune* (26 March).

———— ([1944b] 1986). "Merce Cunningham." In *Dance Writings*, edited by Robert Cornfield and William MacKay. New York: Alfred A. Knopf, 207–208. Originally published in the *New York Herald Tribune* (6 April).

———— ([1944c] 1986). "Pearl Primus on Broadway." In *Dance Writings*, edited by Robert Cornfield and William MacKay. New York: Alfred A. Knopf, 247–248. Originally published in the *New York Herald Tribune* (5 October).

———— (1944d). "The Dance: Dunham in Full Bloom." *New York Herald Tribune* (27 December): 10.

———— ([1945] 1986). "Cunningham Solo." In *Dance Writings*, edited by Robert Cornfield and William MacKay. New York: Alfred A. Knopf, 279–280. Originally published in the *New York Herald Tribune* (10 January).

———— ([1946] 1986). "The Four Temperaments." In *Dance Writings*, edited by Robert Cornfield and William MacKay. New York: Alfred A. Knopf, 414–415. Originally published in *Dance News* (December 1946).

———— ([1947] 1986). "Ballet: The American Position." In *Dance Writings*, edited by Robert Cornfield and William MacKay. New York: Alfred A. Knopf, 507–517. Originally published in *Town and Country* (April 1947).

———— ([1948] 1986). "A Briefing in American Ballet." In *Dance Writings*, edited by Robert Cornfield and William MacKay. New York: Alfred A. Knopf, 517–527. Originally published in *Kenyon Review* (Autumn 1948).

——— ([1949a] 1986). "Against Meaning in Ballet." In *Dance Writings*, edited by Robert Cornfield and William MacKay. New York: Alfred A. Knopf, 527–531. Originally published in *Ballet* (March 1949).

——— (1949b). *Looking at the Dance*. New York: Pellegrini & Cudahy.

——— ([1952] 1986). "A Letter on New York City's Ballet." In *Dance Writings*, edited by Robert Cornfield and William MacKay. New York: Alfred A. Knopf, 415–430. Originally published in *Ballet* (August 1952).

——— ([1953] 1986). "Some Thoughts about Classicism and George Balanchine." In *Dance Writings*, edited by Robert Cornfield and William MacKay. New York: Alfred A. Knopf, 433–440. Originally published in *Dance Magazine* (February 1953).

——— (1965). *Dancers, Buildings and People in the Streets*. New York: Popular Library.

Denning, Michael (1996). *The Cultural Front*. London: Verso.

Dennis, James M. (1998). *Renegade Regionalists: The Modern Independence of Grant Wood, Thomas Hart Benton and John Steuart Curry*. Madison: University of Wisconsin Press.

Desmond, Jane, ed. (2001). *Dancing Desires: Choreographing Sexualities On and Off the Stage*. Madison: University of Wisconsin Press.

Diggins, John Patrick (1988). *The Proud Decades: America in War and Peace, 1941–1960*. New York: W. W. Norton.

"Doom Eager Dance" (1944). *Newsweek* (17 January): 85.

Doss, Erika (1991). *Benton, Pollock, and the Politics of Modernism from Regionalism to Abstract Expressionism*. Chicago: University of Chicago Press.

Drake, St. Clair (1981). Foreward to *Katherine Dunham: Reflections on the Social and Political Contexts of Afro-American Dance*, by Joyce Aschenbrenner. *Dance Research Annual XII*, edited by Patricia A. Rowe. New York: Congress on Research in Dance.

Drown, Marilyn Vaughan (1997). "Merce Cunningham and Meaning: The Zen Connection." *Choreography and Dance* 4, 3: 17–28.

Dudziak, Mary L. (2000). *Cold War Civil Rights: Race and the Image of American Democracy*. Princeton, N.J.: Princeton University Press.

Duell, Daniel, et al. (1987). "Celebrating *The Four Temperaments*—1." *Ballet Review* (Winter): 12–35.

Dunham, Katherine ([n.d.] 1978). "Statement." In *KAISO! Katherine Dunham, an Anthology of Writings*, edited by Vèvè A. Clark and Margaret B. Wilkerson. Berkeley: University of California, Institute for the Study of Social Change.

——— ([1941a] 1978). "The Negro Dance." In *KAISO! Katherine Dunham, an Anthology of Writings*, edited by Vèvè A. Clark and Margaret B. Wilkerson.

Berkeley: University of California, Institute for the Study of Social Change, 66–74. Originally published in *The Negro Caravan*, edited by Sterling A. Brown, Arthur P. Davis, and Ulysses Lee. New York: Dryden Press.

———— ([1941b] 1978). "Thesis Turned Broadway." In *KAISO! Katherine Dunham, an Anthology of Writings*, edited by Vèvè A. Clark and Margaret B. Wilkerson. Berkeley: University of California, Institute for the Study of Social Change, 55–57. Originally published in *California Arts and Architecture* (August).

———— ([1941c] 1978). "Form and Function in Primitive Dance." In *KAISO! Katherine Dunham, an Anthology of Writings*, edited by Vèvè A. Clark and Margaret B. Wilkerson. Berkeley: University of California, Institute for the Study of Social Change, 192–196. Originally published in *Educational Dance* (October).

———— ([1951] 1978). "Program: *Southland*." In *KAISO! Katherine Dunham, an Anthology of Writings*, edited by Vèvè A. Clark and Margaret B. Wilkerson. Berkeley: University of California Press, 117–120.

———— (1994). *A Touch of Innocence*. Chicago: University of Chicago Press.

Dunning, Jennifer (1985). *But First a School: The First Fifty Years of the School of American Ballet*. New York: Viking Press.

———— (1996). *Alvin Ailey: A Life in Dance*. New York: Addison-Wesley.

Emery, Lynne Fauley (1988). *Black Dance from 1619 to Today*. 2nd ed. Pennington, N.J.: Princeton Book.

Erdman, Jean (1948). "Young Dancers State Their Views: As Told to Joseph Campbell." *Dance Observer* (April): 40–41.

———— (1994). *The New Dance Group Gala Concert* (video). Interview with Jean Erdman. American Dance Guild Production.

Fanon, Frantz (1967). *Black Skin, White Masks*. New York: Grove Press.

Feuer, Jane (1993). *The Hollywood Musical*. 2nd ed. Basingstoke, U.K.: Macmillan Press.

Fonaroff, Nina (1948). "Young Dancers State Their Views: As Told to Mary Phelps." *Dance Observer* (May): 52, 63.

Foner, Eric (1998). *The Story of American Freedom*. New York: W. W. Norton.

Foote, Horton (1944). "The Long, Long Trek." *Dance Observer* (October): 98–99.

———— (1945a). "Pearl Primus and Group." *Dance Observer* (April): 43–44.

———— (1945b). "Notes for the Future." *Dance Observer* (May): 56.

Foster, Susan Leigh (1986). *Reading Dancing: Bodies and Subjects in Contemporary American Dance*. Berkeley: University of California Press.

————, ed. (1995). *Choreographing History*. Bloomington: University of Indiana Press.

———— (2001). "Closets Full of Dances: Modern Dance's Performance of Masculinity and Sexuality." In *Dancing Desires: Choreographing Sexualities On and*

Off the Stage, edited by Jane Desmond. Madison: University of Wisconsin Press.

Foulkes, Julia L. (2002). *Modern Bodies: Dance and American Modernism from Martha Graham to Alvin Ailey*. Chapel Hill: University of North Carolina Press.

Franko, Mark (1995). *Dancing Modernism/Performing Politics*. Bloomington: University of Indiana Press.

——— (2002). *The Work of Dance: Labor, Movement, and Identity in the 1930s*. Middletown, Conn.: Wesleyan University Press.

Frascina, Francis, ed. (1985). *Pollock and After: The Critical Debate*. London: Paul Chapman Publishing.

Frascina, Francis, and Charles Harrison, eds. (1987). *Modern Art and Modernism: A Critical Anthology*. New York: Harper and Row.

Fraser, Steve, and Gary Gerstle, eds. (1990). *The Rise and Fall of the New Deal Order, 1930–1980*. Princeton, N.J.: Princeton University Press.

Freedley, George (1944). "Pearl Primus—in Two Parts." *New York Morning Telegraph* (10 October): 2.

Fried, Richard (1990). *Nightmare in Red: The McCarthy Era in Perspective*. New York: Oxford University Press.

Fromm, Erich (1947). *Man for Himself: An Inquiry Into the Psychology of Ethics*. New York: Rinehart.

——— (1950). *Psychoanalysis and Religion*. New Haven: Yale University Press.

——— (1955). *The Sane Society*. New York: Rinehart & Co.

Gaddis, John (1972). *The United States and the Origins of the Cold War, 1941–1947*. New York: Columbia University Press.

——— (1997). *We Now Know: Rethinking Cold War History*. Oxford: Oxford University Press.

Garafola, Lynn (1989). *Diaghilev's Ballets Russes*. Oxford: Oxford University Press.

——— (2002). "Dollars for Dance: Lincoln Kirstein, City Center, and the Rockefeller Foundation." *Dance Chronicle* 25, 1: 101–114.

Garafola, Lynn, with Eric Foner, eds. (1999). *Dance for a City: Fifty Years of the New York City Ballet*. New York: Columbia University Press.

García-Márquez, Vicente (1990). *The Ballets Russes: Colonel de Basil's Ballets Russes de Monte Carlo, 1932–1952*. New York: Alfred A. Knopf.

Gellhorn, Martha (1947). "Cry Shame . . . !" *New Republic* (6 October): 20–21.

Giddings, Paula (1992). "The Last Taboo." In *Race-ing Justice, En-gendering Power: Essays on Anita Hill, Clarence Thomas and the Construction of Social Reality*, edited by Toni Morrison. New York: Pantheon Books.

Gifford, Joseph (1945). "Smoke Gets in Our Eyes." *Dance Observer* (June–July): 65–66.

Gilbert, James (1986). *A Cycle of Outrage: America's Reaction to the Juvenile Delinquent in the 1950s*. New York: Oxford University Press.

Gillmor, Daniel S. (1948). "Guilt by Gossip." *New Republic* (21 May): 15–19.

Gilman, Sander L. (1985). *Difference and Pathology: Stereotypes of Sexuality, Race and Madness*. Ithaca, N.Y.: Cornell University Press.

Gitelman, Claudia (2000). "From Bauhaus to Playhouse: Tracing the Aesthetic of Alwin Nikolais." Conference proceedings, *Dancing in the Millennium* (19–23 July), Washington, D.C.

Goff, Eleanor Anne (1946). "Pearl Primus." *Dance Observer* (June–July): 76–77.

Goffman, Erving (1959). *The Presentation of Self in Everyday Life*. New York: Doubleday.

———— (1963). *Behavior in Public: Notes on the Social Organization of Gatherings*. New York: Free Press.

———— (1979). *Gender Advertisements*. Cambridge, Mass.: Harvard University Press.

Goodman, Paul (1960). *Growing Up Absurd: Problems of Youth in the Organized Society*. New York: Random House.

Gottschild, Brenda Dixon [Stowell] (1988). "Black Dance and Dancers and the White Public: A Prolegomenon to Problems of Definition." In *The Black Tradition in American Modern Dance*, Gerald E. Myers and Stephanie Reinhart, project directors. Durham, N.C.: American Dance Festival.

———— (1996). *Digging the Africanist Presence in American Performance: Dance and Other Contexts*. Westport, Conn.: Praeger.

Goulden, Joseph (1975). *The Best Years: 1945–1950*. New York: Scribner.

Graff, Ellen (1985). "*The Four Temperaments* and *Orpheus:* Models of a Modern Classical Tradition." *Ballet Review* 3 (Fall): 54–59.

———— (1997). *Stepping Left: Dance and Politics in New York City, 1928–1942*. Durham, N.C.: Duke University Press.

Graham, Martha ([1937] 1985). "Graham 1937" and "Affirmations 1926–1937." In *Martha Graham: The Early Years*, edited by Merle Armitage. Reprint, New York: Da Capo Press.

———— ([1941] 1980). "A Modern Dancer's Primer for Action." In *The Dance Anthology*, edited by Cobbett Steinberg. New York: New American Library. Originally published in *Dance: A Basic Educational Technique*, edited by Frederick R. Rogers. New York: Macmillan.

———— (1973). *The Notebooks of Martha Graham*. New York: Harcourt, Brace Jovanovich.

———— (1991). *Blood Memory: An Autobiography*. New York: Simon and Schuster.

Gramsci, Antonio (2000). *The Antonio Gramsci Reader*, edited by David Forgacs. New York: New York University Press.

Grauert, Ruth (1999). Unpublished interview conducted by Claudia Gitelman. Typescript from audio recording. New York: Collection of Claudia Gitelman.

Green, Richard C. (2002). "(Up)Staging the Primitive: Pearl Primus and 'the Negro Problem' in American Dance." In *Dancing Many Drums: Excavations in African American Dance*, edited by Thomas F. DeFrantz. Madison: University of Wisconsin Press.

Greenberg, Clement ([1939] 1986a). "Avant-Garde and Kitsch." In *Clement Greenberg: The Collected Essays and Criticism*, vol. 1, edited by John O'Brian. Chicago: University of Chicago Press. Originally published in *Partisan Review* (Fall 1939).

——— ([1940] 1986b). "Towards a Newer Laocoon." In *Clement Greenberg: The Collected Essays and Criticism*, vol. 1, edited by John O'Brian. Chicago: University of Chicago Press. Originally published in *Partisan Review* (July–August 1940).

——— ([1945] 1986c). "Review of the Ballet *Dim Luster* by Antony Tudor." In *Clement Greenberg: The Collected Essays and Criticism*, vol. 2, edited by John O'Brian. Chicago: University of Chicago Press. Originally published in the *Nation* (3 November 1945).

——— ([1950] 1993a). "The European View of American Art." In *Clement Greenberg: The Collected Essays and Criticism*, vol. 3, edited by John O'Brian. Chicago: University of Chicago Press. Originally published in the *Nation* (25 November 1950).

——— ([1960] 1993b). "Modernist Painting." In *Clement Greenberg: The Collected Essays and Criticism*, vol. 4, edited by John O'Brian. Chicago: University of Chicago Press. Originally published as a pamphlet in *Forum Lectures*. Washington, D.C.: Voice of America.

Greene, Jonnie (1997). "Classic Black." *Dance Magazine* (February): 86–88.

Griffith, Robert (1981). "Harry S Truman and the Burden of Modernity." *Reviews in American History* 9 (September): 295–306.

Guilbaut, Serge (1983). *How New York Stole the Idea of Modern Art*. Chicago: University of Chicago Press.

———, ed. (1990). *Reconstructing Modernism: Art in New York, Paris, and Montreal, 1945–1964*. Cambridge, Mass.: MIT Press.

Hamby, Alonzo (1976). *Beyond the New Deal: Harry S Truman and American Liberalism*. New York: Columbia University Press.

Hammonds, Evelynn M. "Toward a Genealogy of Black Female Sexuality: The Problematic of Silence." In *Feminist Theory and the Body: A Reader*, edited by Janet Price and Margrit Shildrick. New York: Routledge.

Harrison, Charles, and Paul Wood (1993). *Art in Theory: 1900–1990*. Oxford: Blackwell.

Haskins, James (1982). *Katherine Dunham*. New York: Coward, McCann and Geoghegan.

——— (1990). *Black Dance in America: A History through Its People*. New York: HarperCollins.

Helpern, Alice (1991). "The Technique of Martha Graham." *Studies in Dance History* 2, 2: 1–59.

Hering, Doris (1947). "The Workshop, A New Perennial." *Dance Magazine* (July): 19–21.

——— (1948). "Reviewers' Stand." *Dance Magazine* (December): 10, 35.

——— (1949). "The Season in Review: 1st Season: New York City Ballet Company." *Dance Magazine* (January): 12–13, 32–34.

——— (1950). "The New York City Ballet Company Season." *Dance Magazine* January): 12, 47–48.

——— (1952). "Meet John Martin." *Dance Magazine* (November): 20–23, 38–39, 45.

——— (1953a). "José Limón and Company." *Dance Magazine* (February): 53–54, 56, 58.

——— (1953b). "New York City Ballet." *Dance Magazine* (March): 10, 60.

——— (1955). "An Evening of Dance Works by Anna Sokolow." *Dance Magazine* (April): 75–77.

——— (1956). "Geoffrey Holder and Louis Johnson." *Dance Magazine* (January): 76–78.

——— (1958). "Anna Sokolow Dance Company." *Dance Magazine* (April): 26–27.

——— (1959). "Anna Sokolow Dance Company." *Dance Magazine* (February): 28.

——— (1960). "Talley Beatty and Guest Performers." *Dance Magazine* (January): 80–81.

Higham, John (1989). "The Collapse of Consensus History." *Journal of American History* (September): 460–466.

Hill, Constance Valis (1994). "Katherine Dunham's *Southland:* Protest in the Face of Repression." *Dance Research Journal* 26, 2 (Fall): 1–10.

Hill, Martha (1965). *Martha Hill.* Audio interview conducted by Billy Nichols for National Education Network. Dance Collection, New York Public Library.

——— (1990). *Martha Hill Video Project* (video). Dance Collection, New York Public Library.

Hinz, Berthold (1979). *Art in the Third Reich.* Translated by Robert and Rita Kimber. New York: Random House.

Hodson, Millicent (1978). "How She Began Her Beguine: Dunham's Dance Literacy." In *KAISO! Katherine Dunham, an Anthology of Writings,* edited by Vèvè A. Clark and Margaret B. Wilkerson. Berkeley: University of California, Institute for the Study of Social Change, 196–198.

Hoelterhoff, Manuela (1975). "Art of the Third Reich: Documents of Oppression." *Artforum* (December): 55–62.

Horosko, Marian (1991). *Martha Graham: The Evolution of Her Dance Theory and Training, 1926–1991.* Chicago: A Cappella Books.

Horst, Louis (1940). *Pre-Classic Dance Forms.* New York: The Dance Observer.

———— (1943). "Katherine Dunham and Company." *Dance Observer* (October): 90.

———— (1946). "Choreographers' Workshop." *Dance Observer* (December): 124.

———— (1947). "Choreographers' Workshop." *Dance Observer* (February): 20.

———— (1958a). "Anna Sokolow Dance Company." *Dance Observer* (April): 55.

———— (1958b). "Juilliard Dance Theater." *Dance Observer* (June–July): 86.

———— (1959). "Juilliard Dance Theater, Geoffrey Holder & Co., and Midi Garth." *Dance Observer* (March): 39.

Horst, Louis, and Carroll Russell ([1961] 1987). *Modern Dance Forms in Relation to the Other Modern Arts.* Reprint, Princeton, N.J.: Princeton Book Co.

Hurok, Sol, with Ruth Goode (1947). *Impresario, a Memoir.* London: Macdonald and Co.

———— (1953). *S. Hurok Presents: A Memoir of the Dance World.* New York: Hermitage House.

Jackson, Naomi (2000). *Converging Movements: Modern Dance and Jewish Culture at the 92nd Street Y.* Middletown, Conn.: Wesleyan University Press.

Jacoby, Russell (1987). *The Last Intellectuals: American Culture in the Age of Academe.* New York: Basic Books.

Janson, H. W. (1946). "Benton and Wood, Champions of Regionalism." *Magazine of Art* 39, 5 (May): 184–186, 198–200.

Jay, Martin (1996). *The Dialectical Imagination: A History of the Frankfurt School and the Institute of Social Research.* Berkeley: University of California Press.

Jenkins, Nicholas (1998). "The Great Impresario." *New Yorker* (13 April): 48–61.

Jezer, Marty (1982). *The Dark Ages: Life in the United States, 1945–1960.* Boston: South End Press.

Joel, Lydia (1957). "Close-Up of Modern Dance Today: The Non-Objective Choreographers." *Dance Magazine* (November): 20–23.

"John Martin Is Dead at 91; *Times* Critic 35 Years" (1985). *New York Times* (21 May): B6.

Johnson, Harriet (1948). "Talley Beatty and Company." *Dance Observer* (November): 122.

Johnston, Jill (1955). "Thoughts on the Present and Future Directions of Modern Dance." *Dance Observer* (August–September): 101–102.

———— (1957a). "The Modern Dance—Directions and Criticisms." *Dance Observer* (April): 55–56.

———— (1957b). "Abstraction in Dance." *Dance Observer* (December): 151–152.

———— (1960). "Talley Beatty, Louis Johnson, Ernest Parham." *Dance Observer* (June–July): 89.

———— (1968). "Not in Broad Daylight." *Village Voice* (21 November): 32–33.

Jones, Bill T., with Peggy Gillespie (1995). *Last Night on Earth.* New York: Pantheon.

Jordan, Stephanie (2000). *Moving Music: Dialogues with Music in Twentieth-Century Ballet*. London: Dance Books.

Jordan, Stephanie, and Helen Thomas (1994). "Dance and Gender: Formalism and Semiotics Reconsidered." *Dance Research* 12, 2 (Autumn): 3–14.

Jowitt, Deborah (2004). *Jerome Robbins: His Life, His Theater, His Dance*. New York: Simon and Schuster.

Jung, Carl (1971). *The Portable Jung*. Edited, with an introduction by Joseph Campbell. New York: Viking Press.

Kinsey, Alfred, Wardell B. Pomeroy, and Clyde E. Martin, (1948). *Sexual Behavior of the Human Male*. Philadelphia: W. B. Saunders.

Kinsey, Alfred, et al. (1953). *Sexual Behavior of the Human Female*. Philadelphia: W. B. Saunders.

Kirstein, Lincoln (1934a). "Revolutionary Ballet Forms." *New Theatre* (October): 12–14.

———— ([1934b] 1983). "Prejudice Purely." In *Ballet: Bias & Belief; "Three Pamphlets Collected" and Other Dance Writings of Lincoln Kirstein*. Introduction and comments by Nancy Reynolds. New York: Dance Horizons. Originally published in *New Republic* (11 April 1934).

———— ([1937] 1983). "Blast at Ballet." In *Ballet: Bias & Belief; "Three Pamphlets Collected" and Other Dance Writings of Lincoln Kirstein*. Introduction and comments by Nancy Reynolds. Reprint, New York: Dance Horizons.

———— (1939). *Ballet Alphabet: A Primer for the Layman*. New York: Kamin Publishers.

———— (1945). "Art in the Third Reich—Survey 1945." *Magazine of Art* 28, 6 (October): 223–242.

———— (1947a). "Balanchine Musagète." *Theatre Arts* (November): 37–41.

———— (1947b). "Balanchine and the Classic Revival." *Theatre Arts* (December): 37–41.

———— (1948). "The State of Modern Painting." *Harper's* (October): 47–53.

———— ([1953] 1983). "Alec: Or the Future of Choreography." In *Ballet: Bias & Belief; "Three Pamphlets Collected" and Other Dance Writings of Lincoln Kirstein*. Introduction and comments by Nancy Reynolds. New York: Dance Horizons. Originally published in *Dance News Annual*, vol. 1, edited by Winthrop Palmer and Anatole Chujoy. New York: Alfred A. Knopf.

———— ([1959] 1983). "What Ballet Is About: An American Glossary." In *Ballet: Bias & Belief; "Three Pamphlets Collected" and Other Dance Writings of Lincoln Kirstein*. Introduction and comments by Nancy Reynolds. Reprint, New York: Dance Horizons.

———— (1970). *Movement and Metaphor: Four Centuries of Ballet*. New York: Praeger.

———— (1973). *The New York City Ballet*. New York: Alfred A. Knopf.

—— (1983). *Ballet: Bias & Belief; "Three Pamphlets Collected" and Other Dance Writings of Lincoln Kirstein*. Introduction and comments by Nancy Reynolds. Reprint, New York: Dance Horizons.

—— (1991). *By With To & From: A Lincoln Kirstein Reader*, edited by Nicholas Jenkins. New York: Farrar, Straus and Giroux.

—— (1994). *Mosaic: Memoirs*. New York: Farrar, Straus and Giroux.

Klosty, James (1975). *Merce Cunningham*. New York: Saturday Review Press.

Kochno, Boris (1954). *Le Ballet*. Paris: Hachette.

Korff, William (1993). "History of the New Dance Group from the 1930s to the 1970s." In printed program for the video recording of *The New Dance Group Gala Concert*. American Dance Guild Production. New York: American Dance Guild.

Kostelanetz, Richard, ed. (1978). *Esthetics Contemporary*. Buffalo, N.Y.: Prometheus Books.

——, ed. (1991). *John Cage: An Anthology*. New York: Da Capo Press.

——, ed. (1992). *Merce Cunningham: Dancing in Space and Time*. Chicago: A Cappella Books.

Kowal, Rebekah (1999). *Modern Dance and American Culture in the Early Cold War Years*. Ph.D. dissertation, New York University.

Krevitsky, Nik (1948). "Choreographers' Workshop." *Dance Observer* (May): 56–57.

—— (1949). "American Dance Festival." *Dance Observer* (August–September): 98.

—— (1951a). "Merce Cunningham and Company." *Dance Observer* (March): 41–42.

—— (1951b). "Jean Erdman and Company." *Dance Observer* (March): 42.

—— (1951c). "Jane Dudley, Sophie Maslow, William Bales and Company." *Dance Observer* (March): 42–43.

Kriegsman, Sali Ann (1981). *Modern Dance in America: The Bennington Years*. Boston: G. K. Hall.

Kuznick, Peter J., and James Gilbert, eds. (2001). *Rethinking Cold War Culture*. Washington, D.C.: Smithsonian Institution Press.

Laban, Juana de (1945). "What Tomorrow?" *Dance Observer* (May): 55–56.

Lacey, Michael, ed. (1990). *The Truman Presidency*. Cambridge: Cambridge University Press.

Langer, Susanne (1953). *Feeling and Form: A Theory of Art*. New York: Scribner.

Laqueur, Thomas (1987). "The Politics of Reproductive Biology." In *The Making of the Modern Body: Sexuality and Society in the Nineteenth Century*, edited by Thomas Laqueur and Catherine Gallagher. Berkeley: University of California Press.

Larkey, Joan (1949). "Jean Erdman and Company." *Dance Observer* (December): 151–152.

Lash, Scott, and Sam Whimster, eds. (1987). *Max Weber, Rationality and Modernity*. London: Allen and Unwin.

Lawson, Steven F. (1976). *Black Ballots: Voting Rights in the South, 1944–1969*. New York: Columbia University Press.

Lears, Jackson (1989). "A Matter of Taste: Corporate Cultural Hegemony in a Mass-Consumption Society." In *Recasting America: Culture and Politics in the Age of Cold War*, edited by Lary May. Chicago: University of Chicago Press.

LeClercq, Tanaquil (1982). "Tanaquil LeClercq." In *Striking a Balance: Dancers Talk about Dancing*, edited by Barbara Newman. Boston: Houghton Mifflin.

Lehmann-Haupt, Hellmut (1954). *Art Under a Dictatorship*. New York: Oxford University Press.

Leuchtenburg, William (1973). *A Troubled Feast: American Society since 1945*. Boston: Little, Brown.

Limón, José (1951). "The Virile Dance." In *The Dance Has Many Faces*, edited by Walter Sorell. New York: World Publishing.

——— (1999). *José Limón: An Unfinished Life*. Middletown, Conn.: Wesleyan University Press.

Lippincott, Gertrude (1946). "Pilgrim's Way." *Dance Observer* (August–September): 84–85.

——— (1948). "Freedom and the Arts." *Dance Observer* (April): 44–45.

Lipsitz, George (1981). *Class and Culture in Post War America: A Rainbow at Midnight*. New York: Praeger.

——— (1989). "Land of a Thousand Dances: Youth, Minorities, and the Rise of Rock and Roll." In *Recasting America: Culture and Politics in the Age of Cold War*, edited by Lary May. Chicago: University of Chicago Press.

Litz, Katherine (1949). "Young Dancers State Their Views: As Told to Nik Krevitsky." *Dance Observer* (May): 67.

Lloyd, Margaret (1949). *The Borzoi Book of Modern Dance*. New York: Alfred A. Knopf.

Louis, Murray (1960). "The Contemporarry Dance Theatre of Alwin Nikolais." *Dance Observer* (January): 5–6.

——— (1973). Audio interview conducted by Tobi Tobias. Dance Collection, New York Public Library.

——— (1980). *Inside Dance: Essays*. New York: St. Martin's Press.

Lowe, Roberta (1943). "Dunham Dancers Evoke Applause in B'way Opening." *Amsterdam News* (25 September): 9-B.

Macdonald, Dwight (1962). *Against the American Grain*. New York: Random House.

MacKay, William (1986). "Edwin Denby, 1903–1983." In *Edwin Denby: Dance Writings*, edited by Robert Cornfield and William MacKay. New York: Alfred A. Knopf.

Manchester, P. W. (1958). "Anna Sokolow Dance Company." *Dance News* (April): 9.

——— (1959a). "Juilliard Dance Theatre, Midi Garth, Geoffrey Holder & Co." *Dance News* (March): 7.

——— (1959b). "Donald McKayle, Kevin Carlisle and Dance Companies at YM-YWHA." *Dance News* (June): 14.

——— (1960a). "Talley Beatty." *Dance News* (January): 7.

——— (1960b). "Talley Beatty, Louis Johnson, Earnest Parham." *Dance News* (March): 10–11.

Manning, Susan (1993). *Ecstasy and the Demon: Feminism and Nationalism in the Dances of Mary Wigman.* Berkeley: University of California Press.

——— (2004). *Modern Dance, Negro Dance: Race in Motion.* Minneapolis: University of Minnesota Press.

Marcuse, Herbert ([1955] 1974). *Eros and Civilization: A Philosophical Inquiry into Freud.* Reprint, Boston: Beacon Press.

——— ([1964] 1991). *One-Dimensional Man.* Reprint, Boston: Beacon Press.

——— (1968). *Negations: Essays in Critical Theory.* Boston: Beacon Press.

——— (1978). *The Aesthetic Dimension: Toward a Critique of Marxist Aesthetics.* Boston: Beacon Press.

Martin, John ([1933] 1972). *The Modern Dance.* Reprint, Princeton N.J.: Dance Horizons.

——— (1936). *America Dancing: The Background and Personalities of the Modern Dance.* New York: Dodge Publishing Co.

——— (1937). "The Dance: New Ballets." *New York Times* (2 May): X 7.

——— ([1939] 1965). *Introduction to the Dance.* Reprint, Princeton N.J.: Dance Horizons.

——— (1940a). "Negro Dance Art Shown in Recital." *New York Times* (19 February): 23.

——— (1940b). "The Dance: A Negro Art." *New York Times* (25 February): 114.

——— (1943a). "The Dance: Five Artists" *New York Times* (21 February): X 5.

——— (1943b). "Katherine Dunham Gives Dance Revue." *New York Times* (20 September): 24.

——— (1944a). "New Voodoo Dance in Dunham Revue." *New York Times* (27 December): 15.

——— (1944b). "Brilliant Dancing by Pearl Primus." *New York Times* (5 October): 18.

——— (1945). *The Dance.* New York: Tudor Publishing Co.

——— (1949). "The Dance: Newcomer." *New York Times* (27 February): X 9.

——— (1950). "Maslow's Dances Given at Festival." *New York Times* (19 August): 8.

——— (1952). *The World Book of Modern Ballet.* Cleveland: World Publishing.

———— (1953). "The Dance: Diagnosis, A Few Notes Concerning the Strength as Well as Weakness in Modern Field." *New York Times* (June 28): X 3.

———— (1955a). "Dance: Study in Despair." *New York Times* (16 May): 26.

———— (1955b). "The Dance: Modern, Time for Serious Study of Basic Theories." *New York Times* (5 June): X 8.

———— (1956a). "The Dance: New Life." *New York Times* (19 February): X 9.

———— (1956b). "The Dance: Bright Augury." *New York Times* (26 February): X 6.

———— (1959). "Dance: Good Job." *New York Times* (6 December): X 18.

———— (1963). *John Martin's Book of the Dance*. New York: Tudor Publishing.

———— (1989). *John Martin: The Dance in Theory*. Princeton, N.J.: Dance Horizons.

Martin, Richard (1987). *Fashion and Surrealism*. New York: Rizzoli.

Maslow, Sophie (1984). *Dance and Social Consciousness in the 1930s and '40s* (video). Interview with Sophie Maslow and Anna Sokolow. Produced by ARC Videodance as part of the television series *Eye on Dance*, WNYC, New York. Dance Collection, New York Public Library.

Mauss, Marcel ([1934] 1973). "Techniques of the Body." Translated by Ben Brewster. *Economy and Society*, 2, 1 (February): 70–88.

May, Elaine Tyler (1988). *Homeward Bound: American Families in the Cold War Era*. New York: Basic Books.

May, Lary, ed. (1989). *Recasting America: Culture and Politics in the Age of Cold War*. Chicago: University of Chicago Press.

McDonagh, Don (1970). *The Rise and Fall and Rise of Modern Dance*. New York: New American Library.

———— (1973). *Martha Graham, a Biography*. New York: Praeger.

McKayle, Donald (n.d.). Draft for an autobiography, *I Will Dance with You*. Donald McKayle Papers, Special Collections and Archives, UCI Libraries, Irvine, California.

———— (1965). "Donald McKayle." In *The Modern Dance: Seven Statements of Belief*, edited by Selma Jeanne Cohen. Middletown, Conn.: Wesleyan University Press.

———— (1966). "The Negro Dancer in Our Time." In *The Dance Has Many Faces*, edited by Walter Sorell. 2nd ed. New York: Columbia University Press.

———— (1993). *Speaking of Dance: Donald McKayle* (video). Interview with Donald McKayle. American Dance Festival production, directed and produced by Douglas Rosenberg. Dance Collection, New York Public Library.

———— (2000). *Images and Reflections: Celebration of a Masterpiece, Donald McKayle's* Rainbow Round My Shoulder (video). American Dance Legacy Institute Production, American Dance Legacy Institute.

———— (2002). *Transcending Boundaries: My Dancing Life*. London: Routledge.

Meldon, John (1943). "The Dance." *Daily Worker* (23 September): 7.

Mercer, Kobena (1994). *Welcome to the Jungle: New Positions in Black Cultural Studies*. London: Routledge.

Mills, C. Wright (1951). *White Collar: The American Middle Classes*. London: Oxford University Press.

———— (1956). *The Power Elite*. London: Oxford University Press.

———— (1959). *The Sociological Imagination*. London: Oxford University Press.

Morris, Gay, ed. (1996). *Moving Words: Re-writing Dance*. London: Routledge.

———— (2001). "What He Called Himself: Issues of Identity in Early Dances by Bill T. Jones." In *Dancing Desires: Choreographing Sexualities On and Off the Stage*, edited by Jane Desmond. Madison: University of Wisconsin Press.

Moulton, Robert D. (1957). *Choreography in Musical Comedy and Revue on the New York Stage from 1925 to 1950*. Microfilm, New York Public Library.

Myers, Gerald E. (1988). "Ethnic and Modern Dance." In *The Black Tradition in American Modern Dance*, Gerald E. Myers and Stephanie Reinhart, project directors. Durham, N.C.: American Dance Festival.

Myers, Gerald E., and Stephanie Reinhart, project directors (1988). *The Black Tradition in American Modern Dance*. Durham, N.C.: American Dance Festival.

———— (1993). *African American Genius in Modern Dance*. Durham, N.C.: American Dance Festival.

Myrdal, Gunnar ([1944] 1999). *An American Dilemma: The Negro Problem and Modern Democracy*. Reprint, London: Transaction Publishers.

Nabokov, Ivan, and Elizabeth Carmichael (1961). "Balanchine: An Interview by Ivan Nabokov and Elizabeth Carmichael." *Horizon* (January): 44–56.

Nadeau, Maurice (1989). *The History of Surrealism*. Cambridge, Mass.: Harvard University Press.

Nash, Joe (1992). "Talley Beatty." In *African American Genius in Modern Dance*, Gerald E. Myers and Stephanie Reinhart, project directors. Durham, N.C.: American Dance Festival.

Navasky, Victor (1980). *Naming Names*. New York: Viking Press.

Nettleton, Sarah, and Jonathan Watson, eds. (1998). *The Body in Everyday Life*. London: Routledge.

Newman, Barbara (1982). *Striking a Balance: Dancers Talk about Dancing*. Boston: Houghton Mifflin.

Nikolais, Alwin (1957). "Dance: Semantics." *New York Times* (18 August): 31.

———— (1958). "The New Dimension of Dance." *Impulse:* 43–46.

———— (1961a). "Dance, Sexual Dynamics in Contemporary." In *The Encyclopedia of Sexual Behavior*, vol. 1. New York: Hawthorn Books.

———— (1961b). "Growth of a Theme." *Dance Magazine* (February): 30–34.

———— (1965). "No Man from Mars." *The Modern Dance: Seven Statements of Belief*, edited by Selma Jeanne Cohen. Middleton, Conn.: Wesleyan University Press.

———— (1968). "Lecture on Avant-Garde Dance." Aural Recording. Dance Collection, New York Public Library of the Performing Arts.

———— (1971a). *Nik—A Documentary*. Edited, with an introduction by Marcia B. Siegel. *Dance Perspectives:* 48.

———— (1971b). "Interview with Alwin Nikolais." Elinor Rogosin, interviewer. Aural recording. *Dance Focus*, Radio Station WBAI, New York. Dance Collection, New York Public Library of the Performing Arts.

———— (1973). "Interview with Alwin Nikolais," James Day, interviewer. Audio portion of television broadcast *Day at Night*. WNET/Channel 13, New York. Dance Collection, New York Public Library of the Performing Arts.

———— (1973–74). "A Conversation with Alwin Nikolais," by Roger Copeland. *Dance Scope*, 8, 1 (Fall–Winter): 41–46.

Oakley, J. Ronald (1986). *God's Country: America in the Fifties*. New York: Dembner Brooks.

Ocko, Edna (1948). "Dance: Anna Sokolow." *Masses & Mainstream* 1, 1 (March): 95–96.

O'Donnell, Mary P. (1940). "Katherine Dunham and Group." *Dance Observer* (December): 148.

O'Neill, William (1986). *American High: The Years of Confidence, 1945–1960*. New York: Free Press.

Orme, Frederick L. (1938). "The Negro in the Dance: As Katherine Dunham Sees Him." *The American Dancer* (March) 10, 46.

Ortner, Sherry (1974). "Is Female to Male as Nature Is to Culture?" In *Woman, Culture & Society*, edited by Michelle Rosaldo and Louise Lamphere. Palo Alto, Calif.: Stanford University Press.

Palatsky, Eugene (1958). "Backstage at New York City Ballet." *Dance Magazine* (December): 64–67, 101.

Palmer, Winthrop (1949). "Structure and Forms of Writing for the Theatre." *Dance Observer* (October): 112.

Patterson, James T., ed. (1975). *Paths to the Present*. Minneapolis: Burgess Publishing.

———— (1996). *Grand Expectations: The United States, 1945–1974*. New York: Oxford University Press.

Pells, Richard H. (1989). *The Liberal Mind in a Conservative Age: American Intellectuals in the 1940s and 1950s*. Middletown, Conn.: Wesleyan University Press.

Perlmutter, Donna (1991). *Shadowplay: The Life of Antony Tudor*. New York: Viking Press.

Perloff, Majorie (1989). *Postmodern Genres*. Norman: University of Oklahoma Press.

Perpener, John O. (2001). *African American Concert Dance: The Harlem Renaissance and Beyond*. Urbana: University of Illinois Press.

Phelps, Mary (1946a). "Pearl Primus." *Dance Observer* (February): 24.

———— (1946b). "Dancers or Donkeys?" *Dance Observer* (November): 110–111.

———— (1947). "Choreographers' Workshop." *Dance Observer* (June–July): 65.

———— (1948). "Valerie Bettis and Company." *Dance Observer* (February): 19.

Pierre, Dorathi Bock (1941). "A Talk with Katherine Dunham." *Educational Dance* (August–September): 7–8.

———— (1947). "Katherine Dunham: Cool Scientist or Sultry Performer?" *Dance Magazine* (May): 11–13.

Polenberg, Richard (1991). *One Nation Divisible: Class, Race, and Ethnicity in the United States since 1938*. New York: Viking Press.

Preston-Dunlop, Valerie (1995). *Dance Words*. Chur, Switzerland: Harwood Academic Publishers.

Prevots, Naima (1985). "Zurich Dada and Dance: Formative Ferment." *Dance Research Journal* 17, 1 (Spring–Summer): 3–8.

———— (1998). *Dance for Export: Cultural Diplomacy and the Cold War*. Middletown, Conn.: Wesleyan University Press.

Prickett, Stacey Lee (1992). *Marxism, Modernism and Realism: Politics and Aesthetics in the Rise of the American Modern Dance*. Ph.D. dissertation, The Laban Centre for Movement and Dance, London.

Revill, David (1992). *The Roaring Silence: John Cage; A Life*. New York: Arcade Publishing.

Reynolds, Nancy (1977). *Repertory in Review: 40 Years of New York City Ballet*. New York: Dial Press.

———— (1983). Introduction and comments. In *Ballet: Bias & Belief; "Three Pamphlets Collected" and Other Dance Writings of Lincoln Kirstein*. New York: Dance Horizons.

Richter, Hans (1965). *Dada: Art and Anti-Art*. New York: McGraw-Hill.

Riesman, David (1950). *The Lonely Crowd*. New Haven, Conn.: Yale University Press.

Robinson, Harlow (1994). *The Last Impresario: The Life, Times, and Legacy of Sol Hurok*. New York: Viking Press.

Rosaldo, Michelle, and Louise Lamphere, eds. (1974). *Woman, Culture & Society*. Palo Alto, Calif.: Stanford University Press.

Rosenbaum, Ruth (1943). "Dancers' Debit." *Dance Observer* (August): 78.

Rouzeau, Edgar T. (1940). "A Word about Katherine Dunham." *Norfolk Journal and Guide* (9 March): 17.

Rubin, William (1968). *Dada, Surrealism, and Their Heritage*. New York: Museum of Modern Art.

Rudko, Doris (1956). "The Playhouse Dance Company." *Dance Observer* (February): 28.

Runciman, W. G., ed. (1978). *Weber: Selections in Translation*. Cambridge: Cambridge University Press.

Sabin, Robert (1944). "Ballet Russe de Monte Carlo." *Dance Observer* (October): 101.

—— (1945a). "Valerie Bettis and Group." *Dance Observer* (June–July): 70.

—— (1945b). "Ballet Russe de Monte Carlo." *Dance Observer* (October): 97–98.

—— (1946). "Dance Critics in America: John Martin of *The New York Times*." *Dance Observer* (June–July): 72–73.

—— (1950). "Choreographers' Workshop." *Dance Observer* (May): 71.

—— (1952). "Janet Collins." *Dance Observer* (January): 10–11.

Saunders, Frances Stonor (1999). *The Cultural Cold War: The CIA and the World of Arts and Letters*. New York: New Press.

Sawin, Martica (1997). *Surrealism in Exile, and the Beginning of the New York School*. Cambridge, Mass.: MIT Press.

Schlesinger, Arthur M., Jr. ([1949] 1998). *The Vital Center: The Politics of Freedom*. With a new introduction by the author. New Brunswick, N.J.: Transaction Publishers.

Severin, Reed (1948). "The Ballet Society." *Dance Magazine* (March): 7, 42–46.

"The Shape of Things" (1947). *Nation* (29 March): 345–347.

"She is Priestess of Intellectual Ballet" (1947). *Life* (17 March): 101–104.

Siegel, Frederick (1984). *Troubled Journey: From Pearl Harbor to Ronald Reagan*. New York: Hill and Wang.

Siegel, Marcia B., ed. (1971). *Nik—A Documentary*. With an introductory essay. *Dance Perspectives*: 48.

—— (1979). *The Shapes of Change: Images of American Dance*. Boston: Houghton Mifflin.

—— (1987). *Days on Earth: The Dance of Doris Humphrey*. New Haven, Conn.: Yale University Press.

—— (1997). "Using Lexicons for Performance Research: Three Duets." *New Approaches to Theatre Studies and Performance Analysis: Papers Presented at the Colston Symposium, Bristol, England, 21–23 March*. Tübingen: Max Niemeyer Verlag.

Silk, Mark (1988). *Spiritual Politics: Religion and America since World War II*. New York: Simon and Schuster.

Simon, Henry (1943). "The Tropics Invade Broadway." *PM* (20 September): 22.

Sitkoff, Harvard (1993). *The Struggle for Black Equality, 1954–1992*. New York: Hill and Wang.

Skolnick, Arlene (1991). *Embattled Paradise: The American Family in an Age of Uncertainty*. New York: HarperCollins.

Smith, Cecil (1947). "The Maze of the Heart." *Theatre Arts* (May): 29–32.

—— (1948). "Talley Beatty and Company." *Musical America* (15 November): 10.

Soares, Janet (1992). *Louis Horst: Musician in a Dancer's World*. Durham, N.C.: Duke University Press.

Sokolow, Anna (1965). "I Hate Academies . . . " *Dance Magazine* (July): 38–39.

——— (1974). Unpublished interview with Barbara Newman. Typescript from audio recording. Oral History Archives, Dance Collection, New York Public Library.

Sorell, Walter, ed. (1951). *The Dance Has Many Faces*. New York: World Publishing.

——— (1956). "The Playhouse Dance Company." *Dance Magazine* (July): 70.

——— (1958). "Close-Up of Modern Dance Today: The Henry Street Playhouse Produces a Major Dance School, Workshops and Company." *Dance Magazine* (January): 49–52.

——— (1962). "Donald McKayle and Company." *Dance Observer* (June–July): 91.

——— (1966). *The Dance Has Many Faces*. 2nd ed. New York: Columbia University Press.

Stahl, Norma Gengal (1954). "The First Lady of the Metropolitan Opera Ballet: An Interview with Janet Collins." *Dance Magazine* (February): 27–29.

Staples, Robert (1982). *Black Masculinity: The Black Man's Role in American Society*. San Francisco: Black Scholar Press.

Steinberg, Cobbett, ed. (1980). *The Dance Anthology*. New York: New American Library.

Steuben, Francis [Edna Ocko] (1943). "Katherine Dunham's Revue." *New Masses* (2 November): 26.

——— (1944). "Pearl Primus Dance." *New Masses* (31 October): 28.

Steyn, Mark (1997). *Broadway Babies Say Goodnight: Musicals Then and Now*. London: Faber and Faber.

Stich, Sidra (1990). *Anxious Visions: Surrealist Art*. New York: Abbeville Press.

Stuckey, P. Sterling (2002). "Christian Conversion and the Challenge of Dance." In *Dancing Many Drums: Excavations in African American Dance*, edited by Thomas F. DeFrantz. Madison: University of Wisconsin Press.

Suskind, Peter (1943). "A Plug for One of 'Little Folks.'" *Norfolk Journal and Guide* (27 February): 14

Suzuki, Daisetz, T. ([1934] 1964). *An Introduction to Zen Budhism*. Reprint, New York, Grove Press.

Sydie, R. A. (1987). *Natural Women, Cultured Men: A Feminist Perspective on Sociological Theory*. New York: New York University Press.

Tallchief, Maria (1997). *Maria Tallchief: America's Prima Ballerina*. New York: Henry Holt.

Taper, Bernard (1984). *Balanchine: A Biography*. New York: Times Books.

Taylor, Paul (1987). *Private Domain*. New York: Alfred A. Knopf.

Telberg, Lelia K. (1959). "Murray Louis and Group." *Dance Observer* (May): 73.

Terry, Walter (1940a). "Dunham Dancers." *New York Herald Tribune* (19 February): 13.

——— (1940b). "The Negro Dances." *New York Herald Tribune* (28 April): VI 10.

——— (1941). "Balanchine and Graham." *New York Herald Tribune* (26 January): VI 10.

——— (1947a). "Initial Ballet Society Works Stress Variety of Form, Style." *New York Herald Tribune* (19 January): V 4.

——— (1947b). "Lo! The Poor Dancer." *Dance Magazine* (March): 25–28.

——— (1951a). "The Dance World: A Jewish Community in Dance." *New York Herald Tribune* (4 February): IV 7.

——— (1951b). "The Ballet: Absorbing Revival." *New York Herald Tribune* (23 November): 17.

——— (1955). "American Dance." *New York Herald Tribune* (16 May): 12.

——— ([1956] 1971). *The Dance in America*. Reprint, New York: Harper and Row.

——— (1978). *I Was There: Selected Dance Reviews and Articles 1936–1976*. New York: Marcel Dekker.

Thomas, Helen (1995). *Dance, Modernity and Culture: Explorations in the Sociology of Dance*. London: Routledge.

——— (1996). "Do You Want to Join the Dance? Postmodernism, Poststructrualism, the Body, and Dance." In *Moving Words: Rewriting Dance*, edited by Gay Morris. London: Routledge.

Tomkins, Calvin (1976). *The Bride and the Bachelors: Five Masters of the Avant-Garde; Duchamp, Tinguely, Cage, Rauschenberg, Cunningham*. New York: Penguin Books.

——— (1980). *Off the Wall: Robert Rauschenberg and the Art World of Our Time*. New York: Doubleday.

Vaughan, David (1957). "Close-Up of Modern Dance Today: The Non-Objective Choreographers." *Dance Magazine* (November): 20–23.

——— (1958). "Dissenting View on Graham." *Dance Magazine* (July): 26–27.

——— (1997a). *Merce Cunningham: Fifty Years*. New York: Aperture.

———, ed. (1997b). *Merce Cunningham: Creative Elements. Choreography and Dance* 4: 3.

Volkov, Solomon (1985). *Balanchine's Tchaikovsky: Conversations with Balanchine on His Life, Ballet and Music*. New York: Doubleday.

Warren, Larry (1998). *Anna Sokolow: The Rebellious Spirit*. Amsterdam: Harwood Academic Publishers.

Washington, Fredi (1944). "Pearl Primus Captures Broadway; Josh White Added Attraction." *People's Voice* (21 October): 29.

Watts, Alan (1957). *The Way of Zen*. New York: Mentor Books.

Weber, Max ([1904–1905] 1999). *The Protestant Ethic and the Spirit of Capitalism*. With an introduction by Anthony Giddens. London: Routledge.

———— (1946). *From Max Weber: Essays in Sociology.* Edited by H. H. Gerth and C. Wright Mills. New York: Oxford University Press.

———— (1978). *Weber: Selections in Translation.* Edited by W. G. Runciman. Cambridge: Cambridge University Press.

Weber, Nicholas Fox (1992). *Patron Saints: Five Rebels Who Opened America to a New Art, 1928–1943.* New York: Alfred A. Knopf.

Werth, Alexander (1948a). "The 'Reform' of Soviet Music." *Nation* (10 April): 393–395.

———— (1948b). "Culture and Commissars: The Dilemma of Soviet Artists." *Nation* (21 August): 207–209.

Whitfield, Stephen (1991). *The Culture of the Cold War.* 2nd ed. Baltimore: Johns Hopkins University Press.

Whyte, William H., Jr. (1956). *The Organization Man.* Garden City, N.Y.: Doubleday.

Wiebe, Robert H. (1990). *The Search for Order: 1877–1920.* New York: Farrar, Straus and Giroux.

Wiggins, Elizabeth (1946). "The Pilgrim Again Waylaid." *Dance Observer* (December): 125.

Wilde, Patricia, et al. (1987). "Celebrating *The Four Temperaments—1.*" *Ballet Review* (Winter): 12–35.

Wilder, Lucy (1952). "Stage for Dancers." *Dance Observer* (April): 58.

Wilkins, Darrell (1993). "*The Four Temperaments,* an Interpretation." *Ballet Review,* 21, 2 (Summer): 81–87.

Williams, Raymond (1983). *Keywords: A Vocabulary of Culture and Society.* New York: Oxford University Press.

Williams, Simon J., and Gillian Bendelow (1998). *The Lived Body: Sociological Themes, Embodied Issues.* London: Routledge.

Wolfson, Bernice J. (1947). "A Time to Speak and Dance." *Dance Observer* (October): 88–89.

Wollf, N. S. (1944). "Pearl Primus." *Dance News* (November): 7.

INDEX

Page numbers in *italic* represent illustrations.

ABOUT THE AUTHOR

Gay Morris is a dance and art critic whose work has appeared in numerous publications, including *Dance Research*, *Art in America*, and *Body and Society*. For the past three years she has been a research fellow in sociology at Goldsmiths College, University of London. She is the editor of the anthology *Moving Words, Rewriting Dance* (1996).